PERSPECTIVES ON MUSIC

PERSPECTIVES ON MUSIC

*Essays on Collections
at the
Humanities Research Center*

Edited by
Dave Oliphant & Thomas Zigal

Humanities Research Center • The University of Texas at Austin

215333

Cover illustration: Ludwig van Beethoven. Lithograph with stenciled color, n.d. 37.5 × 29.5 cm. Printed in Berlin. *HRC Iconography Collection.*

Contents

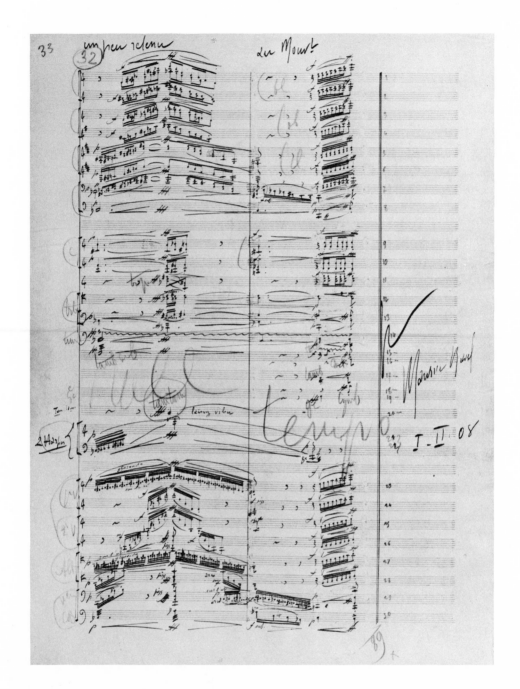

Last manuscript page of Maurice Ravel's *Rapsodie espagnole*, signed by the composer and dated 1 February 1908. *HRC Collections*.

Introduction

Musicians, music historians, and music publishers are beginning to recognize what literary scholars have known for years—that the Humanities Research Center is a treasure house of manuscripts, correspondence, and early printed editions, with significant representation in many areas of study. The HRC's music collection contains rare music manuscripts that are now being noted, discussed, and utilized for their unique characteristics. Many of these manuscripts carry important emendations that are essential for the understanding of a given composer's elaboration of ideas or the composer's solution to specific technical problems. Publishers and performers can now correct, or at least come to terms with, errors in the printed editions of works by preeminent composers; and with the aid of letters, essays, monographs, business files, and general memorabilia in its music and related literary collections, the Center can thus serve as an important source for initiating up-to-date critical editions. In a world where authenticity is paramount, to make these manuscripts and early editions available to performers and publishers is to offer direction and validity to musical interpretation.

The HRC's Carlton Lake Collection is a prominent archive of nineteenth- and twentieth-century French materials, including music manuscripts by George Auric, Hector Berlioz, Ernest Chausson, Paul Claudel, Claude Debussy, Gabriel Fauré, Franz Liszt, and Erik Satie. Among other items of interest are the documents relating to Germaine Albert-Birot's music for Guillaume Apollinaire's surrealist play *Les Mamelles de Tirésias*, and a mock-up for Jean Cocteau's book on music, *Le Coq et l'arlequin*. The papers of Henri-Pierre Roché, author of *Jules et Jim*, contain correspondence with Auric, Darius Milhaud, Albert Roussel, and Satie; and the papers of Edouard Dujardin—novelist, music critic, and a student of Debussy—are particularly rich in correspondence with Paul Dukas, the Wagner family, Maurice Ravel, Olivier Messiaen, and others. Three essays in this volume make use of·the Lake Collection—Robert Orledge's overview of several Gabriel Fauré manuscripts, Susan Youens's discussion of the third and final version of Claude Debussy's *Trois Ballades de François Villon*, and Marie Rolf's delineation of Debussy's settings of Verlaine's "En sourdine." In recent months the HRC has acquired eighty-nine additional autograph music manuscripts by Fauré, Ravel, Debussy, Roussel, and Dukas, preserved intact over several generations but previously unavailable for examination. With this acquisition the HRC now offers a major collection of work by French composers which will afford the scholar a deeper, more extensive look at the original sources of modern French music.

Other HRC archives also possess unexpected caches of music material. This is true especially of the Edith Sitwell and Ezra Pound collections, which have furnished the manuscripts, letters, and miscellanea discussed in Stewart Craggs's "*Façade* and the Music of Sir William Walton" and in Archie Henderson's "*Townsman* and Music: Ezra Pound's Letters to Ronald Duncan." Likewise, in "Paul Bowles: Lost and Found," Bennett Lerner outlines this writer's early career as he developed as both a novelist and a composer of art songs and chamber music scores. The Edwin Bachmann Collection, as noted in Ronald D. Clinton's essay, makes available numerous early printed editions of chamber works by such composers as Mozart, Haydn, and Beethoven. Though the music portions of these collections are incidental to their larger value as literary archives, they nevertheless provide the music historian with essential, sometimes overlooked, information.

Of course the HRC houses a number of significant collections that were acquired solely for their music content. The Alfred Cortot Collection, primarily sacred vocal music from the sixteenth to the nineteenth century, is important for its examples of changing styles and practices, as surveyed here by Dell Hollingsworth. The Ross Russell Collection, its provenance described by Richard Lawn in "From Bird to Schoenberg," affords jazz scholars and aficionados an opportunity to pore over a wealth of books, periodicals, programs, letters, photographs, phonograph records, cassette tapes, catalogues, and the business files of Dial Records.

In addition to the music collections analyzed in the present volume, there are others in a variety of forms, from classical to popular, which represent work from several major countries over a period of four centuries. The Theodore M. Finney Collection contains forty-five bound volumes of seventeenth-, eighteenth-, and nineteenth-century music manuscripts from Italy, France, England, and Germany, done by various hands, including anthems, glees, accompanied secular songs, operatic arias, and music for keyboard, harp, and mandolin. Over 3,800 Italian opera libretti, from the seventeenth through the mid twentieth century, came to HRC as a gift from H.P. Kraus, along with his collection of cantatas, serenatas, oratorios, dialogues, and passions. The manuscripts and correspondence files of the Russian-born composer Nicolas Nabokov are a recent acquisition that covers twenty-two years of Nabokov's career, 1955–77, and includes exchanges with W.H. Auden, George Balanchine, Robert Oppenheimer, Henry Miller, Isaiah Berlin, Igor Stravinsky, and many other composers, musicians, performers, and writers, as well as works by some of Nabokov's contemporaries, notably Stravinsky. In popular music, the David Guion Collection includes more than 100 autograph manuscripts for his concert arrangements of cowboy and frontier songs and hillbilly spirituals.

Robert B. Lynn's "A Progress Report on the 'Trumpet Tablature' at HRC" calls attention to one of several isolated items from the early periods of music history. The oldest music-related holding at HRC is the Bede Manuscript, containing paste-down leaves of music from the fourteenth and fifteenth centuries. A number of works from the Reformation Era pertain to religious music—separate leaves of Gregorian chant for the Mass and the Holy Office, probably dating from the sixteenth century; leaves from a large Dominican choirbook with music for the Office; and five illuminated Spanish liturgical music manuscripts, dating from the late fifteenth or early sixteenth century, with unorthodox arrangements. The Gostling Manuscript, published in facsimile by the University of Texas Press in 1977, is comprised of the collected compositions of the contemporaries of the Reverend John Gostling (d. 1733), the celebrated bass soloist. In this bound manuscript Gostling copied the music of some of the finest composers of his time.

William Penn's "The Music for David O. Selznick's Production No. 103," an essay on music in cinema, demonstrates that the HRC's Theatre Arts Collection is an excellent source for research in popular music. It is estimated that the Theatre Arts sheet music collection numbers 4,000 to 6,000 pieces; in addition, there are some 250 pieces of Ziegfeld Follies and Frolics music and an extensive collection of popular sheet music that was used to accompany the showing of silent films in the Interstate Theatre Chain. The T.E. Hanley Collection is important to music history for its approximately 200 pieces of illustrated sheet music of Victorian song, over half of which was intended for performance in minstrel shows. Audio material is available in a collection of more than 5,000 original cast recordings of musical comedies and other performances, including plays, jazz, and British music hall events. Any sampling of HRC music manuscripts from the world of show business should mention George and Ira Gershwin's layout of songs and themes from *Porgy and Bess* and their original typescript of the 1926 published version of *Porgy*; Cole Porter's working manuscript of his song "Oh, I Just Must Get That Man"; Jule Styne's original scores, publicity material, photographs, and correspondence; papers concerning the concert appearances of Burl Ives between 1944 and 1963; the manuscripts and typescripts of over thirty songs by Paul Anka; and the pages of manuscript music and lyrics for *Mary Poppins*, as well as related publicity items. These materials are but a few of the voluminous, eclectic music holdings in the HRC Theatre Arts Collection.

The essays in *Perspectives on Music* reflect the richness and diversity of the music collections at the Humanities Research Center. From European sacred music of the sixteenth century to jazz, this volume establishes the breadth and depth of scholarship that can derive from examination of the Center's music materials. With so many areas still unexplored, the HRC will remain a valuable resource for research and publication in the field of music history.

—*The Editors, with the assistance of*
Cathy Henderson, HRC Research Librarian

Edwin Bachmann. Charcoal portrait by Bettina Steinke, ca. 1938. From *The NBC Symphony Orchestra* (New York: NBC, 1938). *University of Texas Fine Arts Library.*

The Edwin Bachmann Collection: Perspectives on Early Editions of Solo and Chamber Music with Keyboard

By Ronald D. Clinton

In 1958, The University of Texas at Austin acquired approximately 10,000 volumes from the noted New York collector Edwin Bachmann. Interest in the Bachmann Collection was first aroused by the many reference and bibliographical books it contained, and in fact its acquisition formed the first major bibliographical reference collection at the Humanities Research Center, providing it with such important books and journals as *The Colophon* and *The Book Collector*. In addition to reference works, the Bachmann Collection features nineteenth- and twentieth-century English and American literature; many examples of fine printing; publications by the Grolier, Caxton, and Roxburghe clubs; historical works on book collecting and the antiquarian book trade; catalogues of important libraries sold at public auction; and early printers' manuals and examples of works printed at the Ashendene, Doves, Essex House, and Kelmscott presses. One of the least well known and appreciated areas of this collection is the more than 600 printed editions of music by such composers as Albrechtsberger, C.P.E. Bach, J.S. Bach, Mozart, Haydn, Beethoven, Chopin, Liszt, Franck, Schumann, Brahms, Schubert, Dvorak, Gluck, Handel, Verdi, Wagner, Weber, and others. Also included with the many first and early editions of music by these composers is a scattering of autograph letters and manuscripts. The Bachmann Collection is particularly valuable for the study of music history because it enlarges the repertoire of available music for analysis and performance and provides rare source material for original research, primarily in the area of eighteenth- and nineteenth-century music.

As a concert violinist, Edwin Bachmann gathered materials for his music collection during more than forty years of touring Europe, the United States, South America, and the Middle East. Born in Budapest in 1890, Bachmann grew up in a musical family: his mother was a celebrated concert pianist and his father a prominent cantor. After completing his own studies at the Budapest Conservatory of Music, Edwin was appointed concertmaster of the Budapest Symphony Orchestra. Three years later, in 1911, he moved to the United States and joined the New York Russian Symphony. Subsequently he played with the New York Symphony Orchestra under the direction of Walter Damrosch. In 1928 Bachmann was invited by Joseph Hofmann to take over the class of Carl Flesch at the Curtis Institute, where he taught violin with such noted teachers and performers as Leopold Auer and Efrem Zimbalist.[1] In 1933 he joined the NBC Symphony Orchestra at the invitation of Arturo Toscanini, remaining as a member of the orchestra for the next seventeen years.[2] It was during this period that Bachmann added significantly to his already extensive collection of music. The orchestra's tours throughout Europe, the United States, and South America increased his opportunities to meet musicians and music dealers in many parts of the world. In 1950 he left the NBC Orchestra, but since that time he has continued to pursue his interests as a collector.[3]

Notable items in the Bachmann Collection include the first edition of the full score of J.S. Bach's *Grosse Passionsmusik nach dem Evangelium Matthaei,* one of a limited number of copies published for subscribers in 1830; one of fifty copies on papier de Hollande of Debussy's *Cinq Poèmes de Charles Baudelaire,* inscribed to René Chansarel by the composer; a copy of the 1800 edition of Haydn's *The Creation;* the first complete edition of the full score of Handel's *Messiah;* the first editions of Leopold Mozart's *Versuch einer grundlichen Violinschule* and Charles Burney's *An Account of the Musical Performances in Westminster-Abbey . . . in Commemoration of Handel;* first editions of Mozart's operas *Don Giovanni, Idomeneo, Zaide, Die Entfuhrung aus dem Serail,* and *Le Nozze de Figaro;* and first editions of Mozart's *Symphony No. 40 in G Minor,* Beethoven's *Symphony No. 5 in C Minor,* and Brahms's *Ein Deutsches Requiem.* Of special interest to students of keyboard music are the eighteenth- and nineteenth-century editions of piano works by such composers as J.S. Bach, Handel, Haydn, Mozart, Mendelssohn, Schubert, Schumann, Franck, and Weber. Also included are thirty-two early editions of piano works by Chopin and more than sixty by Beethoven. Since modern editions of early music often differ greatly from the original publications, the Bachmann Collection offers an historical context within which to observe editorial changes that have taken place in the editions of important works by these eighteenth- and nineteenth-century composers. In the case of Beethoven it is especially valuable to have these early editions when the original manuscripts have not survived. By comparing more recent editions with the first or early printed edition of a Beethoven work for keyboard, it is possible to observe editorial changes which may depart significantly from the composer's original conception.

[1]Nellie and Margaret Bok, *Overtones, Fiftieth Anniversary Issue, The Curtis Institute of Music* (Philadelphia: Drake Press, 1974), p. 40.

[2]Philip Kerby, *The NBC Symphony Orchestra* (New York: National Broadcasting Company, 1938), p. 22.

[3]Mr. Bachmann currently lives in New York City and, at age ninety-four, collects rare books, letters, and paintings.

The period during which many of the Bachmann editions were published, the eighteenth and nineteenth centuries, has often been referred to as "the age of engraving," and the majority of early editions of keyboard music contained in the Bachmann Collection were printed using this method. First applied to the printing of music in 1581, engraving had been used prior to that time only in the area of the visual arts and, more especially, in the printing of maps.[4] Although the preparation of the plate used for printing required a great deal of skill on the part of the engraver, once prepared, it provided a reliable medium for the printing of large quantities of music and could be stored and used repeatedly. With the use of an awl or punch, characters were etched into a metal plate, usually of copper or pewter, and the plate was in turn covered with ink and pressed onto paper to create an impression.[5] This technique of pressing the engraved plate on paper leaves a very distinguishable margin on the page of printed music where the edge of the plate is transferred to the paper. As one of the visual characteristics of music that has been printed by the engraving method, this plate outline is present in numerous musical scores in the Bachmann Collection.

Earlier printing practices involved the use of carved wooden blocks and the "movable type" process, first employed by Ottaviano de Petrucci in 1501 in Venice, for the printing of polyphonic music. The engraving method proved superior to Petrucci's "triple impression," which was both time-consuming and costly and required separate impressions for the staff lines, the music, and the text.[6] After Petrucci, other printers reduced this technique to two impressions, one for the words and one for the music, but the technical problems were still far from simple, as the following account illustrates:

> The printer had to devise a system for correlating staves, notes and text. . . . Using for the staves a block of metal or occasionally separate lengths of rules, the printer set this material together with the words of the text in the form, and printed both at the first impression. He then removed all this type from the form and replaced it with the type required for the second impression. This comprised the clefs, and the notes set with such meticulous spacing that each would leave its impression right on the centre of the

[4]A. Hyatt King, *Four Hundred Years of Music Printing* (London: British Museum, 1964), p. 17.

[5]H. Edmund Poole, "Music Engraving Practice in Eighteenth-Century London," *Music and Bibliography, Essays in Honour of Alec Hyatt King*, ed. Oliver Neighbor (New York: Clive Bingley, 1980), pp. 103–107.

[6]Donald J. Grout, *A History of Western Music*, 3rd ed. (New York: W. W. Norton & Co., 1980), p. 172.

appropriate line of the stave, and stand in an equally exact vertical relation to the syllables of the text printed beneath.[7]

This method of printing continued throughout the sixteenth and seventeenth centuries and experienced a brief rebirth even as late as the 1750s when Johann Gottlob Immanuel Breitkopf, after much research and experiment, overcame many of its inherent limitations, namely, its clumsiness and lack of flexibility when used for the printing of chords and florid music.[8] As early as the sixteenth century, however, with the rapid development of new musical styles and forms, this type of music printing began to show signs of inadequacy. The more florid keyboard and stringed instrumental styles, with their use of faster tempi and more varied rhythms, placed demands for a greater variety and quantity of new symbols which ultimately proved too complex for the movable type process because of its technical limitations.[9] In addition, the rise of Italian opera, as well as other large-scale vocal forms, created the need for printing music in full score.[10]

During the seventeenth century, the engraving process was used alongside the older and more established movable type process. By the beginning of the eighteenth century, however, engraving had become the dominant form of printing throughout Europe.[11] This dominance continued until the middle part of the nineteenth century when Alois Sennfelder's "lithographic transfer" process gained ascendancy.[12] This process, perfected by Sennfelder in 1797, involved the technique of chemically coating a stone plate in such a way that an impression was left which could then be taken directly from the stone. The main advantage of this method was that it was relatively inexpensive compared with the engraving process. Other developments in the lithographic method simplified the technique even further through the use of metal plates instead of stone. In response to the growing number of musical amateurs and an increasing demand for greater quantities of new and less expensive music, the lithographic method outstripped the slower and more costly engraving process and remained the dominant medium until the advent of the newer photographic processes developed in the early twentieth century.

The prominence of musical engraving around the turn of the eighteenth century was paralleled by the rise of new publishing centers and an unprecedented proliferation of publishing firms. London, Paris, Vienna, and

[7] King, p. 10.
[8] Ibid., p. 23.
[9] Ibid., p. 16.
[10] H. Edmund Poole and Donald W. Krummel, "Printing and Publishing of Music," *The New Grove Dictionary of Music and Musicians*, ed. Stanley Sadie (London: Macmillan, 1980), 15:248.
[11] King, p. 18.
[12] Ibid., pp. 27–30.

Leipzig became the leading centers of publishing activities during this time, encouraged by a steady stream of instrumental music which emanated first from Italy, and later in the century from Germany and Austria.[13] In Paris, after 1750, several publishing firms began to specialize in the publication of instrumental chamber music. They used the oblong format, first established by Estienne Roger in Amsterdam in 1690,[14] which became the most popular for instrumental music during the course of the eighteenth century, a format employed in the majority of eighteenth- and nineteenth-century piano scores found in the Bachmann Collection. The most important French publishing firms represented in the Bachmann Collection arose in the early nineteenth century, and these included the firms of Richault, Maurice Schlesinger, Troupenas, and Brandus, all of which were active in the publication of Chopin's music.

During the second part of the eighteenth century, Germany became more active in the music publishing industry. In Leipzig, Breitkopf began to publish music using the modified typesetting process, a procedure that was unique to Breitkopf, since other German firms continued to use the engraving process already established in Italy, England, and France. It was Vienna, however, which became the most important center for the publication of works by the great "classical" masters and, especially, the works of Haydn, Mozart, and Beethoven. The Artaria Company, founded in 1778, began this Viennese reign but was soon followed by several important competitors, two of which were employees and later partners in the original Artaria firm: Tranquillo Mollo (founded in 1798) and Giovanni Cappi (1800).[15] Other Viennese publishers were the firms of F.A. Hofmeister (1784) and Carlo and Pietro Mechetti (1798). In 1801, the Kunst und Industrie Comptoir (Bureau d'Arts et d'Industrie) opened for business and published numerous first editions of Beethoven. Their firm, however, was relatively shortlived and eventually taken over by S.A. Steiner. After 1820 Steiner's firm, along with that of Anton Diabelli, emerged as the most important of the Viennese publishers. They were, in turn, followed by S.A. Spina (Diabelli's successor) and Tobias Haslinger (Steiner's successor) in the 1830s.[16] Many of Haslinger's reprints of the original Steiner editions of Beethoven's piano sonatas are found in the Bachmann Collection. In Leipzig after 1820, H.A. Probst (1823) and Bartholf Senff (1844) became notable firms along with the great Breitkopf. Leipzig eventually overshadowed Vienna and became the center of music publishing in Germany during the time of Schumann, Mendelssohn, and Liszt.

[13] Poole, "Printing and Publishing of Music," 15:265.

[14] Ibid., p. 267.

[15] Alexander Weinmann, "Tranquillo Mollo," *The New Grove Dictionary of Music and Musicians*, ed. Stanley Sadie (London: Macmillan, 1980), 12:471.

[16] Poole, "Printing and Publishing of Music," p. 269.

Other firms represented by editions contained in the Bachmann Collection and deserving mention are A.M. Schlesinger (1810) and Bote & Bock (1838), both of Berlin. Two Swiss firms, Hans-Georg Nägeli in Zurich (1791) and Rieter-Biedermann in Winterthur (1849), are also represented by publications of Beethoven and Brahms. The edition of J.S. Bach's *Clavier Sonaten mit Obligater Violine* contained in the Bachmann Collection, published by Nägeli in 1804, provides an excellent example of the older "hand engraved" edition. The notes, ledger lines, and musical symbols are highly irregular in shape, and the spacing between notes changes noticeably from measure to measure.

The firm of Artaria and Company, with its offshoot companies of Giovanni Cappi and Tranquillo Mollo, was the most important publisher of Beethoven's early works, and the Kunst und Industrie Comptoir and the firm of Breitkopf and Härtel became the dominant publishers of his middle period works. With the exception of the firms of Steiner and Schlesinger, which published many of the important works of Beethoven's late period, the composer's later works were published by a greater number of publishers than in the preceding early and middle periods. As his fame and notoriety increased throughout the course of his career, demonstrated by the great number of publishing firms that clamored for his compositions, Beethoven did not need to rely upon the largest and most established firms for publication but was free to seek the highest bidder for each work.[17] Beethoven relied exclusively on Viennese publishers for the first publications of his early period, although reprints of his works did appear elsewhere during this time. Because of the close connection between Viennese and Leipzig publishers, some of whom had branches in both cities, works which first appeared in Vienna were soon published in Leipzig as well.[18] As early as 1801 Hofmeister began the practice of simultaneously publishing editions in both cities, a practice which Beethoven turned to his advantage in his later years.[19] As his fame as a composer grew, his works also began to appear with increasing frequency in England, France, and Italy.

In his later period, Beethoven tended to have new works published by foreign firms. This preference can be explained in part by his desire to appeal to a more international audience. Evidence indicates, however, that his practice of dealing with several publishers at once for the publication of a given work, which culminated in the scandalous episode over the publication of the *Missa Solemnis* in 1821, lessened his credibility among the

[17] See Beethoven's letter to Breitkopf and Härtel in *Beethoven's Letters*, trans. J.S. Shedlock (London: J. M. Dent & Sons, 1926), p. 41.

[18] Alexander Thayer, *Life of Beethoven*, ed. Elliott Forbes (Princeton: Princeton University Press, 1964), p. 264.

[19] Alexander Weinmann, "Hofmeister, Franz Anton," *The New Grove Dictionary of Music and Musicians*, ed. Stanley Sadie (London: Macmillan, 1980), 8:628–30.

First page of Sonata no. 4 from J.S. Bach's *Clavier Sonaten mit Obligater Violine*, a hand-engraved edition published in Zurich by Hans-Georg Nägeli, 1804. *HRC Collections*.

important German firms of Steiner, Artaria, Peters, and Simrock.[20] Because of this incident, in which Beethoven promised the work to each one of these publishers and even went so far as to receive payment from Simrock without delivering the work, Beethoven's future relations with these firms was seriously damaged. Additionally, in his later years Beethoven owed a sizable financial debt to Artaria and Steiner. His income had diminished as a result of the limited compositional output of his last few years, and pension payments from princely admirers had fallen off, so he was compelled to borrow substantial sums totaling more than 4,000 florins from these two firms. This debt has also been suggested as providing a further incentive on his part to seek other publishers who would pay "hard cash" for his works instead of merely reducing the size of his debt, as was the procedure with Artaria and Steiner.[21]

Although this conduct on the part of Beethoven toward the German publishing firms may account for his preference in later years for foreign publishers, the shift in his choice of publishers that occurred between his early and middle period publications was caused by events which took place in 1801–02. It was during these two years that Beethoven had his last significant dealings with Artaria and Mollo, the firms which dominated his early period publications, because of an incident concerning the publication of Beethoven's Violin Quintet in C Major (op. 29), a composition which he had sold to Breitkopf and Härtel to be published in Leipzig. The manuscript, which had been lent to Count Moritz von Fries, was stolen by Artaria and published simultaneously in Vienna by Artaria and Mollo without Beethoven's knowledge or consent.[22] Beethoven ultimately forced a retraction of this edition as well as a public apology from Artaria, although this did not repair the damage done to their relationship. It was not until 1806 that Artaria published another original Beethoven edition. By this time Beethoven's relationship with the Leipzig firms and the Kunst und Industrie Comptoir in Vienna had been well established; consequently, Artaria never regained the dominance which it had exercised over the publication of the composer's early works.

Although first and early editions of Beethoven's music are known to contain numerous errors, as evidenced by comparisons with existing manuscripts and letters written by Beethoven himself on this subject,[23] these editions are the primary source for such authoritative editions as the Henle Verlag Urtext of 1974.[24] For example, since the manuscript for Beet-

---

[20] Thayer, pp. 787–95.

[21] Ibid., p. 795.

[22] Ibid., pp. 310–11.

[23] See Beethoven's letter to Steiner & Co. in *Beethoven's Letters*, trans. J.S. Shedlock, pp. 207–208. Also, his letter to Breitkopf & Härtel, pp. 169–72.

[24] Ludwig van Beethoven, *Sonaten für Klavier und Violine*, 2 vols., ed. Siegherd Brandenburg (Munchen: G. Henle Verlag, 1974).

hoven's First Sonata for Violin and Piano (op. 12, no. 1) has not survived, the Henle Verlag edition was based on the original edition by Artaria, published in 1799. The HRC's Bachmann Collection contains the second edition of this sonata, which was published by Breitkopf and Härtel in 1818.[25] A comparison of this edition with the Henle Verlag shows that the first movements found in these two editions are identical, with the exception of phrasing discrepancies in measures 9–12, measure 42, measures 81–82, and their corresponding measures in the recapitulation. Additionally, the Breitkopf and Härtel edition uses the older symbols for the separation and accentuation of notes (i.e., wedges and *Einschnitts*).[26]

This First Sonata for Violin and Piano by Beethoven has suffered severe neglect in the sizable amount of literature that has been written about his music. In the few studies which deal with the violin and piano sonatas, the great portion of writing is devoted to only a few of the more popular sonatas, such as the Kreutzer (op. 47), the Spring (op. 24), and the C Minor Sonata (op. 30, no. 2).[27] The opus 12, no. 1 sonata is given no more than a brief paragraph or two and remains virtually eclipsed by these larger works. This situation is due partly to the fact that many musicians consider the earlier sonatas to have less musical and esthetic significance than the later ones. Also, the opus 12, no. 1 is less well known because of a lack of historical references to its composition and the circumstances surrounding its first performance.

Written probably in the years 1797–1798, the sonata was composed in Vienna, where Beethoven had moved from his native city of Bonn.[28] In Vienna he studied with several renowned teachers: Haydn, Albrechtsberger, and Salieri. The opus 12 sonatas were dedicated to Salieri and their publication announced in the *Wiener Zeitung* on 12 January 1799.[29] However, there seems to be an earlier mention of these sonatas in a program which has been preserved in the archives of the Gesellschaft der Musikfreunde. This program announces that "a sonata with accompaniment is to be played by Beethoven."[30] The concert to which this announcement refers took place on 29 March 1798 and was a benefit for the singer Josefa Duschek. Anton Schuppanzigh, a violinist and close friend of Beethoven, participated in this concert, and because of this it is assumed that the sonata played that

---

[25] Ludwig van Beethoven, *Trois Sonates pour le Pianoforte avec accompagnement de Violon obligé, Op. 12* (Leipzig: Breitkopf and Härtel, 1818).

[26] Willi Apel, *Harvard Dictionary of Music*, 2nd ed. (Cambridge: Belknap Press of Harvard University, 1970), p. 806.

[27] Examples include S. Midgley's *Handbook to Beethoven's Sonatas for Violin and Pianoforte* (London: Breitkopf, 1911) and Joseph Szigeti's *The Ten Beethoven Sonatas for Violin and Piano* (Urbana, Ill.: American String Teachers Assn., 1965).

[28] Thayer, pp. 214–15.

[29] Ibid.

[30] Ibid., p. 204.

evening was a violin sonata. Since this concert took place not in a small salon but in a public concert hall, it can be further conjectured that the work performed was the first of the opus 12 sonatas because of its overtly virtuosic and extroverted character.[31] This sonata was much better suited for playing in a large concert hall than in the small, intimate surroundings of the salon.

The critical reception of the opus 12 sonatas is expressed in a review found in the *Allgemeine Musikalische Zeitung* in 1799. In it, the critic reflected on the great difficulty of the works, which caused him to feel

> like a man who expected to take a stroll through an inviting wood with a congenial friend, but who found instead only hostile entanglements, and finally emerged from the thicket exhausted and disheartened.[32]

He goes on to say that

> Undeniably Herr van Beethoven is going his own way, but what an eccentric, tortuous way it is! Intellect, intellect, and more intellect, but without nature, without song! Indeed, there is nothing in the music but a mass of learning without even a good method of conveying it. It is dry and uninteresting, a forced attempt at strange modulations, an aversion to the conventional relationships, a piling up of difficulty upon difficulty until one finally becomes impatient and loses all pleasure in the task.

The critic seems to be reacting to a certain aspect of Beethoven's compositional style which was as evident in his early works as in his later—his capacity for developing the inherent possibilities of his motivic material at what was often considered the expense of the singing melodic style that was popular at the time. This tendency appeared forced and unnatural to a musical public whose tastes had not yet made the transition from an essentially "rococo" conception of art, which stressed the qualities of elegance and suave expressiveness, to the coming "romantic" style.

Changes in editorial taste that have occurred in various editions of op. 12, no. 1 since its original publication in 1799 can be observed by comparing the Breitkopf and Härtel edition in the Bachmann Collection with two "modern" printings of this work: the Augener edition (1911)[33] and the Schirmer edition

[31] Ibid.

[32] Anton Schindler, *Beethoven As I Knew Him* (Raleigh: North Carolina State University Press, 1966), p. 77.

[33] Ludwig van Beethoven, *Beethoven Violin Sonatas*, ed. Fritz Kreisler (London: Augener, 1911).

Page of Beethoven's First Sonata for Violin and Piano (op. 12, no. 1), published by Breitkopf and Härtel, 1818. *HRC Collections.*

(1973).[34] The greatest differences between the Breitkopf and Härtel edition and the two modern ones are in the area of phrasing. As noted earlier, discrepancies between the Breitkopf and Härtel edition and the original Artaria edition occur also in the area of phrasing, but these are limited to some half-dozen measures. The modern editions, however, reveal discrepancies which are far more pervasive and more at variance with the original edition.

The late eighteenth century showed a marked preference for short phrases, as opposed to the longer phrases which became more characteristic of the nineteenth century. The longer phrases which do occur in the late eighteenth century are almost never indicated by long phrase marks. They are composed of a series of highly articulated and compact one- or two-bar motivic units juxtaposed in such a way as to create a symmetrically balanced longer phrase. As Charles Rosen has suggested in his book *The Classical Style*, the phrase syntax of the period in which Beethoven composed the op. 12, no. 1 was one in which the unity and balance of the longer periodic phrase was achieved through the use of an ingenious variety of shorter phrases which served as building blocks for the overall phrase structure.[35]

The opening theme of the first movement of op. 12, no. 1 provides an excellent example of a longer phrase which has been built out of a series of highly differentiated shorter ones. The opening twelve-bar phrase is made up of no less than four short and highly contrasting phrases, each having its own distinct motivic material and character. This opening phrase begins with a bombastic chord, followed by two measures of trumpetlike arpeggios, then proceeds with a long, flowing melodic figure which ends with a short, staccatolike cadence. As contrasting as these motives and textures are, they are still linked in such a way as to comprise a unified musical phrase—a unity achieved in spite of the diversity of the individual parts. Both the Augener and Schirmer editions reflect the modern inclination toward highlighting the longer phrase by placing less emphasis on the visual articulation of the shorter phrases; i.e., by the use of slurs. In the Breitkopf and Härtel edition, measures 5 through 13 show slur marks over two bars, a slur over the next two bars, then a slur over three bars, followed by two short slurs over beats 1 and 2 and 3 and 4 of the last measure of the phrase. Expressed numerically, the pattern is 2-2-3-½-½. This particular phrasing scheme does justice to the diversity inherent in the smaller units, which comprise the larger periodic phrase of the opening theme, and thus highlights these smaller units so that they stand out in musical relief. In the Augener edition, however, these short phrases are obscured by placing a

[34] Ludwig van Beethoven, *Violin Sonatas*, ed. Adolph Brodsky and Max Vogrich (New York: G. Schirmer, 1973).

[35] Charles Rosen, *The Classical Style* (New York: W. W. Norton & Co., 1972), p. 147.

long slur over six bars (1-6-½-½), and in the Schirmer edition the short phrases are dispensed with altogether by placing a long slur over the entire eight measures. Additionally, there are instances in both the Augener and Schirmer editions where the editors have chosen to carry a slur across the bar-line (i.e., measures 166–67), a practice almost unknown in Beethoven's early works.

Aside from differences in phrasing and dynamics found between the Breitkopf and Härtel and the Augener and Schirmer editions, there are other distinguishing characteristics: the addition of fingerings, bowings, and harmonics in both of the two modern editions, some of which are highly romanticized and therefore questionable within the context of the classical style; indications concerning the use of the pedal in the Schirmer edition; and an error in pitch which occurs in both the Augener and Schirmer editions (violin, m. 205). The deviations which occur between the Breitkopf and Härtel edition and the two modern editions are entirely editorial and cannot be attributed to errors in copying. In general, the deviations found in these editions can be viewed as reflecting the personal tastes of the editors and their attempt to bring an earlier musical style into conformity with contemporary performance practices. By comparing modern editions with early ones, such as the Breitkopf and Härtel edition of the op. 12, no. 1 and the many others like it in the Edwin Bachmann Collection, performers and scholars alike will gain important insights into the musical style of the eighteenth and early nineteenth centuries.

Alfred Cortot, n.d. Photograph © Karsh, Ottawa.

Sacred Vocal Music from the Collection of Alfred Cortot

BY DELL HOLLINGSWORTH

Alfred Cortot (1877–1962) is best known today as one of the great interpreters of romantic music. As a conductor, he was a leading figure in French musical life when he was not yet thirty, conducting many of the first performances in France of works by Wagner, Beethoven, Brahms, and contemporaries such as Chausson and Roussel. As a pianist and editor, Cortot left behind a legacy of exquisite recordings and study editions of Chopin, Schumann, and others which reveal his intimate understanding of their styles. He published four books between 1928 and 1949: two on aspects of piano technique and interpretation, one on Chopin, and a three-volume work on modern French piano music, which he championed both in writing and in performance. As a teacher—first at the Paris Conservatoire and later at the École Normale de Musique, which he founded—Cortot influenced and encouraged countless young musicians, and his classes became legendary. Cortot the collector is less known, though indeed he was "the last of the great music collectors whose libraries aimed, within certain limits, at universality in their representation of music and musical history, and who could achieve their aim to a remarkable degree, thanks to the conjunction of availability of the material and the means to acquire it."[1] The only professional musician among the notable twentieth-century music collectors,[2] Cortot was a firm believer in the need for basing interpretive ideas on a familiarity with original sources. He himself organized and catalogued his vast music library, classifying the music and the books on music into twenty-three different categories.[3]

---

[1] Albi Rosenthal, "Alfred Cortot as Collector of Music," *Music and Bibliography* (New York: K. G. Saur, 1980), p. 212.

[2] Ibid., p. 210.

[3] These main categories are: Théorie musicale, Esthétique musicale, Histoire de musique, Méthodes, Histoire des instruments, Bibliographie musicale, Dictionnaires, Catalogues, Périodiques, Biographie, Mémoires & correspondances, Ouvrages relatifs à la musique, Notation, Musique instrumentale antérieure à 1800, Musique vocale religieuse, Liturgie, Musique vocale profane, Folklore, Musique dramatique, Danse, Interprétation, Facsimilés, and Iconographie. Cortot's catalogue of the theoretical works in his library was published under the title *Bibliothèque Alfred Cortot: Première partie: Traités et autres ouvrages théoriques* (Paris: R. Coulouma, 1936).

After Cortot's death, the major portion of his library was acquired by the London firm of Otto Haas. From there, part of the collection went to the British Museum, the University of California at Berkeley, the Newberry Library in Chicago, and the University of Kentucky.[4] In 1980 the Humanities Research Center acquired parts of the categories designated as "Musique vocale religieuse" and "Liturgie," which had not been offered for sale before that time and which comprise eighty-two items illustrating various facets of the development of European sacred music. The majority of the items were published in France, but England, Italy, Germany, Belgium, the Netherlands, Switzerland, and Spain are also represented. The works range in date from the sixteenth to the nineteenth centuries, with two twentieth-century imprints being facsimiles of earlier items. The music itself is of course of great interest to musicians and musical scholars, showing as it does the dissemination of certain types of music and the continuity or the changing of styles and practices. But the collection contains an important body of additional information—in the form of prefaces and introductory matter—on performance practices, educational practices, and social conditions during four centuries of European history. The collection also sheds light on the development of music printing and publishing. Although related items held by the HRC will be mentioned here, this is meant as no more than an introduction to the Center's holdings in vocal literature. As an aid to interested scholars and students, a short-title list of the Cortot Collection follows at the end of the article.

The group of psalm books and hymnals in the vernacular, which makes up a sizeable portion of the collection, illuminates a significant chapter in the history of Protestant church music, along with the Catholic reaction to it. Beginning with a limited edition facsimile of the famous "Constance Songbook" of 1540, the *Nüw Gsangbüchle von vil schönen Psalmen und geistlichen Liedern,* many of the major developments in Reformed church music are represented. The *Nüw Gsangbüchle,* commissioned by the Swiss city of Constance and compiled by Ambrosius Blaurer and Johannes Zwick, was an important catalyst in the spread of congregational singing throughout northern Switzerland, where it was eventually to become a national pastime. Despite the efforts of the Swiss reformer Ulrich Zwingli to do away with all music in the service, congregational singing continued to grow in popularity, largely because of Johannes Zwick's preface to the Constance Songbook, which was "the most important defense of singing at the service in southwest Germany during the century of the Reformation" and "offered a challenge to Zwingli's musical views, carefully thought out and nobly formulated."[5] The

[4] See articles in *The British Museum Quarterly* 1, nos. 1-2 (1966) and *University of Kentucky Library Notes* 1, no. 3.

[5] Walter Blankenburg, "Church Music in Reformed Europe," in Friedrich Blume, *Protestant Church Music* (New York: Norton, 1974), p. 562.

music consists of unaccompanied melodies taken from both secular songs and older sacred sources such as Gregorian chant, for there was a tendency from the very beginning of the Reformation to sing the new vernacular psalms and hymns to familiar tunes.

Zwingli's counterpart in French-speaking Switzerland and France, John Calvin, was a little less strict with regard to music in the service: he allowed congregational psalm singing, unaccompanied and in unison. His steps toward creating a complete rhyming psalter culminated in 1562 with the publication by Antoine Vincent of what is generally known as the Genevan Psalter. The result of one of the most ambitious publishing ventures of all time, this psalter was brought out simultaneously in Geneva, Paris, Lyons, and a number of other cities by a total of fifteen printers. The first complete collection containing all 150 psalms, it quite literally took Europe by storm. Within three years there were no fewer than sixty-three editions, an event unparalleled in the history of Protestant hymnals.[6] Although the Genevan Psalter was the exclusive official hymnbook among French Reformed congregations, its use was not limited to this group: everyone loved singing these psalms, Catholics and Protestants alike, in churches, in homes, at court, and at school. In *Protestant Church Music*, Walter Blankenburg states that "never again, at any time or place in the history of Protestant hymnals based on Calvin's principles, would there be a treasury of poems and songs, of sheer ecumenical significance, equal to the Genevan Psalter in unity, durability, and, eventually, wide dissemination."[7] The texts were translated by Clément Marot and Théodore de Bèze, and the melodies were created and assembled by a variety of composers from various sacred and secular sources. Rhythmically and melodically simple but lovely and lyrical, these melodies were more accessible than the heavier Lutheran tunes, and they still charm the ear today as they did in the sixteenth century.

The Cortot Collection includes two of the "simultaneous first editions" of 1562, both of which contain Calvin's preface of 1543 and his *La Forme des Prières Ecclésiastiques*. There are also editions of 1611, 1656 (with an added title page dated 1661), 1684, and 1722. (Outside the Cortot Collection, the HRC also holds a 1675 edition.) The 1722 edition—in French but published in London—has added under each melody a bass line adapted from the four- and five-part settings of the composers Goudimel and Le Jeune. The preface explains that this work was produced under the auspices of the Society of Protestant Refugees in London, and it discusses the performance of psalms in church and at home.

Despite the strict limitation of Calvinist service music to unaccompanied unison singing, a number of polyphonic psalm arrangements were created,

---

[6] Ibid., p. 519.
[7] Ibid., p. 530.

Page from *Les Pseaumes de David*, 1611. *HRC Collections*. An example of the printer's stock border, with its strange Bosch-like figures.

some based on the original Genevan tunes, others not. These polyphonic settings were provided by Protestant composers for the use of their congregations outside the service—for singing and playing at home and for other occasions—and also by Catholic composers for use within and outside of their services. Claude Le Jeune, one of the most important and influential arrangers of the Genevan Psalter, published a number of polyphonic settings in different styles. His four- and five-part arrangements of the complete psalter, first published in Paris in 1601, comprised "the most widely disseminated polyphonic arrangement of the Huguenot Psalter after the one by Goudimel of 1565."[8] These settings are based on the original melodies, which often appear in the tenor voice.

One of the most impressive items in the Cortot Collection is a 1627 Geneva edition of Le Jeune's 1601 psalm arrangements. It is made up of five part books bound together in a later (probably nineteenth-century) binding. Since music in parts was most often published not in score but in separate part books, which easily become separated over time, it is rare to find complete copies of sixteenth- and early seventeenth-century music. Aside from lacking the first eight pages of the tenor part, which have been replaced in manuscript, the Cortot copy is in excellent condition. Preceding each part book is a leaf of contemporary manuscript music, entitled "Fugue à l'unisson après deux tens—Canon à cinq." Each title page is inscribed "J. R. Clerici" (could this perhaps be the composer Giovanni Clerici, and might the "Canon à cinq" be his?). Included in the fifth part book is a set of psalms "à cinq et à six parties . . . nouvellement adjoustez aux douze de Claudin Le Jeune par Jean Le Grand."

The Catholics could not remain indifferent to the tremendous success of the Protestant psalter. The Abbé Philippe Desportes created a new paraphrase of the psalms intended to counterbalance the success of the Genevan Psalter. In the Cortot Collection there are two settings of this translation, one to unaccompanied melodies by Denis Caignet, published in 1624, and another in four and five parts by Signac, published in 1630. Although Signac did not use the traditional melodies, his style was inspired by that of the Protestants.[9] Antoine Godeau, bishop of Grasse and Vence, also translated the psalms anew to help offset the popularity of the Protestant version. The first published setting of his texts was the four-voice version by the Catholic composer Jacques de Gouy. This printing contains only the first fifty psalms, and although Gouy had the remaining 100 ready for publication, he was not allowed to publish them, since his first efforts were held to be too difficult and too far from Godeau's intentions (as one can read in the

[8] Blankenburg, *Protestant Church Music*, p. 541.
[9] Édith Weber, *La Musique protestante de langue française* (Paris: H. Champion, 1979), p. 110.

publisher's preface to the setting by Aux-Cousteaux, discussed below). This set of part books, first published in Paris in 1650, is Gouy's only surviving publication. The Cortot Collection contains the "Taille" (tenor) part book of this edition, which bears the bookplate of Thomas Bever, LL. D. (1725-1791), English judge, professor of law, and amateur musician.

Artus Aux-Cousteaux, director of music at Sainte-Chapelle in Paris, succeeded in "coming a little closer" to Godeau's desire "to have the psalms on everyone's lips, after the example of those who are separated from the church," by returning to simple unaccompanied tunes.[10] Pierre Le Petit, the publisher of Aux-Cousteaux's *Paraphrase des pseaumes de David*, goes on to say in his preface that Thomas Gobert, director of music for the King's chapel, assisted with this edition, modifying some of the settings. Three years later, in 1659, Le Petit asked Gobert to make a new setting of the texts, and the publisher wrote in his preface to this new work that Aux-Cousteaux's version "did not have all the grace desired for such admirable verses." Le Petit had asked Gobert to set the psalms for two voices in simple counterpoint, thereby realizing completely Godeau's wishes for a harmonized version easy enough for those with a limited knowledge of music. Along with suggestions for performance, Le Petit makes it clear that the upper part (Dessus) could be sung either alone or with the bass part. In addition to a Dessus part book of the Gobert setting, the HRC's Cortot Collection contains a setting of Godeau's texts by the Protestant Antoine Lardenois, a member of the Reformed Church of Nîmes. The Cortot copy is a second edition (1658); outside the Cortot Collection, the HRC also holds the first edition of 1655. Lardenois's setting is monophonic and his melodies derive from the Genevan tunes. The settings by Gobert, Aux-Cousteaux, and Lardenois all contain Godeau's lengthy preface explaining his views on the psalms, on his work and sources, on the function of music, and his opinion of Desportes's paraphrases.

Toward the end of the seventeenth century, Protestants in French-speaking territories began to tire of the sixteenth-century psalm translations, and a new version of the Genevan Psalter was generally accepted in 1679. Although this new psalter featured texts revised by Valentin Conrart, it retained the original unaccompanied tunes, which were still as popular as ever.[11] The original tunes are present as well in the two most recent French psalters in the Cortot Collection: an edition of 1803 and one of 1837. However, both have new texts; a special note in the 1803 edition states that the texts have been "reviewed and approved by the pastors and professors of the church and of the Academy of Geneva." Both editions contain hymns as

---

[10] Artus Aux-Cousteaux, *Paraphrase des pseaumes de David*, 4th ed. (Paris: Pierre Le Petit, 1656), from the preface by Pierre Le Petit. All translations from works in the Cortot Collection are my own.

[11] Weber, *La Musique protestante*, p. 57.

well as psalms, which was the result of a relaxation of restrictions regarding service music.

Two other French Calvinists are represented in the Cortot Collection by rare and interesting items. There is an original 1564 edition of Pierre de Courcelles's rendering in French verse of Solomon's Song of Songs and the Lamentations of Jeremiah. An exquisitely printed little volume, it is dedicated to Louis de Bourbon, Prince de Condè, one of the most valiant leaders of the Calvinist movement. The volume also includes a double sonnet to Courcelles by Théodore de Bèze. The musical settings are monophonic. Louis Des Masures, secretary to the cardinal of Lorraine, published his *Tragédies sainctes* in Geneva in 1566. The Cortot copy is an edition of 1583 which includes the tragedy *Josias* (published under the pseudonym "Philone") and the *Bergerie spirituelle* and *Eclogue spirituelle*, plays which had been published separately from the 1566 edition.[12] According to Albi Rosenthal, this work is "of great rarity and significance as one of the earliest publications of plays on Old Testament subjects with music."[13] The settings are in four parts, in choir-book format.

In the Netherlands, where the Genevan Psalter had been translated into Dutch in 1568, the Reformed churches did not officially introduce a new edition until 1773. This version comprised selections from various translations, and remained in use until 1949. The Cortot copy of *Het Boek der Psalmen* is the 1777 edition and includes the 1773 "Acte van Consent" and "Verklaaring." In addition to the monophonic psalm melodies, there are four four-part psalm settings (arranged in table-book format), twelve four-part canons, and a section of monophonic songs. The catechism is bound in at the end. A notable feature is the inclusion of solfa letters beside the notes of each first verse.

In Germany, the Genevan Psalter had been translated by Ambrosius Lobwasser, a Lutheran law professor in Königsberg. First published probably in 1572,[14] Lobwasser's version became popular among German-speaking congregations. Some editions of this translation retained the Genevan tunes in their unaccompanied form, while others adopted the homophonic settings of Goudimel. The Cortot Collection includes a 1683 monophonic edition of the Lobwasser psalter, and bound with it is the *Neu vermehrtes volständiges Gesangbuch*—containing songs by Martin Luther and others—which is without music, followed by the catechism. Outside the Cortot Collection, the HRC holds two other monophonic editions of the

[12] J.-C. Brunet, *Manuel du libraire*, 5th ed., vol. 2 (Paris: Dorbon-Aîné, n.d.), columns 636-37.

[13] See the short-title catalogue compiled by Albi Rosenthal (of Otto Haas) to accompany the HRC's Cortot Collection.

[14] Blankenburg, *Protestant Church Music*, p. 549.

Lobwasser psalter, one published in 1595 by Christof Raben, and the other published by Christoph Saur in Germantown, Pennsylvania, in 1772.[15]

The Lobwasser psalter found its strongest competitor in the Latin psalm translations by the Scottish scholar George Buchanan. This psalter was first published in 1585 by Nathan Chytraeus, with simple four-part settings composed and arranged by Statius Olthof. Widely used in the Protestant Latin schools that proliferated during the period of the Counter-Reformation, Buchanan's psalter constituted "Lutheranism's conscious self-defense against the infiltration of Calvinist ideas."[16] The Cortot copy of this work was published in London in 1648.

In England in 1636, George Sandys, son of the archbishop of York, published his own psalm paraphrases, which in 1638 were set to music in two parts by Henry Lawes. The Cortot Collection contains the 1676 edition, "carefully revised and corrected from many errors which passed in former impressions, by John Playford." In its other collections the HRC holds the first edition of 1638 and the second edition of 1648. Sandys's version of the psalms was one of several new, freer translations that sought to replace the old Sternhold and Hopkins version of 1562, and Lawes's setting "is somewhat outside the mainstream. The metres of Sandys's version are various and subtle: the tunes, all new, lack popular characteristics and seem designed for solo singing."[17] The Cortot Collection contains three other, perhaps more typical, representatives of English psalmody. Holdroyd's *Spiritual Man's Companion* (fifth edition, 1753) and Gilmour's *Psalm-Singer's Assistant* (second edition, 1793) are representative of eighteenth-century rural parish psalmody, while Knibb's *Psalm Singer's Help* (1770?) is aimed at "the churches and dissenting congregations in London." The latter two are tune-books, with no text, or only key words, included.

Along with the rise of psalm singing in the sixteenth century came the creation, in French-speaking territories, of the *chanson spirituelle,* or *cantique,* a secular song in which the secular text is replaced with moralistic or sometimes scriptural words. If the text was a Christmas text, the song was called a *noël.* Written chiefly at first by Protestant sympathizers, both the *cantique* and the *noël* were soon taken up by Catholics as well, and over the next two centuries were particularly cultivated by the Jesuits. Both monophonic and polyphonic settings were used, and some songbooks contain a mixture of adapted and newly composed music. Sometimes the term *cantique* was also applied to newly composed works more on the order

---

[15] The title of the latter work is *Neu-vermehrt-und vollständiges Gesang-Buch worinnen sowohl die Psalmen Davids, nach D. Ambrosii Lobwassers, uebersetzung hin und wieder verbessert, als auch 730 . . . geistreichen Liedern begriffen sind. . . .*

[16] Friedrich Blume, *Protestant Church Music*, p. 145.

[17] Nicholas Temperley, "Psalms, metrical, III," in *The New Grove Dictionary of Music and Musicians,* vol. 15 (London: Macmillan, 1980), p. 370.

One of the four-voice settings in table-book format from *Het Boek der Psalmen*, 1777. *HRC Collections.* Two parts are printed upside down, so that the book can be read by singers facing each other across a table.

of *petits motets,* with alternating solos, choruses, and instrumental inter-
ludes, such as Pascal Collasse's *Cantiques spirituels.*

As late as 1772, the lengthy and enlightening preface to the *Opuscules
sacrés et lyriques* explains the practice of fitting new, moralistic words to
secular tunes in terms that, surprisingly, echo early Lutheran sentiments:

> We have endeavored to purify and consecrate these tunes, as they
> purified the temples of the idols to consecrate them to the cult of the
> true God. . . . Many people sing *chansons* only because of the
> music which pleases them. We want to engage them to substitute
> pious words for the profane and often dissolute *chansons;* our
> *cantiques* furnish them the occasion. The music will still be the
> same, but its subject ceases to be dangerous. . . . We would surely
> not have succeeded in setting our *cantiques* to new tunes: if people
> had liked them, they would perhaps have sung them sometimes,
> but without abstaining from the *chansons;* we would even have
> been afraid that they would soon have adapted ours.

A very rare item, and one of the loveliest in the Cortot Collection, the
Opuscules sacrés contains—in addition to its informative preface—a thirty-
six-page bibliography of *cantique* and *noël* collections published between
1586 and 1772. Some ninety-five collections from many different publishers
are described and critiqued, and excerpts of the poetry are often included.
The author of the bibliography (perhaps the publisher, Nicolas Crapart) is
admittedly selective, but he includes a great deal of information and his
biting critiques make entertaining reading in themselves. This two-volume
set (four parts in two volumes) is also a fine example of Fournier's
contributions to music printing: an elegant single-impression type, with
round note heads, designed to look as if it had been engraved. The first
edition of the *Opuscules* had been published in 1768, but the Cortot copy
(1772) is an edition "completely redone." The music is mainly for one to four
voices, unaccompanied, although two pieces include basso continuo and, as
the preface mentions, existing accompaniments for some of the pieces have
been excluded. The texts in parts one and two are by Bonaffos de la Tour,
who set them himself to well-known tunes, while the texts in parts three and
four are by Racine, Voltaire, and others, set to music by Clavis, Dupuy, and
Leemans.

A limited edition facsimile of Martin's *Les Noëlz & chansons* (1555)
represents the earliest of the French songbooks of this type in the Cortot
Collection. Notable for being written in the Savoyard dialect, this work
contains both sacred and secular texts, which have been "newly composed
with their melodies by Nicolas Martin, musician."

Another item, the *Recueil de cantiques spirituels* of 1734, contains texts in

Provençal and is intended "for the use of the missions of Provence." Aside from the *Recueil de pseaumes et de cantiques* (1798), which contains four-voice settings, and Macé's *Cantiques spirituels* (second edition, 1648), which are set for two voices, the remaining *cantique* collections proper contain unaccompanied melodies. The Abbé Pellegrin was one of the most enthusiastic of the adapters, setting whole chunks of the Bible to popular tunes and opera airs by Lully and others.

More elaborate, and newly composed, are the dialogues of Claude Oudot (the first and third editions of 1692 and 1722) for treble and bass soloists, three-part chorus, two violins and basso continuo, and the *Cantiques spirituels* (1695) of Collasse, for similar forces. Collasse's *cantiques* were written for and performed at Saint Cyr, the convent school for poor girls of noble birth, founded by Mme. de Maintenon in 1686. The texts, by Racine, were set by several different composers for the girls at Saint Cyr.[18]

Guillaume Nivers, director of music at Saint Cyr, is represented in the Cortot Collection by two chant books, a 1733 edition of his *Chants et motets* and several of the Lamentations of Jeremiah contained in *Chants divers* (1778). *Chants et motets*, a beautifully engraved two-volume set, contains some chant but mostly motets (some of which are by Clérambault). The majority of the motets are for two-part women's chorus, with interspersed solos and duets. The Cortot copy bears what appears to be an eighteenth-century bookplate of the royal house of France.

The various French sacred songbooks had their counterparts in other countries. There are three Dutch songbooks in the Cortot Collection, two of which (those of Theodatus and Neck) contain unaccompanied melodies either taken from other sources or newly composed. The *Zangwijzen van Stichtelijke Gezangen* (ca. 1760), another exceptionally beautiful engraved volume, contains sacred songs for voice and basso continuo, along with several solo cantatas, by Leonard Frischmuth, Johannes Colizzi, and anonymous contributors. The texts are by Rutger Schutte.

According to Walter Blankenburg,

> Most characteristic for the development of polyphonic sacred music in northern Switzerland in the late 17th century, and the 18th, are mainly three-part works, usually for two high voices and a low one [sometimes with figured bass], products of the German lied-style tradition of the 17th century. They were meant principally, if perhaps not exclusively, as religious music for the home and

[18] The Cortot copy, which lacks the title page and a number of internal pages, bears a label identifying it as Moreau's *Cantiques chantez devant le roy*, but it is almost certainly the work by Collasse in the short-title list at the end of this article. I am indebted to Dr. Robert Snow of the University's Department of Music for this information.

became, in the course of time, an important entering wedge for Pietist devotional exercises.[19]

Pietism was a movement among late seventeenth- and early eighteenth-century German-speaking Protestants toward a more intensely personal and emotional display of faith. The songbooks of this type in the Cortot Collection are an 1803 edition of J.C. Bachofen's "distinctly Pietistic" *Musicalisches Halleluja* (first published in 1727)[20] and his settings of B.H. Brockes's *Irdisches Vergnügen in Gott* (a first edition of 1740), and J. Schmidlin's *Singendes und spielendes Vergnügen reiner Andacht* (a first edition of 1752). Bachofen's songs, particularly those in his *Musicalisches Halleluja*, became so popular that in the St. Gall district of Switzerland the term "bachofele" was still used in the nineteenth century to refer to a gathering of singers for rehearsal.[21]

The introduction of organ accompaniment in Protestant churches led to the appearance of a growing number of chorale books (hymnbooks for organists). These at first contained only the melody and figured bass on two staves, perhaps with the other vocal parts on the facing page, as exemplified in Schmidlin's settings of Gellert's *Geistliche Oden und Lieder* (a first edition of 1761). As the practice of figured bass began to die out, this format was replaced by the modern hymn-style format with all four parts on two staves, as represented in the Cortot Collection by Christmann and Knecht's chorale book (a first edition of 1799).

In the Engadine region of Switzerland, religious singing in parts became highly developed among the Reformed congregations. The *Canzuns Spirituaelas*, in the Romantsch language, contains a preponderance of settings for two high voices and a low voice, making it very similar in format to the German-Swiss songbooks. The settings are by "diverse famous authors ancient and modern," revised by several local musicians. G.M. Casini, whose Italian songbook contains unaccompanied tunes and was intended for unison singing by Catholic congregations, "wrote in a highly personal . . . style. The expressive chromaticism and wandering tonality of his motets . . . are found even in his *Canzonette Spirituali* . . .,"[22] of which the Cortot Collection contains a first edition from 1703.

Catholic liturgical books make up the largest group within the Cortot Collection. The majority of these are beautifully printed in red and black, with numerous woodcut initials and vignettes illustrating the text. Among the earliest items are two sixteenth-century Spanish *passionaria*, which contain the passion texts from the four Gospels along with the Lamentations of Jeremiah and various other chants.

---

[19] Blankenburg, *Protestant Church Music*, p. 562.
[20] Ibid.
[21] Peter Ross, "Bachofen, Johann Caspar," in *New Grove*, vol. 1, p. 882.
[22] John W. Hill, "Casini, Giovanni Maria," in *New Grove*, vol. 3, p. 858.

The *Sacerdotale* of 1576 and the *Liber Sacerdotalis* compiled by Albert Castellani in 1537 are early ritual books, predecessors of the modern *Rituale Romanum*. (The Ritual contains all the services a priest needs besides those in the Missal and Breviary.) During this time liturgical books were being revised according to uniform standards, and although the sacerdotals in the Cortot Collection were published without official sanction, they and other books like them were issued in the hope of promoting uniformity.[23]

The impressive *Pontificale Romanum* of 1582 is in its original gold-tooled binding, with the cardinals' device on the covers. The Pontifical is the bishops' book and contains the rites of Confirmation, the coronation of kings and queens, the services for laying foundation stones and consecrating churches, and the myriad other functions a bishop must perform. The *Caerimoniale Episcoporum* (Ceremonial of Bishops) is a book of rubrical directions, many of which are contained in other books such as the Ritual and Pontifical. Despite its title, the Ceremonial has in it much material needed by clerics other than bishops, and it forms an indispensable supplement to the other rubrical books. The version represented in the Cortot Collection by a 1606 edition was first issued (under another imprint) by Clement VIII in 1600. The Cortot edition contains seventy-one large woodcut vignettes.

Another predecessor of the modern Ritual is the *Pastorale*, one of a number of books containing various services (the sacraments, visitation of the sick, burial service, exorcism, etc.) and blessings. The Cortot *Pastorale* (1607) was compiled in 1588 by Joannes Hauchinus, archbishop of Mechlin, and later revised and enlarged by Matthias Hovius, who was archibishop by the time of its publication, for use in the archdiocese of Mechlin.

The *Directorium Chori* gives or indicates all the music of the chants (except for the responsories after the Lessons), the tones of the psalms, the "Te Deum" and Litanies, etc. The Cortot *Cantorinus* of 1566 is of this type and includes a twelve-page introduction to the singing of plainchant. The *Directorium Chori* of Giovanni Guidetto, chaplain to Pope Gregory XIII, is an eighteenth-century edition of his most important chant manual, published originally in Rome in 1582. Guidetto's manuals are the most complete and authoritative from the period following the Council of Trent. His *Directorium Chori* provides a standardized church calendar and plainsóng formulae based on older traditions, although he did advocate rhythmically differentiated notation.[24]

Other early items are the *Chantepleure d'eaue vive*—a book of excerpts of chant from the Office, of Bible passages, and of homilies of Saint Gregory, compiled by Johannis Coignet—the *Psalmi et Hymni Ecclesiastici*, and Sergius's *Libellus Omnes Psalmos*. The latter two, very rare items, have been

---

[23] Adrian Fortescue, "Ritual," in *The Catholic Encyclopedia*, vol. 13 (New York: Encyclopedia Press, 1913), p. 89.

[24] Lewis Lockwood, "Guidetti, Giovanni Domenico," in *New Grove*, vol. 7, p. 802.

printed with blank staves so that clerics in different localities could add in manuscript the chants peculiar to their services. Sergius's book has very little chant added, but bound with it is a *Brevia Gregoriani sive Choralis* in which the chant has been added throughout. The *Psalmi et Hymni* is a special copy in a lovely original binding with metal clasps. Much of the chant has been added, and full-page engravings have been inserted, their versos bearing versicles and responses in a beautiful contemporary hand; there are, in addition, fourteen pages of manuscript chant and text bound in at the end.

The various chants needed for the Mass and for the Divine Office are provided by different books. The Antiphonary, represented in the Cortot Collection by the *Antiphonarium* printed in Paris in 1660, contains all the antiphons, hymns, and responses for the Office; that is, the entire musical service other than the Mass. That part of the Mass which is sung by the choir is contained in the Gradual. In the Cortot Collection are three Graduals: one, printed in 1674, was intended for the use of the Carthusian Order; the other two are eighteenth-century Graduals, one of which was for the use of the diocese of Clermont-Ferrand. The last section of the Gradual, containing the chants for the Ordinary of the Mass and known as the Kyriale, was (and still is) often printed separately. The *Cantus Diversi* of 1675 is an example of such an independent volume. The seventeenth-century *Missae Novae* contains supplements to the Missal of newly approved Ordinaries not restricted to one particular place or order.

There are five processionals in the Cortot Collection, all from the eighteenth century. The Processional is the book containing the chants, rubrics, and prayers appropriate to liturgical processions. The material is taken out of the Ritual, Missal, and Pontifical, and is put together in one place for convenience. Processionals were often adapted for particular local uses, and indeed, three of the Cortot processionals are for particular orders: one is Dominican—for the use of the Couvent de St. Jacques in Paris, one Carmelite, and another, bound with Hermann Mott's *Musices Choralis Medulla*, was intended for the novices of the Franciscan Recollets in the province of Cologne. All three are beautifully engraved.

The late seventeenth century in France saw a surge of interest in both the new composition of plainsong and the adaptation of existing melodies to accord with contemporary views. Guillaume Nivers was one of several composers who sought to breathe new life into the ancient chants, and his very rare and important *Passiones Domini N.I.C.* (represented in the Cortot Collection by a first edition from 1683) helped to lay the foundation for this evolution.[25] In the process of accommodating the chants to the taste of the day, these composers utlimately distorted them—sometimes beyond recognition—by admitting chromatic alterations, mensural values, and embel-

[25] Karl Fellerer, "Der Cantus Gregorianus im 17. Jahrhundert," *Geschichte der katholischen Kirchenmusik*, vol. 2 (Kassel: Barenreiter, 1976), p. 120.

LECTIO III. *Iob* 10.

Manus tue Domine fecerunt me / et plasmaue-
runt me totum in circuitu / et sic repente pre-
cipitas me ﹖ Memento / queso / quod sicut lutum fe-
ceris me / et in puluerem reduces me. Nonne sicut lac
mulsisti me / et sicut caseum me coagulasti ﹖ Pelle
et carnibus vestisti me / ossibus et neruis compegisti
me. Uitam / et misericordiam tribuisti mihi / et vi-
sitatio tua custodiuit spiritum meum.

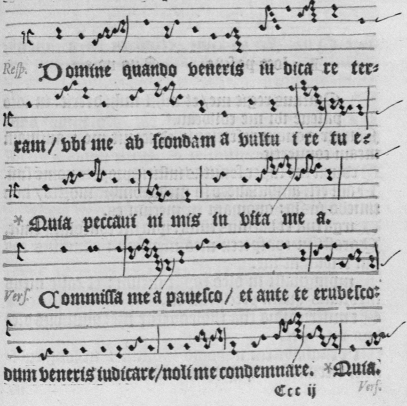

Resp. Domine quando veneris iu dica re ter-

ram / vbi me ab scondam a vultu i re tu e-

* Quia peccaui ni mis in vita me a.

Vers. Commissa me a pauesco / et ante te erubesco﹖

dum veneris iudicare / noli me condemnare. *Quia.

Page from *Psalmi et Hymni Ecclesiastici*, 1609. *HRC Collections.* The text was printed; the musical notation has been added in manuscript.

Dominus, & Rex magnus super
omnes Deos : quoniam non
repellet Dominus plebem su-
am quia in manu ejus sunt omnes fines terræ, & altitu-
dines montium ipse con-
spicit.

Quoniam ipsius est ma-
re, & ipse fecit illud, & a-
ridam fundaverunt manus e-
jus : venite adoremus, &
procidamus ante Deum : plo-
remus coram Domino qui fecit
nos, quia ipse est Dominus De-
us noster : nos autem po-pu-
lus ejus & oves pascuæ
ejus.

Hodie si vocem ejus
audieritis, nolite obdurare
corda vestra, sicut in exacer-
batione secundum diem ten-
tationis in deserto : ubi tenta-
verunt me patres vestri, pro-
baverunt & viderunt o-
pera mea.

Quadraginta annis proxi-
mus fui generationi huic,
& dixi, semper hi errant cor-
de : ipsi vero non cognove-
runt vias meas, quibus jura vi
in ira mea, si introi-
bunt in requiem meam.

Gloria Patri, & Filio:

Page from Demotz de la Salle's *Bréviaire Romain*, 1727, showing his system of chant notation. *HRC Collections.*

lishments. On the other hand, their devotion helped to keep the chant alive in France into the eighteenth century. A processional by Nivers is one of the five mentioned above; some of his chants are also included in the *Chants divers* of 1778, along with those of other composers such as Chabert. Santeul's *Hymni sacri* (1698) contains some plainsong hymns by Dumont, Le Bègue, and others from the same circle. Plainsong masses by Dumont show up also in J. & M. Delporte's twentieth-century hymnal and chant book, but with an interesting disclaimer to the effect that they are not part of the Gregorian repertoire proper. Guichard's late eighteenth-century *Essais de nouvelle psalmodie* should be mentioned here, as it too reflects an interest in the ancient song of the church. A collection of settings of the Magnificat, this work harks back to the style of the fifteenth- and sixteenth-century *falsobordoni* (simple homophonic chant harmonizations with a preponderance of triads).

It remains to mention those chant books devoted primarily to teaching purposes. From the seventeenth century come the little pamphlet of the Abbé Cerne and the *Manuale* of Coferati, a famous Florentine teacher whose plainsong methods were very popular. From the eighteenth century come Mott's *Musices Choralis Medulla*, with a later supplement, and the fascinating *Bréviaire Romain* "notated according to a new system of chant" by the Abbé Demotz de la Salle. Demotz's system of notation eliminates staff lines and inserts directly into the text a special character whose position—vertical, horizontal, or inclined to right or left—determines the degree of raising or lowering of the pitch. Although this system was not a new idea—several seventeenth-century musicians had proposed similar methods, intended to make it easier for those knowing little about music to sing the chants in church—Demotz de la Salle had greater success with it, having his system approved twice by the Academy of Sciences and publishing three books using this notation.[26] From the nineteenth century comes Gomant's *Manuel du chantre*, which contains a "New Method of Plainchant" and "The Elements of Music and of Musical Plainchant Compared" and a collection of various chants, many of them newly composed.

Many of the items in the Cortot Collection represent the only copy of a particular work in the United States. Examples include Le Jeune's *Pseaumes* (1627), Lobwasser's *Psalmen Davids* (1683), and Oudot's *Stances chrestiennes* (1692). Even among those items which are not unique there is a wealth of valuable material in this small but choice collection—material which will benefit not only students of sacred music but of secular music as well, for in the past, as the Cortot Collection makes apparent, there was a vital interchange between the two.

[26] F.J. Fétis, *Biographie universelle des musiciens*, 2nd ed., vol. 2 (Paris: Didot Frères, Fils et Cie, 1861), p. 466.

This engraving of St. Cecilia, the patron saint of music, forms the frontispiece to part two of *Opuscules sacrés*, 1772. *HRC Collections.*

Items within groups are in chronological order.

The spelling of book titles conforms to that of the original title pages.

I. Metrical Psalters, Other Paraphrases, Etc.

Nüw Gsangbüchle von vil schoenen Psalmen und geistlichen Liedern. . . .
    Zurich: Zwingli Verlag, 1946; after C. Froschouer, 1540.

Marot, Clément & Théodore de Bèze. *Les Pseaumes mis en rime françoise.*
    . . . [Lyons]: Michel Blanchier for Antoine Vincent, 1562.

_____. *Les Cent cinquante pseaumes de David.* . . . Caen: Pierre Le
    Chandelier & Pierre Gondouin for Antoine Vincent, 1562.

Courcelles, Pierre de. *Le Cantique des cantiques de Salomon . . . ensemble,*
    Les Lamentations de Ieremie. . . . Paris: Robert Estienne, 1564.

Des-Masures, Louis. *Tragédies sainctes,* with: Philone. *Iosias, Tragédie.*
    . . . [Geneva]: Gabriel Cartier for Claude d'Augy, 1583.

Marot, Clément & Théodore de Bèze. *Les Pseaumes de David.* . . . Geneva:
    Jean de Tournes, 1611.

Caignet, Denis. *Les CL Pseaumes de David . . . par Ph. Des-Portes.* . . .
    Paris: Pierre Ballard, 1624.

Le Jeune, Claude. *Les Pseaumes de David, mis en musique a quatre & cinq*
    parties. . . . Geneva: Jean de Tournes, 1627.

Signac. *Cinquante Pseaumes de David . . . Premier livre. Haute contre.* . . .
    Paris: Pierre Ballard, 1630.

Buchanan, George. *Psalmorum Davidis Paraphrasis Poetica.* . . . London:
    Edward Griffin, 1648.

Gouy, Jacques de. *Airs en quatre parties sur la paraphrase de pseaumes de*
    Antoine Godeau . . . Première partie. Taille. Paris: Robert Ballard,
    1650.

Aux-Cousteaux, Artus. *Paraphrase des pseaumes de David . . . Quatrième*
    edition. . . . Paris: Pierre Le Petit, 1656.

Lardenois, Antoine. *Paraphrase des pseaumes de David . . . Seconde*
    edition. . . . [n.p.]: Aux despens de l'autheur, 1658.

Gobert, Thomas. *Paraphrase des pseaumes de David . . . Cinquieme*
    edition. . . . Paris: Pierre Le Petit, 1659.

Marot, Clément & Théodore de Bèze. *Les Pseaumes de David.* ...
Charenton: P. Des-Hayes & A. Cellier, 1656; Charenton: Anthoine
Cellier, 1661.

Lawes, Henry. *A Paraphrase upon the Psalms of David, by George Sandys
... revised and corrected ... by John Playford.* London: W. Godbid
for Abel Roper, 1676.

Conrart, Valentin. *Les Pseaumes en vers françois retouchez.* ... Geneva:
Samuel de Tournes, 1679.

Lobwasser, Ambrosius. *Psalmen Davids.* ... Amsterdam: Joachim Nosche,
1683.

Marot, Clément & Théodore de Bèze. *Les Pseaumes de David ... reduits
nouvellement a une ... facile methode pour apprendre le chant.* ...
Amsterdam: G.P. & J. Blaeu, 1684.

—————. *Les Pseaumes de David ... Nouvelle edition.* ... London:
Guillaume Pearson, 1722.

Holdroyd, Israel. *The Spiritual Man's Companion ... Fifth edition.* ...
London: Robert Brown for J. Hinton, 1753.

Knibb, Thomas. *The Psalm Singers Help ... A New edition.* ... London:
George Pearch & Joseph Gurney, [1770?].

Het Boek der Psalmen. ... Amsterdam: Heirs of Hendrik van der Putte,
1777.

Gilmour, Robert. *The Psalm-Singer's Assistant ... Second edition.* ...
Paisley: J. Neilson & sold by the author, 1793.

Les Pseaumes de David. ... Neuchàtel: Louis Fauche-Borel, 1803.

Les Pseaumes de David ... Nouvelle edition. Geneva: Susanne Guers, 1837.

II. Sacred Songbooks, Hymnals, Etc.

Martin, Nicolas. *Les Noëlz & Chansons.* ... Paris: Belin, 1889, after M.
Bonhomme (Lyons), 1555.

Theodatus, Salomon. *Het Paradys der Gheestelycke en Kerckelycke Lof-
sangen ... Vierden druck.* ... Antwerp: Hendrick Aertsens, 1638.

Macé, Denis. *Cantiques spirituels ... par ... Irenee d'Eu ... Seconde
edition.* Paris: Robert Ballard, 1648.

Neck, Pieter van. *Stichtelijcke Bedenckinghe, Onledighe Ledigheydt, Stichtelijcke Tijdtkortinge ... C.J. Wits. Achsten druck.* ... Enchuysen:
Jan Lely-Veldt, 1679.

Oudot, Claude. *Stances chrestiennes de M.L.T.* [*L'Abbé Testu*]. . . . Paris: Christophe Ballard, 1692.

Collasse, Pascal. *Cantiques spirituels tirez de l'Ecriture Sainte.* Paris: Christophe Ballard, 1695.

Casini, Giovanni. *Canzonette spirituali . . . composte dal Padre Bernardo Adimari.* . . . Florence: Pietro Antonio Brigonci, 1703.

Pellegrin, Simon. *Cantiques spirituels.* . . . Paris: Nicolas Le Clerc, 1701. With his *Noëls nouveaux . . . Troisième edition; Chansons spirituelles . . . Troisième edition . . .;* and *Chants des Cantiques.* . . . Paris: Le Clerc, 1704.

_____. *Airs notez des Cantiques . . ., Noëls nouveaux et Chansons spirituelles.* . . . Paris: Nicolas Le Clerc, 1706.

Nouveau Recueil de cantiques spirituelles. . . . Liege: Barthelemi Collette, 1708.

Oudot, Claude. *Stances chretiennes de M.L.T.* . . . *Troisième edition.* . . . Paris: Christophe Ballard, 1722.

Nivers, Guillaume. *Chants et Motets a l'usage de l'eglise et communaute des dames de la royale maison de St. Louis a St. Cyr.* . . . [Paris]: Colin, 1733.

Recueil de cantiques spirituels a l'usage des missions de Provence en langue vulgaire. . . . Avignon: François Joseph Domergue, 1734.

Bachofen, Johann. *Herrn B.H. Brockes . . . Irdisches Vergnügen in Gott.* . . . Zurich: Johann Heinrich Bürckli, 1740.

Schmidlin, Johannes. *Singendes und spielendes Vergnügen reiner Andacht.* . . . Zurich: Bürgklischer Truckerey, 1752.

Mestral, L'Abbé. *Prières et cantiques à l'usage des missions.* . . . Paris: Christophe Ballard, 1759.

Zangwijzen van Stichtelijke Gezangen . . . door Rutger Schutte. . . . Amsterdam: Johannes Cóvens Jr., [ca. 1760].

Schmidlin, Johannes. *Herrn Professor Gellerts geistliche Oden und Lieder.* . . . Zurich: Bürgklischer Truckerey, 1761.

Canzuns Spirituaelas Davart Cristo Gesu il Bun Pastur. . . . Cellerina: Giacomo N. Gadina, 1765.

Opuscules sacrés et lyriques . . . à l'usage de la jeunesse de la paroisse de S. Sulpice. . . . Paris: Nicolas Crapart, 1772.

Recueil de pseaumes et de cantiques à l'usage de l'eglise française de Saint Gall. . . . St. Gall: Jean Zollicofer, 1798.

Christmann, Johann & Justin Knecht. *Vollständige Sammlung . . . vierstimmiger Choralmelodien für das neue Wirtembergische Landgesangbuch.* . . . Stuttgart: Gebrüder Mäntler, 1799.

Bachofen, Johann. *Musicalisches Halleluja.* . . . Zurich: David Bürkli, [1803].

III. Liturgical Books, Plainsong, Etc.

Passionarium cum aliis in horis canonicis necessariis. Logroño: Michael de Eguia for Alfonso de Castella, 1533.

Coignet, Johannes. *Chantepleure d'eaue vive.* . . . Paris: Desiderii Maheu, 1537.

Liber sacerdotalis nuperrime ex libris Sancte Romane Ecclesie. . . . Venice: V. a Rabanis, 1537.

Passionarium. Contenta in hoc volumine: Passio domine nostri . . . exultet . . . kyrieleyson . . . Lamentationes Hieremie . . . punctata melodia . . . summa cura . . . iterum revisa . . . correcta et emendata. Saragossa: Bartholomaeus Nagera, 1563.

Cantorinus pro his, qui cantum ad chorum pertinentem . . . novissime castigatus. . . . Venice: Heirs of L.A. Giunta, 1566.

Sacerdotale ad consuetudinem S. Romanae Ecclesiae. . . . Venice: Guerra Bros., 1576.

Pontificale Romanum . . . revisum, emendatum & impressum. Venice: Giunta, 1582.

Sergius, Johannes. *Libellus omnes psalmos, hymnos, responsoria brevia.* . . . Monasterii Westphaliae [Münster]: Lambertus Raesfeldt, 1598. With: *Brevia Gregoriani sive choralis et plani cantus principia.* . . . Monasterii Westphaliae [Münster]: Lambertus Raesfeldt, 1596.

Missae Novae, Festis solemnioribus decantandae. . . . Leyden: de Does, [1600s].

Caerimoniale Episcoporum. Iussu Clementis VIII . . . novissime reformatum. . . . Rome: Lepidus Fatius, 1606.

Pastorale, ad usum romanum accommodatum . . . Ioannis Hauchini . . . olim editum nunc . . . Matthaei Hovii . . . auctoritate recognitum. Antwerp: Plantin, 1607.

CANTIQUE XXIII.

Priere à Dieu dans la tentation.

Marqué fans vîteffe.

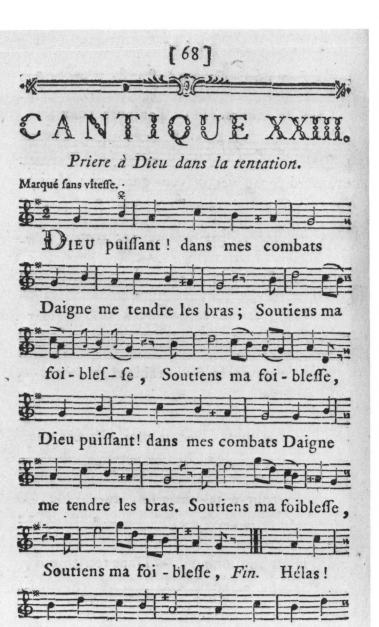

Dieu puiffant! dans mes combats

Daigne me tendre les bras; Soutiens ma

foi - blef - fe , Soutiens ma foi - bleffe,

Dieu puiffant! dans mes combats Daigne

me tendre les bras. Soutiens ma foibleffe ,

Soutiens ma foi - bleffe , *Fin.* Hélas !

je veux être à toi : Mais tout s'arme

Page from *Opuscules sacrés*, 1772. *HRC Collections*. Fournier's single-impression music type with round note heads was praised by contemporaries as being more elegant and easier to read than the older diamond-shaped notes.

Psalmi et Hymni Ecclesiastici cum officio defunctorum. Ad Romani Breviarii nuperrime correcti. . . . Louvain: Joh. Masius, 1609.

Antiphonarium Romanum juxta breviarium . . . pars hyemalis. Paris: Ballard, 1660.

Graduale recens impressum missis conventualibus tam de tempore . . . ad usum sacri ordinis Cartusiensis. . . . Lyons: Gregoire, 1674.

Cantus Diversi . . . ex graduali Romano. . . . Lyons: Bachelu, 1675.

Nivers, Guillaume. *Passiones Domini N.I.C. cum Lamentationibus Jeremiae . . . ad usum sacri & canonici praemonstratensis ordinis.* . . . Paris: Leonard, 1683.

Cerne, L'Abbé. *Les Principes du plain-chant.* . . . Paris: Simon Langronne [printed by Christophe Ballard], 1688.

Coferati, Matteo. *Manuale degli Invitatori co suo Salmi . . . opera raccolta.* . . . Florence: Vincenzio Vangelisti, 1691.

Santeul, Jean de. *Hymni Sacri et Novi . . . editio novissima.* . . . Paris: Dionysium Thierry, 1698.

Mott, Hermanus. *Musices choralis medulla . . . editio secunda.* . . . With: *Processionale ad Normam missalis ac ritualis.* . . . Köln: Johann Wilhelm Friess, 1704.

Processionale usibus ac ritibus S. Romanae Ecclesiae . . . nova editione . . . emendatum. . . . Paris: P. de Launay [in fine: Lud. Sevestre], 1709.

Mott, Hermanus. *Additiones Breves ad musices choralis medullam . . . ad usum Fratrum Minorum Recollector.* . . . Köln: J.E. Fromart, 1725.

Demotz de la Salle, L'Abbé. *Bréviaire Romain noté selon un nouveau système de chant.* . . . Paris: Quillan fils, 1727.

Graduale Romanum, juxta missale . . . cui additus est cantus missarum . . . . Grenoble: Faure, 1730.

Nivers, Guillaume. *Processional avec les saluts suivant l'antiphonaire des religieuses.* . . . Paris: J.-B. Christophe Ballard, 1736.

Guidetto, Giovanni. *Directorium Chori . . . olim editum . . . Francisco Pelichiari.* . . . Rome: Salvioni, 1737.

Processionale ordinis Carmelitarum . . . de novo correctum annotatum et sculptum. . . . Lyons: Casimir Viri, 1739.

Graduale Claromontense . . . Francisci-Mariae le maistre de la Garlaye . . . autoritate, ac . . . editum. . . . Clermont-Ferrand: Boutaudon, 1744.

Processionale sacri ordinis FF. Praedicatorum Jussu R.P.F. Antonini Cloche . . . editum. . . . With: *Officium defunctorum* . . . With: *Officium Hebdomadae sanctae.* . . . Paris: [n.p.], [ca. 1760].

Chants divers extraits de l'antiphonaire romain . . . nouvelle edition . . . augmentée d'une nouvelle methode pour apprendre le plainchant. . . . Avignon: Jean-Joseph Niel, 1778.

Guichard, François. *Essais de nouvelle psalmodie, ou Faux-Bourdons.* . . . Rome & Paris: Nyon, 1783.

Gomant. *Manuel de chantre . . . cinquième edition.* . . . Paris: Garnier, [after 1834].

Delporte, J. & M. *Manuel de chant complet . . . conforme aux instructions du Saint Siège.* . . . Tournai & Paris: Desclée & Cie, [1919].

Gabriel Fauré, n.d. Photograph autographed for Georges Jean-Aubry. *HRC Photography Collection*.

From a Vision of Death to the Genesis of "Pénélope": The Gabriel Fauré Manuscript Collection

BY ROBERT ORLEDGE

The Carlton Lake Collection, which forms an important part of the manuscript holdings at the Humanities Research Center, is particularly well endowed with French music of the late nineteenth and early twentieth centuries, making it an invaluable primary source which no scholar of this period can afford to ignore. As well as containing some 126 important letters by Debussy and the earliest known libretto for his unfinished Poe opera, *The Fall of the House of Usher*, the HRC also possesses several manuscripts by Gabriel Fauré and seventy-one letters and other documents by this composer.

Perhaps the most valuable Fauré manuscript is the neat five-page copy of "O mort, poussière d'étoiles," the tenth and final song of the Charles Van Lerberghe cycle, *La Chanson d'Ève* (op. 95), made for the publishers Heugel et Cie in January 1910. Fauré began what was to grow into his longest song cycle with "Crépuscule" (no. 9) in June 1906, to which he added "Paradis" (no. 1) and "Prima verba" (no. 2) that September. The rest of *La Chanson d'Ève* emerged during gaps in the composition of his opera *Pénélope* (1907–13), comprising "Roses ardentes" (no. 3) and "L'aube blanche" (no. 5) in June 1908; "Comme Dieu rayonne" (no. 4), "Eau vivante" (no. 6), and "Dans un parfum de roses blanches" (no. 8) in the summer of 1909; and finally "Veilles-tu, ma senteur de soleil?" (no. 7) and "O mort, poussière d'étoiles," completed early in 1910. The other nine manuscripts are now in the Bibliothèque Nationale, Paris (MSS 17748 [1–9]), and the covers of "Roses ardentes" and "Comme Dieu rayonne" show that the intended order of performance grew as follows: song numbers 1–3, 5 and 9; then 1–3, 4, 8, 6, 5, and 9. The final ordering (1–10) is to be found only on the cover of the HRC manuscript, and it was in this form that the complete cycle was first performed at the inaugural concert of the Société Musicale Indépendante, Paris, on 20 April 1910 by its dedicatee, Jeanne Raunay, with the composer at the piano. On the day after the successful premiere, Ravel wrote to Fauré:

My dear teacher,

How I would have wished to express my joy to you yesterday, as deeply as I felt it, after the performance of *La Chanson d'Ève!* I was too moved, and besides, how was I to do it amid all the jostling? But you certainly understood me. One feels so close at these magnificent moments.[1]

The final ordering of *La Chanson d'Ève* seems to have been chosen for esthetic rather than chronological reasons, Eve's character gradually deepening as she uncovers alone more and more of the natural secrets of God's universe. She sees her days of innocence in the Garden of Eden drawing to an end in "Crépuscule," and finally in "O mort, poussière d'étoiles" the mood changes again and she looks forward to death as an immortal, transfiguring, and inevitable force. Both of these poems appropriately came from the fourth and final section of Van Lerberghe's collection, subtitled "Twilight," and as they were only published in 1904 they show Fauré characteristically turning to the best, most modern poetry available, as he had done in his earlier Verlaine settings.

"O mort, poussière d'étoiles" comes at the other end of the spectrum from the beauty and stillness of night as evoked in the "Nocturne" from *Shylock* or "La Lune blanche" from *La Bonne Chanson*, and from Fauré's view of death as a gentle release in his *Requiem*. "O mort" derives some of its somber blackness from its contrast with the rest of the cycle, which is often focused in the treble register with thin, linear scoring. Now, for the first time, we encounter thick tenor and bass registers, and the frequent recourse to the tonic chord of D flat major helps contribute to its leaden feeling, as do the intense chromaticism, halting rhythms, and elliptical phrases, which gradually sink with the vocal line in the final bars (fig. 1). For once, Fauré's confidence in an ideal world created through art comes close to annihilation in this powerful and moving vision, which is worlds apart from the sensuous warmth of "Prima verba," or the freshness and luminous grace of "Eau vivante" encountered earlier in the cycle.

The HRC manuscript shows little evidence of any struggle during composition, but because Fauré destroyed his sketches for the cycle, a firm conclusion cannot be drawn. In his fair black ink copies, the composer crossed out whole passages that contained even the minutest error, so that the amendments appear to be far more extensive than is actually the case. Probing beneath the blocked-out passage at the top of page 4 (fig. 1), we find only a slight rhythmic alteration in the vocal line to the words "Un vin de flamme et d'arome divin," though the change of note from F sharp to D sharp on "d'*arome*" (final version), instead of on "flam*me* d'arome" (first

[1] Gabriel Fauré, *Correspondance*, ed. Jean-Michel Nectoux (Paris: Flammarion, 1980), pp. 278–79. All translations are my own.

Fig. 1

version), better reflects the natural stresses of Van Lerberghe's powerful poem. Similarly, the alterations on page 5 (fig. 2) all involve the vocal line, which Fauré appears to have written first. The accompaniment throughout is exactly as in the printed version, apart from the missing tenor A flat in the final chord, which must have been added by Fauré at the proof stage.

The two other HRC manuscripts are early works from the École Niedermeyer period (1860–65). The first, a three-page *Fugue à 3 parties* in F major, written in black ink in 3/2 time on soprano, alto, and bass clefs, is probably one of the fugues written for the composition prize at the École Niedermeyer and may date from 1861 or 1863. The parts enter *(Moderato)* from the bass upwards (fig. 3), employing a real answer and a regular counter-subject. There are the usual episodes and middle entries in nearly related keys during its 119 bars, and Fauré makes skillful use of inverted entries and stretti in all three parts during the final tonic entries, further intensifying his final climax by a long dominant pedal in the bass. On the

Fig. 2

Fig. 3

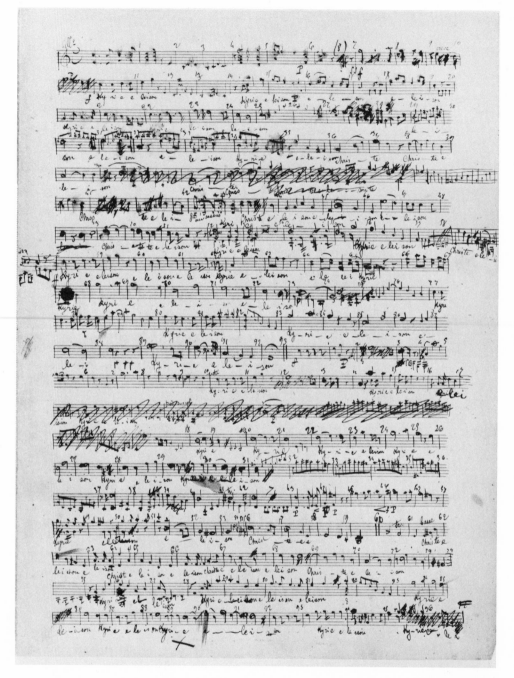

Fig. 4

verso of one page of the fugue there are extensively corrected vocal parts (with instrumental cues) for a Mass in C (*Allegro*, 4/4 time) in the Classical manner. As they are written on the same paper, they probably date from the early 1860s too, though little else is known about them. Figure 4 shows a soprano part with the underlay "Kyrie eleison, Christe eleison," and the bars carefully numbered from 1 to 96. As the instrumental cues are often altered or crossed out altogether and the whole is untidy and sketchlike, it seems unlikely that Fauré was copying out the work of another composer, or his own arrangement of someone else's Mass. But on the other hand, there is nothing that stylistically suggests Fauré's authorship either, and perhaps readers may be able to suggest answers to this seemingly insoluble problem.

The two other HRC manuscripts, which were originally classed in good faith as being by Fauré, have since turned out to be by another composer, though that composer still remains anonymous. Both works are settings of poems—one by Jean Moréas, alias Ioannes Papadiamantopoulos (1856–1910), and the other by Paul Fort (1872–1960). Moréas's poem from his *Le Pèlerin passionné* (1891) is entitled "Chanson" and is set for soprano or tenor in A minor, with some rather dubious prosody in places. The setting of Fort's poem from his *Ballades françaises* (1897) is a particularly poignant one for mezzo-soprano or baritone in G minor, with intense dissonances which enhance the overall mood of premature tragedy, and a piano accompaniment of stark simplicity. The power and concentration of the latter suggests that it could well be an unknown work by a composer of some importance.[2] The reason I too originally believed these settings to be by Fauré lies in the third stanza of the manuscript song entitled "Les Courlis dans les roseaux," which is a setting of Moréas's "Chanson." Here the accompaniment contains a rising figure that closely resembles the start of Fauré's "Chanson de Mélisande" (1898),[3] which coincidentally became the start of "Crépuscule," the song with which he began *La Chanson d'Ève* in 1906.

The majority of the seventy-one letters and other autograph documents by Fauré in the HRC are addressed to two of the composer's biographers: Gabriel Faure (1877–1962) and Émile Vuillermoz (1878–1960). Quite a few of the thirty-five letters to Fauré's virtual namesake have been published in

[2] Both the manuscripts are discussed in Robert Orledge, *Gabriel Fauré* (London: Eulenburg, 1979), pp. 209–11. If any readers know of a single composer who set both "Les Courlis dans les roseaux" from Jean Moréas's *Le Pèlerin passionné* (1891) and "Cette fille, elle est morte" from the first collection of *Ballades françaises* (1897) by Paul Fort, probably in the 1920s, I should be glad to hear from them. Neither the Société des Auteurs et Compositeurs in France nor any libraries I have consulted possess printed versions of either song in the HRC.

[3] "Chanson de Mélisande" comes from act 3, scene 1 of Maeterlinck's play *Pelléas et Mélisande*, set by Fauré in English on 31 May 1898 and later scored for flute, clarinet, and strings. This formed part of his incidental music for Sir Johnston Forbes-Robertson's production of the play, which opened at the Prince of Wales' Theatre, London, on 21 June 1898 with Fauré conducting the orchestra.

Faure's slim biography, an unpretentious chronicle of a friendship which began around the turn of the century.[4] The HRC letters mostly cover the period 1909–22, and with the extra letters found in Faure form essentially a complete correspondence,[5] though Faure's replies were unfortunately not retained by Fauré, who showed a royal disregard for manuscript material.

Gabriel Auguste Faure was a prolific author and poet who specialized in stylish literary accounts of the Italian landscape and civilization.[6] As Fauré invariably spent the summer months composing in either the Italian or Swiss Alps, the two sometimes met, and by 1909 they were on sufficiently intimate terms for Fauré to write freely about his compositions, or his everyday life and problems. Thus, in 1911, we find Fauré installed in his favorite Grand Hôtel Métropole et Monopole in Lugano, picking up the threads of the first act of his opera *Pénélope* from the point where he had had to abandon it in the summer of 1908 in order to return to Paris and his onerous duties as Director of the Conservatoire. On 22 September 1911 he wrote to Faure, who had sent him the itinerary for an excursion around the Italian lakes:

> Wisdom, that is to say *Pénélope*, has prevailed; the tempting project that you so kindly and carefully drew up has not become a reality. My only escapade has been to take the boat to Menaggio as far as Como and to return from there by train. I had lunch on the bridge of the boat and took photos during the trip. It was a straightforward excursion, without surprises, but delightful all the same. Apart from this it is work, work, and more hard work! I should manage, above all, to take back to Paris [on 5 October] the parts [of my opera] which have remained incomplete, so that the process of publishing can recommence and everything be linked together.[7]

This last observation was made because Fauré had not composed *Pénélope* in its performance order. The problem had arisen from the long act 2 duet between Ulysses and Penelope, whose contrived situation—Penelope does

[4]Gabriel Faure, *Gabriel Fauré* (Paris: B. Arthaud, 1945). On pages 34–35, Faure recounts the confusion that this homonym created with regard to wrongly directed letters, wrongly attributed photographs in the press, etc. But the confusion that most upset Fauré was with the baritone Jean-Baptiste Faure (1830–1914), who was also a composer: his inferior songs are still sometimes confused with the masterpieces of Fauré.

[5]See the facsimiles of Fauré's letter of 2 February 1923 thanking Faure for his article in *Le Figaro* (Faure, *Gabriel Fauré*, p. 101), and the touching card sent from Annecy-le-Vieux late in September 1924, a month before Fauré's death (p. 109).

[6]See *Heures d'Ombrie* (Paris: E. Sansot, 1908); *Autour des lacs italiens: Côme, Majeur, Lugano, Orta, Varèse, Iseo, Garde* (Paris: E. Sansot, 1912); *Heures d'Italie* (Paris: E. Fasquelle, 1921); and *L'Amour sous les lauriers-roses; roman des lacs italiens* (Paris: Bibliothèque Charpentier, 1919).

[7]See Faure, *Gabriel Fauré*, p. 77, whose cited text of this letter bears no date and is slightly at variance with the HRC original, from which the present translation derives.

not recognize her husband on his return, disguised as a beggar—Fauré found hard to handle. In August 1911 Fauré felt obliged to rewrite the music he had composed for this duet in 1909, and then he had to fill the gaps left earlier in act 2 and complete the end of act 1. After a great effort, Fauré was able to put the finishing touches to the first act on 3 October 1911, leaving only one day before he was obliged to return to Paris.

Fauré spent the following Easter at Hyères on the Côte d'Azur, where he composed half of act 3 of *Pénélope* between 2 and 24 April 1912.[8] During the ensuing Conservatoire exams he managed to find time to correct the publisher's proofs for acts 1 and 2 of the vocal score, and by 24 July he was back in Lugano. Here, however, he was troubled by a dispute between the Opéra and the Opéra-Comique over who should mount the Paris premiere of *Pénélope*,[9] and was interrupted by a visit from the Conservatoire adminis-trator Fernand Bourgeat to discuss the admission exams for the coming October. But Fauré still remained his optimistic and equable self, as is shown in one of the letters to Faure housed in the HRC:

> Here [in Lugano], I have rediscovered the clear sky that you love, and a more clement temperature. I cannot say that I am recovering from fatigue, for, thank God, I bore the [Conservatoire] examina-tions period very well, without weariness, and above all without any boredom. I took up my labor where I had left it [in the middle of act 3] and I hope to see the end very soon, at least as far as the composition is concerned. . . . I work as hard as I can. I am taken more than ever with Lugano; I have even taken root here![10]

The beneficial effect of Lugano and the encouragement of friends like Faure spurred on the composer to complete the orchestration of act 1 of *Pénélope* that summer, with acts 2 and 3 being orchestrated in Monte Carlo the following winter (with assistance from Fernand Pécoud). Despite the artistic success of the 1913 Paris performances, both *Pénélope* and Debussy's ballet *Jeux* were overshadowed by the *succès de scandale* of Stravinsky's *Rite of Spring* by Diaghilev's Ballets Russes on 29 May, and Astruc's revival of *Pénélope* in October 1913 was less carefully prepared than the May

[8] See Gabriel Fauré, *Lettres intimes* (Paris: Bernard Grasset, 1951), pp. 201–203, for an account of this busy "vacation." Fauré's letters to his wife Marie from his visits to Lugano in 1911 and 1912 are given on pages 194–200 and 204–11 respectively.

[9] In the end, the official premiere took place at Gabriel Astruc's newly founded Théâtre des Champs-Élysées on 10 May 1913 with Lucienne Bréval as Penelope and Lucien Muratore as Ulysses. The actual premiere occurred in Monte Carlo on 4 March 1913, when Charles Rousselière sang the role of Ulysses.

[10] Letter dated "Dimanche," probably from mid-August 1912, as Fauré finished act 3 of *Pénélope* on 31 August 1912. Faure wrongly implies that the letter was written prior to the letter of 22 September 1911 by quoting from it on page 76 of his biography.

performances due to his impending bankruptcy. However, the performances at the Théâtre de la Monnaie in Brussels in December 1913 were enthusiastically received, and the opera finally reached the stage of the Paris Opéra-Comique on 20 January 1919, though the intervention of the War had by then somewhat dimmed its initial appeal. *Pénélope* was revived in the more suitable Paris Opéra on 14 March 1943 with Germaine Lubin in the title role, and though its libretto has weaknesses (as Fauré realized during his struggle with act 2), the score represents the best of Fauré in its balance of power and serenity. Perhaps the recent recordings of the complete opera will give the work the attention it so richly deserves.[11]

The other HRC letters to Faure discuss a wide range of subjects, from Conservatoire personnel (2 December 1910), to family worries, to Fauré's triumphant reception on a concert tour to Leningrad (then St. Petersburg). On 15 November 1910 the composer wrote to Faure from the Hôtel Societetshuset in Helsinki (then Helsingfors)—where Fauré enjoyed a similar acclaim—"I believe that God the Father was never received more gloriously!" But earlier that summer in Bad Ems in Germany, Fauré had been worried by the serious illness of his eighty-six-year-old father-in-law, the sculptor Emmanuel Fremiet, to such an extent that he only composed four piano preludes (op. 103, nos. 4–7) in what should have been a productive period for *Pénélope*. While Fauré was pleased that the city of Lille had commissioned a replica of Fremiet's famous statue of Joan of Arc in the Place des Pyramides, Paris, he was angry about the covert hostility of the Ministry of Fine Arts towards what might be his father-in-law's last work, a statue of his teacher François Rude (1784–1855), which Fauré wished to see inaugurated in the gardens of the Louvre during Fremiet's lifetime. Fauré complained to Faure that

> Certain people have taken exception to the too intimate nature of this statue of Rude, which in the Salon was a great success with the press, artists, and public alike. There is, it appears, a certain pipe which has greatly offended. They do not wish to remember that Fremiet was the nephew of Rude, that he was his favorite pupil, or that he lived close to him in a family atmosphere. It is therefore natural that he has represented what he saw a hundred times. . . .
> In these times of charlatans and *arrivistes*, the career of my father-in-law has been so pure, noble, and disinterested that one should, in all fairness, leave no stone unturned to separate any affliction

[11] Erato STU 71387-9 and Discoreale DR 10012-14, both issued in 1981. The Erato recording is a fine new version in which the Orchestre Philharmonique de Monte Carlo is conducted by Charles Dutoit and Penelope is sung by Jessye Norman. The accompanying brochure by Jean-Michel Nectoux is an excellent resource for anyone wishing to know more about the opera and its background.

whatsoever from his last days, or, at the very least, from an old age which has remained so active.[12]

Later, during the War, Fauré was also to write with concern about his son Philippe, who had voluntarily enlisted and had been posted to Thessaloníki, Greece, on 19 July 1916. The letter to Faure of 3 August, now housed at HRC, reveals that Fauré as yet had no news and was angry that communication by telegraph was "forbidden" to ordinary soldiers "when civilians are using it to order themselves pairs of suspenders!" Fauré was very grateful to his friend for giving a description of his son to General Sarrail, and when Philippe returned to France and was awarded the Croix de Guerre at Verdun, Fauré was overjoyed. As he told Faure on 3 January 1918, "I am very proud of him, and I am above all very happy about the strong physique that outdoor life has given him."

The twenty-six letters to Émile Vuillermoz cover the period 1899–1923, though the majority date from 1921–23 when Fauré fortunately developed the practice of precisely dating all his correspondence. Vuillermoz was a respected music critic who became editor-in-chief of the *Revue musicale* in 1911 and wrote frequently for journals like *L'Illustration, L'Éclair, Comoedia,* and *Excelsior.* He had wide interests which included the cinema and gramophone, as well as the championship of contemporary composers like Debussy, Ravel, and, of course, Fauré, of whom he later wrote a perceptive and comprehensive biography.[13]

In 1909 Vuillermoz played an important part in setting up the Société Musicale Indépendante (SMI), of which Fauré was the first president. This group broke away from the Société Nationale, which Ravel, Koechlin, Caplet, Schmitt, and other SMI founding members considered had become too biased towards Vincent d'Indy and the Schola Cantorum. Their aim was to "make known through performance French or foreign modern music, published or unpublished, without exceptions of genre or style."[14] One of Fauré's duties as president was to use his influence as Conservatoire Director to mobilize official support for the SMI, and thus on 28 February 1913, only four days before the premiere of *Pénélope,* he wrote to Vuillermoz from the Hôtel de Helder, Monte Carlo:

> As to the request of the SMI, I have addressed it to M. Bérard [Under-Secretary of State for Fine Arts] through the immediate intermediary of his Head of Cabinet, Maurice Reclus, in such a way

[12]Letter from Das Römerbad, Bad Ems, "Lundi," probably mid-August 1910. HRC Collections.

[13]Émile Vuillermoz, *Gabriel Fauré* (Paris: Flammarion, 1960).

[14]Advertisement in *Le Guide du concert* on 17 December 1910.

that it will not lie about in offices; I have also coupled it with a most pressing letter. I stressed the merit not only of the importance of the mission proposed by the SMI, but also the especially lively and affectionate interest which the members of its committee inspire in me (almost all of them my old pupils), together with my role as president.

It is unfortunately true that, ignoring the financial difficulties of the Society, I have insisted, when *breaking away* from the recommendation for the "Salon des Musiciens," that the Conservatoire should not remain at the fore in all competitions. Only I find that people are all too ignorant about what I have been able to say in this respect. In reality, I dread the invasion of the "Quatuors Parent"[15] and other invalids!

I can add personally that no one from the Ministry of Fine Arts has made *any reply* to me, and on my return to Paris I shall ask you to be so good as to come and see me.

Fauré then adds in a revealing postscript: "Here [in Monte Carlo] I flounder in a lake of indifference! I firmly believe that *Pénélope* bores almost all those who are occupied with it, with [Raoul] Gunsbourg at their head!" To some extent, Fauré was frustrated once the responsibility for *Pénélope* had passed out of his hands, and he had lamented a week earlier to his wife that "except for [the conductor, Léon] Jéhin and [Charles] Rousselière [Ulysses], no one seems interested in my work."[16] But he had strong grounds for legitimate criticism, for Saint-Saëns wrote to the publisher, Jacques Durand, on 5 March after the premiere that "[the producer] Gunsbourg's conduct had been infamous; he did all he could to thwart *Pénélope* for the benefit of his own opera *Venise*," which was in production at the same time.[17] Saint-Saëns told Fauré on 12 March that the singers could not be heard, the brass was too noisy, and the "suitors lacked youth and distinction!"[18] As Fauré's letter to his wife after the premiere reveals, he regarded Monte Carlo as merely a rehearsal for the true Paris premiere of his opera at the Théâtre des Champs-Élysées two months later.[19]

Other interesting letters concern Fauré's "Chinese" incidental music for Georges Clemenceau's play *Le Voile du bonheur* (op. 88), of which

[15] An established Parisian quartet, founded in 1892, which had done much to popularize the chamber music of Beethoven, Schumann, and Brahms in France. Led by Armand Parent (1863–1924), its other members were M. Loiseau (violin), M. Vieux (viola), and M. Fournier (cello). They also performed contemporary music, including Ravel's *Quartet* in 1909.

[16] Fauré, *Lettres intimes*, p. 215. Letter of 21 February 1913.

[17] "Gabriel Fauré et Camille Saint-Saëns: Correspondance inédite," ed. Jean-Michel Nectoux, in *Revue de musicologie* 59 (1973): 62 n. 1.

[18] Ibid., pp. 62–63.

[19] Fauré, *Lettres intimes*, p. 217. Letter of 5 March 1913.

Gabriel Fauré composing *Pénélope* at the Grand Hôtel Métropole et Monopole in Lugano, 1911. Photograph from the collection of Mme. Philippe Fauré-Fremiet.

Vuillermoz conducted the first performance at the Théâtre de la Renaissance, Paris, on 4 November 1901. Fauré wrote to him on 4 October 1911, a decade later, to ask if the score and parts had been "returned by the theatre at the Porte St. Martin," as Clemenceau needed them for a "performance in Madrid."[20] This shows that Fauré's unusual little score for flute, clarinet, trumpet, gong, tubophone, harp, and strings, with its nine deliberately repetitive and often pentatonic pieces, was much in demand.[21] At times Fauré must have wished that the score had been published, for on 15 May 1922 he was again forced to write to Vuillermoz:

> If [my publisher] Hamelle (22 Blvd. Malesherbes) has not made sweet-wrappers out of it, it is he who is withholding the tiny score of *Le Voile du bonheur* and the instrumental parts. If one could recover them and if I were able to run over them for a moment with the young musician you have spoken to me about, I would most willingly put them at his disposal as soon as he would like me to.

Elsewhere we find Fauré seeking Vuillermoz's assistance in securing another performance of his powerful *Fantaisie* (op. 111), which Alfred Cortot (its dedicatee) had neglected since he premiered it in Paris on 14 May 1919.[22] On 7 March 1921 Fauré writes to Vuillermoz from the Villa Mercédès in Nice:

> I wrote, at the very start of the season, to [the conductor] Rhené Baton to beg him to put my *Fantaisie* for piano and orchestra in one of his programs, and to entrust the piano part to one of my best interpreters, Robert Lortat. If you can possibly help me in the realization of a heartfelt desire, you would greatly oblige your most sincerely and most affectionately devoted
>
> Gabriel Fauré

On 29 August 1922, Fauré wrote to Vuillermoz from Annecy-le-Vieux:

> I have had to prepare the performance of a little Mass.[23] This will

[20] Postcard from Lugano, dated from the postmark. HRC Collections.

[21] The autograph score (28 pages) is now in the Bibliothèque Nationale, Paris (MS 17786), as are the instrumental parts in the hand of a copyist (Vma. MS 920).

[22] The actual premiere had been presented in Monte Carlo by Marguerite Hasselmans on 12 April 1919, when the orchestra was conducted by Léon Jéhin. Since Fauré had done so much to further Cortot's career, he was deeply disappointed by this neglect, though, as often, he only expressed his true feelings in private or in letters.

[23] His *Messe basse* ("Low Mass"), which was originally written with André Messager as the *Messe à l'Association des Pêcheurs de Villerville* in 1881–82 and revised by Fauré alone in December 1906. The 1922 revival in the Church at Annecy was conducted by Albert Bertelin, and the Casino there also mounted a festival of Fauré's works as part of the series of tributes that took place in 1922.

take place on Sunday [3 September] with the help of a group of attractive voices, and the "big wigs" staying in the country beside the lake. And I ought not to forget a little *Sorbonne* in the Casino at Annecy inspired by Henri Malherbe from the Opéra-Comique.[24] There were the Prefect and the Mayor, and some tricolored decorations. The Prefect and the Mayor, no doubt impressed because they had heard about [the larger Sorbonne festival on] 20 June, treated me like a Minister of State! Finally, I have had to write some "Souvenirs" for Henri Prunières.[25] But memories are for relating verbally, they are not to be written down, especially when they are the memories of a life as uneventful as mine. Then I had to repeat the old story of the École Niedermeyer. I fear that the subject will appear to be lacking in contemporary relevance.

The remaining ten Fauré letters and documents in the HRC consist of one letter each to Léon Melchissédec (n.d.), Paul Porel (1889), and Armand Dayot (1907); several to unknown addressees, and eleven lines of poetry signed by the librettist of *Pénélope*, René Fauchois, which come from act 2 of his play *Rivoli* and are dedicated to "Mademoiselle Solange Daniel." There is also a signed photograph of Fauré dedicated "very affectionately" to the writer Georges Jean-Aubry. Two items refer to Fauré's interest in the theatre prior to 1900, which was far more extensive than is generally realized.[26] First comes an undated letter (3 pp.) to an unknown male addressee, probably from the early 1890s. The following appears on pages 1–2:

> My friend [the dramatist, Georges de] Porto-Riche [1849–1930] has misunderstood me if he writes of my desire to undertake a full-scale dramatic work. I have told him that, in a parallel direction to my pure music, it would be agreeable to me to compose either incidental music for a literary work which would require it, or better still, a ballet. I unfortunately don't have enough time to undertake a more extensive theatrical piece, without talking of private ideas which, for the moment at least, are distracting me from this path.

[24] Fauré is here referring to the larger festival organized in his honor by Fernand Maillot at the Sorbonne, Paris, on 20 June 1922 with the orchestra and choir of the Société des Concerts du Conservatoire and such notable performers as Pablo Casals and Alfred Cortot. The conductors included Vincent d'Indy and André Messager.

[25] Published in the special Fauré edition of *La Revue musicale* no. 22 (1 October 1922): 3–9. Vuillermoz also wrote a tribute to Fauré (pp. 10–21), along with others by Ravel, Koechlin, Nadia Boulanger, etc.

[26] See J-M. Nectoux, "Flaubert, Gallet, Fauré ou Le Démon du Théâtre," *Bulletin du Bibliophile* no. 1 (1976): 33–47; and Orledge, *Gabriel Fauré*, pp. 116–18.

This theme of incidental music crops up elsewhere in Fauré's correspond-ence, though without revealing as he does here that he had balletic plans contemporary with his incidental music for *Caligula* and *Shylock* (1888–89). Incidental music provided Fauré with an opportunity both to write for the theatre and to continue to use the smaller forms for which he then knew his musical talents were best suited. As he wrote to Saint-Saëns in October 1893: "If by any chance you wake up one morning with a revulsion for *Antigone* . . . pass it on to me! Incidental music is the only genre that suits my limited abilities!"[27]

Incidental music was also the subject of Fauré's HRC letter to Paul Porel, Director of the Théâtre de l'Odéon, on 6 December 1889.[28] Fauré asks,

> Will you please add to the list I gave you yesterday the name of the *Princesse de Scey-Montbéliard* for a box?[29] She is returning from the country expressly for the premiere of *Shylock* (so she tells me!!) . . . For my part, I shall be very grateful for this. I hope to come to the Odéon tomorrow. Your rehearsals amuse and fascinate me to the highest degree! It is a real treat!

The Princesse's invitation for a holiday to Venice and Florence in 1891 (during which Fauré began his first Verlaine song cycle, the *Cinq mélodies "de Venise"* (op. 58), proved an important turning point in his musical career. As it was her enjoyment of *Shylock* as much as the dedication of Fauré's setting of Richepin's *Larmes* (op. 51, no. 1) to the Princesse in 1888 which was instrumental in securing her valuable patronage, it is evident that the above letter is of greater significance in assessing Fauré's development than might at first appear to be the case. It also reveals his fascination with the theatre— and his charming unpretentiousness which impressed itself on all who knew him well.

[27] "Gabriel Fauré et Camille Saint-Saëns: Correspondance inédite," ed. J-M. Nectoux, *Revue de musicologie* 58 (1972): 211. This letter concerned Saint-Saëns's incidental music for Sophocles' *Antigone* (in a translation by Meurice and Vacquerie), which was revived at the Comédie Française on 21 November 1893.

[28] Paul Porel was a pseudonym for Raoul Parfouru (1843–1917), who commissioned the music for Alexandre Dumas *père's Caligula* (op. 52) and for Edmond Haraucourt's adaptation of Shakespeare's *The Merchant of Venice*, entitled *Shylock* (op. 57), first performed at the Odéon on 17 December 1889. Both scores are dedicated to Porel.

[29] Later the Princesse Edmond de Polignac (1865–1943), who was a wealthy and astute patroness of the arts and the daughter of Isaac Merritt Singer of sewing-machine fame. For further details on the Princesse, see Michael de Cossart, *The Food of Love* (London: Hamish Hamilton, 1978).

From this survey of Fauré manuscripts and letters at HRC it will, I hope, have become clear just how important a source this is for anyone interested in this compelling period in French culture. I predict, however, that those coming to Austin will find themselves hard pressed to stick to a single figure like Fauré when confronted with the veritable gold mine of contemporary source material which the HRC is so fortunate and so justifiably proud to possess.

Claude Debussy. Etching by Yvan Thiele, June 1913. 18.2 x 13.2 cm. *HRC Iconography Collection.*

A *Gradual Diminuendo: Debussy and the*
"Trois Ballades de François Villon"

BY SUSAN YOUENS

PART I

In June 1915, Debussy gave an inscribed copy of the orchestral version of his *Trois Ballades de François Villon*, published by Jacques Durand in 1911, to a friend and fellow composer, André Charles Prosper Messager (1853–1929). The score, now in the Carlton Lake Collection of the Humanities Research Center at The University of Texas at Austin, contains numerous emendations handwritten in red ink and bears the dedication

> pour Messager
> son vieux dévoué
> Claudedebussy[1]
> juin 1915

written in blue ink in the upper left-hand corner of the title page. The emended presentation copy given to Messager is the third and final metamorphosis of these songs, beginning with the autograph manuscript of the original version for voice and piano (1910), now housed in the Bibliothèque Nationale. Durand published the completed *Ballades* in 1910, and they were first performed by the baritone Paule de Lestang on 5 February 1911. A few months before the premiere, in October 1910, Debussy had begun work on an orchestral arrangement of the three songs, which were performed on 5 March 1911 at the Concerts Sechiari with Debussy himself conducting, exactly one month after the initial public presentation of the original version. Four years later, Debussy returned to the orchestral version of the Villon *Ballades* and revised it once more.

We do not know exactly why he made the emendations and then gave the score to Messager—perhaps a definitive answer lies hidden somewhere in the estimated 1,500 or more letters by Debussy still largely unavailable and unpublished. Messager, nine years Debussy's senior and a pupil and friend of Gabriel Fauré, was famous as a composer, particularly of light operas, as a

---

[1] Debussy often signed his name in this fashion.

69

conductor, and as a leading Wagnerite. He served as director of the Société des Concerts du Conservatoire from 1908 to 1919, so it is at least probable that the emended version of the *Trois Ballades* might have been intended as a "conductor's score" for one of those concerts, although there is no mention of any such performance in the reviews, programs, and news items about the Conservatory in *La Revue musicale, Le Ménéstral,* or other sources. Even if the immediate inspiration for the emendations and the dedication to Messager could be attributed to plans for a performance that never took place, other circumstances—personal and historical vicissitudes—intersect at the emended score of the *Trois Ballades:* the problematical relationship between the two contemporaries, Debussy's increasing doubt that any composer could set poetry to music without a perceptible gulf between the two worlds of ordered word and ordered sound, his difficulties with the Villon texts he had chosen for his trilogy, and his philosophical and musical response to World War I.

The *Trois Ballades de François Villon* are among Debussy's most important compositions from the end of the first decade of this century, all the more significant because he wrote so few songs in his later years. He began primarily as a composer of *mélodies* in the 1880s and early 1890s, producing the five Verlaine settings of 1881–82, the *Ariettes* of 1888 (later, the *Ariettes oubliées* of 1903), the *Cinq Poèmes de Baudelaire* of 1889, the *Trois Mélodies* of Verlaine, the *Fêtes galantes,* and many individual songs; but after 1892, works for piano or orchestra and the various dramatic projects, particularly *Pélléas et Mélisande,* took precedence over songwriting, and the lapses of time between songs became longer and longer. In 1903 and 1904, well after the completion of *Pélléas et Mélisande* and after his divorce from Lily Texier, Debussy again became interested in the composition of *mélodies* to texts by Verlaine, Charles d'Orléans, and the early seventeenth-century poet Tristan l'Hermite, evidence of Debussy's increasingly refined but eclectic poetic tastes. After 1904, nearly six years lapsed before he returned to the *mélodie* with two more settings from l'Hermite's long poem *Le Promenoir des deux amants* and the Villon *Ballades.* He wrote only four more songs before his death: the *Trois Poèmes de Stéphane Mallarmé* of 1913 and the "Noël des enfants qui n'ont plus de maison" of 1916 from a poem by Debussy himself, an expression of his sorrow and outrage over the plight of the homeless children of war. Of the late songs, those composed from 1910 to the time of the "Noël," the Villon *Ballades* are the most ambitious and complex.

The *Ballades* also caused Debussy the most trouble. In March 1911, a journalist named Fernand Divoire asked a group of poets—Pierre Louÿs, Henry Bataille, Henri de Regnier, Edmond Haraucourt—and a group of composers, among them Debussy, Dukas, and Ravel—to respond to the same question for the short-lived periodical *Musica:* "Should one set good poetry, bad poetry, free verse, or prose to music?" ("Sous la musique que faut-il mettre: de beaux vers, de mauvais, des vers libres, de la prose?"). Debussy did not reply at length, as one might expect, since he disliked theorizing,[2] but he *did* contribute a brief article. In it, he is particularly concerned with the problems inevitable in any attempt to reconcile the inherent rhythms of great poetry with musical inspiration and with the purely abstract processes of composition. One can perhaps infer from the chronology of Debussy's *mélodies* and the laconic, almost hesitant prose of his response in *Musica*—unlike his usual witty and fluent style—that he had grown more and more aware of this fundamental conflict since the 1880s and 1890s. One of his most important compositions, a setting of Verlaine's "Colloque sentimental" (the third and last song of the *Fêtes galantes II* of 1904), in which we see and hear a stylistic change towards sparer, more modern textures, is in part about the persistence of Romantic illusions, the inexpressibility of feelings, and the futility of words, "choses indicibles."[3]

This basic and ineradicable sense of a rooted conflict at the source of song composition evidently became especially acute with regard to the Villon *Ballades*. Admittedly, these were his latest vocal works—he would naturally think of them first when asked the question by *Musica*, but he does not mention the two songs of *Le Promenoir des deux amants*, also composed in 1910, which are smaller, slighter compositions, lovely and undeservedly little-known but less ambitious and less problematical.

> Oh, lately, I've set to music, I don't know why, three ballades by Villon. Yes, I do know: because I've wanted to for a long time. Well, it's difficult to follow, to "strike" the right meter and still retain some inspiration. If you're just putting things together, content to juxtapose, of course it's not difficult, but then it's not worth the trouble either. Classic poetry has a life of its own, an "inner

---

[2] *Claude Debussy: Lettres 1884–1918*, ed. François Lesure (Paris: Hermann, 1980), p. 148. In a letter of Saturday, 10 March 1906 to his friend Louis Laloy, Debussy makes the characteristic statement: "Vous savez aussi-mieux que moi-combien on écrit sur la musique, puisqu'à notre époque, quand on ne sait plus quoi faire, ni surtout quoi dire, on s'improvise critique d'art!

"D'ailleurs les artistes eux-mêmes se sont mis à rever profondément sur des problèmes d'ésthetique—le plus curieux est qu'ils disent généralement beaucoup plus de bêtises que les autres. . . ." ("You also know—better than I—how much people write about music, since in our times, when one doesn't know what to do or what to say, one improvises art criticism! Besides, artists themselves ponder on problems of esthetics—it is quite curious that they generally say many more inanities than others. . . ."). Unless otherwise stated, all translations are mine.

[3] Susan Youens, "Debussy's Setting of Verlaine's 'Colloque sentimental': From the Past to the Present," *Studies in Music* no. 15 (December 1981): 93–105.

dynamism," as the Germans would say, which has nothing to do with us.[4]

It is hardly surprising that Debussy should have known about Villon's poetry and been attracted to it "for a long time": it had been "in the air" since the second quarter of the century and was part of the cultural *mise-en-scène* throughout the composer's life. This was due in part to reciprocal cultural currents between France and England, where the Pre-Raphaelites had rediscovered Villon—as early as 1870, Dante Gabriel Rossetti translated three of Villon's more rarefied and refined poems, including the "Ballade que Villon feit à la requeste de sa mère pour prier Nostre-Dame"[5]—and in part to the influence of scholarship. In 1873, the famous medievalist Gaston Paris made several archival discoveries regarding Villon's life—his attendance at the Université de Paris, his possible true identity as François Montcorbier— and this spurred on the already-present fascination with the fifteenth-century poet. That same year, in 1873, Theodore de Banville wrote his *Trente-six Ballades Joyevses pour passer le temps composées à la manière de François Villon*, which Debussy surely knew, since he set eleven poems by Banville in the 1880s and also worked on but never completed a setting of Banville's play *Diane au bois*. By "manière" Banville meant both matters of form and meter (ballades with refrains and envois in octosyllabic and decasyllabic lines), as well as subjects inspired by Villon's ballades, if completely unlike them in tone and style: a "Ballade en l'honneur de sa Mie," a "Ballade pour célébrer les pucelles," and a "Ballade à sa mère," in which he praises his mother for recognizing his poetic genius before anyone else.

Such *hommages* and imitations reflect a changed attitude toward Villon— an earlier generation, although impressed by his poetic genius in spite of their differing sensibilities and fascinated by the mysteries of his life, adopted a more disapproving stance. Théophile Gautier (1811–1872), who died just before Gaston Paris's discoveries, wrote a series of essays entitled *Les Grotesques*, which begins with Villon.[6] The Romantic-turned-Parnassian

[4]The responses by Debussy and Pierre Louÿs are reprinted in Henri Borgéaud, ed., *Correspondance de Claude Debussy et Pierre Louÿs* (Paris: Librairie José Corti, 1945), pp. 197–200. The quotation is taken from p. 198.

[5]William M. Rossetti, ed., *The Collected Works of Dante Gabriel Rossetti*, vol. 2 (London: Ellis and Scrutton, 1886), pp. 463–64.

[6]Gautier's *Les Grotesques* was first published in 1844 in Paris by Desessart, rue des Beaux-Arts, and reprinted in new editions several times throughout the next quarter of a century. In the edition of 1859 (Paris: Michel Levy Frères), the essay on Villon appears on pp. 1–39. Gautier speaks of Villon as one of the "minor poets" ("petites poètes") whose strange vision includes those qualities supposedly not to be found among "the aristocrats of art": the fantastic, the trivial, the ignoble, the popular proverb, even bad taste. He also writes, in an incorrect but revealing observation for his time, that "Villon is nearly the only one, among all of the medieval writers ['les gothiques'], who really had ideas."

72

François Villon. Wood engraving by Fritz Eichenberg, ca. 1979. 16.5 x 10.3 cm. *HRC Iconography Collection.*

Gautier could see in the poet of the "Testament" only someone "of the second order," a curiosity to add to his collection of "grimacing heads." The sole poem of which he approves is the prayer for Villon's mother which Debussy later set to music, and even then Gautier praises it in somewhat deprecating terms as something antique and primitive, "like one of those old paintings on a gold background by Giotto or Cimabue . . . its features . . . simple and naive, a little dry like all primitive things."[7] Twenty years later, Jean Richepin, a contemporary of Debussy who was also captivated by Villonesque fact and fiction, wrote a lengthy volume of poems entitled *La Chanson des Gueux* (1876), intended in part as an "imitation" (it could only have been written in the early years of the Third Republic) of Villon's argot poems and bawdier, seamier manner. This book, which earned Richepin a month in jail and a stiff fine for its mildly pornographic passages, was later reprinted in less censorious times in a deluxe illustrated edition.[8] By the end of the century, the Villon vogue was an established fact—there were several editions of Villon's works in France, and many of the medievalizing avant-garde poets acknowledged him in one way or another.

For Debussy, the fact that Villon was a contemporary of one of his favorite poets, Charles d'Orléans (1394–1465), whom Debussy quoted frequently in his letters and whom he called the "doux prince aimé des muses et si gentil français" ("sweet prince beloved of the muses and most noble Frenchman"),[9] must have been an additional attraction; one wonders if Debussy knew that the "Prince amoureux" in the envoi of Villon's "Ballade à s'amye" is probably a reference to Charles d'Orléans.[10] Both were French poets, both wrote in the *formes fixes* of the period, both were at times imprisoned in that violent age, but there were worlds of difference between Charles d'Orléan's twenty-five years of captivity in England and Villon's imprisonment and torture under far less genteel conditions in France—and a corresponding difference in their poetic styles. Debussy had already shown a preference for the "ideal" rather than the "mal" poems of Baudelaire, Verlaine's elegant and often melancholy Symbolist poetry rather than the later, longer, more rhetorical and detailed works, so predictably Debussy stayed away from Villon's vivid

[7] Gautier, pp. 37–38. "Cette dernière stance est délicieuse; on dirait une de ces vieilles peintures, sur fond d'or, de Giotto ou de Cimabue; le linéament est simple et naïf, un peu sec, comme toutes les choses primitives; les tons sont éclatants, sans crudité, quoique les demi-teintes manquent en quelques endroits; c'est de la vraie poésie catholique, croyante et pénétrée, comme un plus grand poète ne saurait la faire maintenant."

[8] Jean Richepin, *La Chanson des Gueux* (Paris: Éditions d'Art Édouard Pelletan, 1910).

[9] This is from a letter written by Debussy on 18 January 1914 to the conductor D.-E. Inghelbrecht. See *The Poetic Debussy: A Collection of His Song Texts and Selected Letters*, collected and annotated by Margaret G. Cobb (Boston: Northeastern University Press, 1982), p. 171.

[10] The editor of the edition Debussy probably used, Paul Lacroix, does not mention Charles d'Orléans in his notes or "éclaircissements" for "Ballade à s'amye."

depictions of the thieves' underworld in late medieval Paris, choosing instead wit ("Ballade des femmes de Paris"), simple but profound piety, and a rejected lover's bitterness. Debussy found the inherent musicality of Charles d'Orléans's verse—

> Par de ça, ne de là, la mer
> Ne sçay dame ne damoiselle
> Qui soit en tous biens parfais telle.
> ("Dieu! qu'il la fait bon regarder!")

> (Nowhere does the sea touch any woman
> married or maiden
> who is in any way more perfect than she.
> ["Lord! how good it is to look at her!"])

—and its prevailing tone of refined understatement closer to his innate preferences than even the gentler side of a *homo duplex* like Villon. The delicacy and recourse to suggestion rather than direct statement in Charles d'Orléans at times approach the reticences and deliberate indirection of Symbolist verse, always Debussy's "home ground," the milieu that most closely shares the techniques and ambience of Debussy's music. But in Villon, there is much less that is incomplete or hinted, and the poetic rhythms are different; he did not take as much delight as did Charles d'Orléans in word-music, the lilt of lines like "Par de ça, ne de là, la mer." Villon's complex and changeable poetic rhythms shift from one decasyllabic or octosyllabic line to the next in a way that challenges comparable periodicity in music. In fact, the rhythms are often somewhat choppy: every syllable seems to demand its due weight and accent, the result in part of the great number of plosive consonants and percussive *t*'s, *d*'s, *k* sounds, and relatively few *l*'s, or liquid, fluent sounds. The sound is quite unlike that of Charles d'Orléans, who creates a particular kind of euphony with the same or similar vowels chiming through the line. Where Villon begins a line with rhyming or euphonious sounds—"Faulse beauté"—he ends once again with the more usual compressed, lively, punctuated language: "tant que ru peult courir," "hypocrite doulceur," "la mort d'ung povre cueur," often throughout entire lines, as in "Sans lesquelz bien ame ne peult merir":

> Mais las! nen-ny: Ce se-roit donc fo-leur,
> Vieil je se-ray; vous laide et sans cou-leur.
> Or, beu-vez fort, tant que ru peult cou-rir.

When Debussy returned to *mélodies* after the Villon *Ballades*, it was with settings of some of Mallarmé's most pensive, elegant, musical poetry, including an evocation of the eighteenth-century world of "fêtes galantes," of

Watteau, Fragonard, and Boucher in "Placet futile." In the *Trois Poèmes de Stéphane Mallarmé*, he returned to the refined, richly allusive, delicate vein he knew best and preferred, the themes, moods, and qualities that he sought in Verlaine, Baudelaire, Charles d'Orléans, Tristan l'Hermite, and Mallarmé. The Villon *Ballades* represent Debussy's attempt (a successful one, for all of his doubts) to set poetry very different in tone and use of language from anything he had set to music before. In Villon's massive "Testament," even though Debussy chose themes nominally similar or related to those he had set to music before—the bitterness of rejected love, an old woman's simple, mystical piety—the compression and the distinctive rhythms of Villon's language posed Debussy problems he knew existed but encountered here in a particularly troubling way.

In *Musica*, Debussy was principally concerned with the difficulty, perhaps the impossibility, of preserving purely musical inspiration—the abstractions of musical laws—while attempting to do justice to the rhythms of language and imposing musical stresses and regular accents upon a language that does not itself possess those qualities. His problems in the Villon *Ballades* were undoubtedly compounded by a less-than-perfect edition, probably that by Paul Lacroix, Conservateur at the Bibliothèque de l'Arsenal.[11] Lacroix based his edition, as he tells the reader in the preface, on the latest information regarding Villon's life and the sources for his poetry, including the archival discoveries of Gaston Paris and Auguste Vitu, as well as a biography of the poet published the same year, 1877.[12] However, the texts are full of errors that Debussy might well have found puzzling—he once asked the musicologist Louis Laloy for the "sens exact" of certain words in Charles d'Orléans's poems,[13] and the "sens exact" of certain lines and phrases in the *Ballades* was difficult to decipher. For example, both Lacroix and Debussy have the line "Nommer te puis de ma deffaçon soeur" ("I could even call you sister of my dishonor") in the "Ballade à s'amye" rather than the correct reading "Nommer que puis de ma deffaçon seur/sur" ("Now certain of my ruin, I can name her"). Villon does just that—name her—in the second stanza, the first letter of the first six lines spelling out the name "MARTHA," just as the initial letters of the first stanza spell out his own name, "FRANÇOYS." The

---

[11] There is an earlier edition by one "Paul Jacob, Bibliophile" (Paris: P. Jannet, 1854), part of the series in the Bibliothèque Elzévirienne. Paul Jacob turns out to be none other than Paul Lacroix, a friend to Gérard de Nerval, among others. This edition was based upon the corrections made in 1835 by a still earlier scholar, Jean-Henri-Romain Prompsault (1798–1858), to his edition of 1832.

[12] Lacroix refers the "curious" to Auguste Longnon's *Étude biographique sur François Villon, d'après les documents inédits conservés aux Archives Nationales* (Paris: Henri Menu, 1877), as well as to Antoine Campaux's *François Villon, sa vie et ses oeuvres* (Paris: A. Durand, 1859) and to Auguste Vitu's biographical-archival study *Notice sur Villon* (Paris: Librairie des Bibliophiles, 1873).

[13] Cobb, *The Poetic Debussy*, p. 143n.

later misreading makes little sense: the poet has just called her far harsher names than "sister of my undoing," and Martha and Françoys were hardly brother and sister, in dishonor or otherwise (unlike Baudelaire, Villon was not given to calling his mistresses "sister," "mother," "child").

There *were* other editions available, including a recent one published in 1892 by the scholar Auguste Honoré Longnon, whose earlier works Lacroix cites in his preface, with the correct "seur" instead of "soeur," "sercher" and "onneur" rather than "crier" and "bonheur" in the lines

> Mieulx m'eust valu avoir esté *crier/sercher* (chercher)
> Ailleurs secours, c'eust esté *bonheur/mon onneur*

from the first *Ballade,* and "J'en risse lors, se tant peusse *mascher*" rather than "marcher." Had Debussy consulted this edition, he would have found the "sens exact" of phrases and lines whose meaning is obscured in Lacroix's edition by incorrect words. However, Lacroix writes in the preface that his texts are taken "d'après un manuscrit du XVᵉ siecle à la Bibliothèque de l'Arsenal," actually, ms. 3523 of the Bibliothèque de l'Arsenal, one of the most reliable of the Villon sources and the only one used by Lacroix, however "fautive." Lacroix goes on to write, "Il n'éxiste aucun texte vraiment authentique et original: ses poésies n'ont été recueillies qu'après sa mort sans doute, et, dans tous les cas, par des éditeurs qui ne les tenaient pas de lui directement, et qui les ont imprimées sur des copies plus ou moins fautives, sans les soumettre à la revision de l'auteur" ("There exists no truly authentic original text: his poems were without doubt gathered together after his death and, in every instance, by editors who did not receive them directly and who printed more or less inaccurate versions, without submitting them to the author for revisions").[14] Furthermore, the edition is quite lovely, and Debussy was partial to fine books.

There are, however, discrepancies between Lacroix's and Debussy's texts, although only one of them is of any consequence. For the line "J'en risse lors, se tant peusse marcher" above, Lacroix has a phrase that resembles Debussy's, but makes no sense: "J'en risse lors, *s'enfant* peusse marcher." The correct reading is an idiomatic expression, "Je m'en risse se tant peusse maschier," *maschier* meaning "to chew"—"I'll laugh if I can open my mouth that far," a link with the first stanza and the line, "Amour dure plus que fer a *maschier*" ("Hard love, harder than iron to chew"). Either Debussy or his editor, confounded by the lack of a "sens exact" in Lacroix's text, might have emended the line so that it acquired meaning, if not precisely according to Villon's intent. The differences in spelling are not that meaningful—Debussy was notoriously unreliable when it came to spelling, and he may have wished

---

[14]Paul Lacroix, ed., *Oeuvres de François Villon* (Paris: Librairie des Bibliophiles, 1877), p. ix.

to modernize some of the words: suys/suis, doibvent/doivent, cher-me/charme, etc. Also, Lacroix is far more liberal with commas than either Debussy or the medieval scribe ("Vierge, portant, sans rompure en-courir . . ."), again, a minor matter.

The strongest argument in favor of the Lacroix edition as Debussy's source has to do with the second *Ballade*, the prayer for Villon's mother. In the second stanza, the old woman speaks with fear of the cleric Theophilus, who sold his soul to the devil and was only saved by the Virgin Mary's intervention, and pleads, "Preservez moy que ne face jamais ce" ("Keep me from ever doing that"). However, both Lacroix and Debussy have the line "Préservez moy que je n'accomplisse ce," which is not to be found in the other contemporaneous editions and is surprisingly awkward. It is inconceiv-able that Villon would have inserted an eleven-syllable line into the middle of a ballade in decasyllabic *vers;* he was not as concerned with the intricacies of courtly versification as other fifteenth-century poets but he would not have made such a basic metrical error.

Perhaps it was Debussy's puzzlement about Villon/Lacroix's correct meaning, as well as problems in translating Villon's complex rhythms into music, that caused what seem to be difficulties with the vocal line. His setting of the line "Nommer te puis de ma deffaçon soeur" in the first *Ballade* is one example: before that point, the musical rhythms and poetic rhythms are in agreement, even though one would certainly place more stress on the first syllable of the word "Faul-se" than Debussy does in the rhythmic pattern ♪♪♪♪ for the initial four syllables ("Faulse beauté"), one that he uses many times in the Villon *Ballades* because of the 4 + 6 disposition of many decasyllabic lines. Within the first vocal phrase, Debussy stresses the word "qui" by setting it as a quarter note rather than an eighth note (not something one would do in speech, but very effective here), then reaches up a fifth from D to A, the higher pitch and larger interval, in graphic illustration of the word "tant." Transposed a third higher, the same gesture is repeated at the words "-te cher," with the last word "cher" sustained in obvious emphasis. The triplet eighth-note figures for the second line of the ballade, "Rude en effect, hypocrite doulceur," are also beautifully calculated, but not the ambiguous fourth line, which Debussy sets as a series of eighth notes:

Nommer te   puis de ma def_fa_çon sœur.

Here, musical inspiration and prosody are at odds with one another. The rising inflection in the melodic line at the word "te," the highest point of the phrase, places an undue emphasis on the word, while the succession of equal eighth notes flattens out the differences in the duration and relative emphasis within the line.

This is always a problem in setting French to music. The variations in the weight and tempo of words in French are greater than those of the durational values in music, with their precise equivalencies—half notes, quarter notes, eighth notes, sixteenths. Debussy is justly praised for vocal writing in which the meter, rhythmic patterns, tessitura, and inflections seem to stem directly from speech, intensified and rhythmically ordered, as in the refrain "En ceste foy je vueil vivre et mourir" in the second *Ballade;* each time it recurs, it is set to the same melodic phrase:

En ces_te foy je vueil vivre et mou _ rir.

Ordinarily the second and weaker syllable of the word "ces-te" with its mute *e* would not be set to a higher pitch than the first syllable and to an equal note value, but here the descending perfect fourth results in an entirely appropriate emphasis on the word "foy" and at the lower tessitura where the elderly woman's most moving and sincere avowals of that faith are set. Those avowals are set as recitation "à voix basse," phrases in which Debussy deliberately chooses to ignore all or most considerations of speech inflection. The effect is that of the humble, low-pitched, near-monotone mutter of someone who feels herself to be worthless, more expressive in this context than a closer approximation of speech inflections would be.

(à voix basse)

je n'en suis menteres _ se.

An eighteenth-century writer, Michel de Chabanon, criticized composers who set lines of verse as a series of notes of equal value, something he considered a condemnable leveling of syllabic quantity,[15] but composers both before and after his day made effective use of precisely that practice; certainly it is commonplace in Debussy's music. His difficulties with certain passages and lines in the *Ballades*—the setting of "Amour dure, plus que fer à mascher"—

with the A of "Amour" elongated beyond speech accentuation and "Amour dure" set as a dactyl—should not obscure the fact that many of the vocal lines have an air of inevitability about them that comes from a perfect marriage of musical inspiration and the demands of poetry.

In *Musica,* Debussy was not as pessimistic as Dukas, who wrote, "Do not fool yourself, poems cannot be set to music. . . . Poetry and music do not mix; they never merge."[16] Debussy merely recommended, tongue-in-cheek, that "we leave the great poets in peace. Besides, they like it better that way . . . in general, they're a bad lot."[17] Both declared a preference for prose or "prose rythmée," although it is difficult to know whether or not Debussy intended a distinction between "prose rythmée" and free verse of the sort that he himself wrote in the "Proses lyriques" of 1892 and "Nuits blanches" of 1899–1902.

> Tout à l'heure ses mains plus délicates que des
> fleurs, se poseront sur mes yeux . . .
>
> Ce soir, il m'a semblé que le mensonge
> Traînait dans les plis de sa jupe
> Et ses petits pieds ont foulé
> Mon coeur sans merci.
>
> (A while ago, her hands, more delicate than
> flowers, were placed upon my eyes . . .

---

[15] Michel Paul Guy de Chabanon, "Lettre sur les propriétés musicales de la langue française," *Mercure de France* (January 1773): 171–91, quoted in Frits Noske, *French Song from Berlioz to Duparc,* trans. Rita Benton, 2nd ed. (New York: Dover Publications, 1970), p. 47.

[16] F. Divoire, "Sous la musique que faut-il mettre? De beaux vers, de mauvais, des vers libres, de la prose?" *Musica* nos. 101–102 (February–March 1911): 38–40, 58–60.

[17] Borgéaud, *Correspondance,* p. 198.

That evening, I felt that falsehood
was caught in the folds of her skirt
and her tiny feet trampled
my heart without mercy.)

Possibly Debussy meant prose poetry after the manner of Pierre Louÿs's *Les Chansons de Bilitis,* the source for one of his most beautiful cycles, or the Symbolist prose of Maeterlinck's *Pélléas et Mélisande.* In either case, the de facto conversion of poetry into prose, the loss of a seen and felt progression from one rhythmically ordered line to the next, is no longer at issue, even if the more basic problem of language into music, in whatever artful arrangement, remains. For Debussy, "musicien français," for whom literature and the French language mattered greatly, who attended Mallarmé's *mardis,* who wrote poetry himself, whose friends were poets, the problem became more and more disturbing. Even though care for the inflections of the poet's text in itself hardly constitutes good music, much less great music, it was of utmost importance in Debussy's conception of French song; his dislike of Reynaldo Hahn's music without a doubt stemmed in part from the fact that Hahn at times does violence to the inherent rhythms of works by some of Debussy's most cherished poets: Verlaine, Charles d'Orléans, Gautier. Yet whatever his doubts expressed in 1911, two years later he composed the *Trois Poèmes de Stéphane Mallarmé.* For all his reservations, setting great poetry to music proved at times, and to our great fortune, irresistible.

Once the 1910 original version of the Villon *Ballades* for voice and piano was completed, Debussy orchestrated the songs but did not change the vocal line at all, and the emendations in 1915 once again have to do only with the orchestral parts. In the several metamorphoses of the *Trois Ballades,* the voice part never changes; however hard-won the reconciliation between Villon's poetic rhythms and melodic composition, Debussy was either reasonably content with the end result or unwilling to tamper with it any longer.

As for Messager, to whom the HRC copy of the *Trois Ballades* is inscribed, . he would most certainly have looked for, understood, and appreciated Debussy's variants and emendations in the orchestration of the *Ballades,* possibly—among other things—a peace offering to an estranged friend in time of war. Messager was known for his attention to matters of orchestration: according to one biographer, he never failed to comment on the orchestration of a work. He praised the "instrumentation d'une richesse et d'une variété incomparable" of Stravinsky's *Petrouchka* and disliked what he characterized as the heavy, unrelenting orchestration of Granados's "Goyes-

André Charles Prosper Messager, n.d. Photograph by Nadar. *HRC Photography Collection.*

cas."[18] Messager and Debussy were at one time fellow Wagnerites, Messager preceding Debussy to Bayreuth in 1886 to hear *Tristan und Isolde* and *Parsifal,* Debussy following later in 1888 and 1889, but while Messager remained a lifelong advocate of *wagnérisme,* Debussy began to resist the charms of "ce vieux Klingsor" almost upon his return from the Bayreuth pilgrimages. Debussy told another of Messager's later biographers that Wagner "n'avait commencé à y voir clair qu'avec *Parsifal,*" always for him the most potent Wagnerian influence.[19] Much of the early history of *Pélléas et Mélisande* is bound up with Messager's directorship of the Opéra-Comique from 1898 to 1903 and his help with the "jeunesse of *Pélléas*"—for example, Debussy entrusted the proofreading of the orchestral parts for the fourth act to Messager.[20] Debussy first confided in Messager about the inception of *La Mer,* and it was at Messager's invitation that Debussy first went to London in 1902.

The closeness did not last. With Debussy's divorce from his first wife, Lily Texier, in 1904, relations between the two composers cooled, since Messager, along with many of Debussy's friends, disapproved of the younger man's actions. The friendship might have been somewhat strained for other reasons as well—according to Fevrier, Debussy once told him "qu'il ignorait tout de la musique de Fauré" ("that he ignored all of Fauré's music"), Messager's beloved master and friend. Not until 1910, the year of composition of the Villon *Ballades,* did the two resume their interrupted friendship when Messager wrote Debussy a letter of condolence on the death of Debussy's father.[21]

Both Messager and Debussy were later asked to take part in the same international project supporting King Albert and the Belgian people against the German invasion. In April 1914, Debussy traveled to Brussels; six months later, in a letter to his publisher and friend, Jacques Durand, written on 9 October 1914, two days after the fall of Antwerp, he mentions a commission for a "Marche héroïque" but does so with a certain fastidious distaste, a feeling that it was hypocritical and absurd for him to "faire de l'héroïsme, tranquillement à l'abri des balles" ("act like a hero, safely out of

---

[18] Michel Augé-Laribe, *André Messager: musicien de théâtre* (Paris: Éditions du vieux colombier, 1951), p. 173.

[19] Henry Fevrier, *André Messager* (Paris: Amiot-Dumont, 1948), p. 109. "Debussy, très paradoxal, me dit une autre fois que Wagner 'n'avait commencé à y voir clair qu'avec *Parsifal*'" ("Debussy, very paradoxically, said to me another time that Wagner 'only began to see his way clearly with *Parsifal*'").

[20] François Lesure, ed., *Claude Debussy: Lettres 1884–1918* (Paris: Hermann, 1980), p. 124. In a letter written on 29 June 1903, Debussy thanks Messager for his undertaking.

[21] Jean André-Messager, ed., *L'Enfance de Pélléas: Lettres de Claude Debussy à André Messager* (Paris: Dorbon-Ainé, n.d.), p. 83. Debussy wrote a brief note to Messager earlier that same year on 2 March 1910; the formality of both notes is quite different in tone from the previous letters.

reach of the bullets").[22] He did, however, write a "Berceuse héroïque" in November 1914 for solo piano, a work first printed that month in *King Albert's Book: A Tribute to the Belgian King and People from Representative Men and Women Throughout the World.* The project was organized by the prolific British writer Sir Hall Caine (1853–1931), a novelist with a pronounced religious bent *(The Eternal City,* "The Christian," *Life of Christ, The Master of Man),* and published by the *London Daily Telegraph* in conjunction with the *Daily Sketch,* the *Glasgow Herald,* and the firm of Hodder and Stoughton. Many prestigious writers, visual artists, and composers from both France and England were contributors, including Rudyard Kipling, Thomas Hardy, Henri Bergson, and Monet. Debussy's "Berceuse" is not a major composition, certainly nothing comparable to the Villon *Ballades;* in fact, none of the works in *King Albert's Book* are more than mediocre *pièces d'occasion.* Debussy spoke of it as a "digression" and admitted that it was very difficult to write,[23] but the delicacy and subtlety of the soft sonorities are nevertheless very moving. Somehow it seems characteristic that he should write such a quiet cradle song/funeral march rather than a military march. The horn-calls might have come from personal experience: in September 1914, Debussy and his family had gone to Angers in western France for refuge because of rumors rather than real danger at that time, and there Debussy heard French soldiers playing "trumpet calls and rhythms which irresistibly remind me of the best themes of the two Richards [Wagner and Strauss]," as he tells Durand, adding tongue-in-cheek, "if you feel inclined to draw morals, you may certainly find one here."[24] Possibly those fanfares found their way in transmuted form into the "Berceuse." Some sonorities are directly reminiscent of Debussy's orchestration for the Villon *Ballades,* such as the muted double-stopped cello

[22]Claude Debussy, *Lettres de Claude Debussy à son éditeur* (Paris: A. Durand et Cie, 1927), p. 128.

[23]Claude Debussy, *Lettres à deux amis* (Paris: Librairie José Corti, 1942), p. 143, letter of 1 January 1915. "Sollicité par le *Daily Telegraph,* j'ai dû écrire quelque chose pour *le Livre du Roi Albert.* Ça a été très dur, d'autant plus que la Brabançonne ne verse aucun héroïsme dans le coeur de ceux qui n'ont pas été élevés 'avec'.

"Le résultat de ces divagations prend le titre de 'Berceuse héroïque' . . . . c'est tout ce que j'ai pu faire, le voisinage encore si proche des hostilités me gênant physiquement. Il faut y ajouter mon inferiorité militaire, car je ne saurais me servir d'un fusil. . . ." ("Approached by the *Daily Telegraph,* I was obliged to write something for *King Albert's Book.* It was quite hard, particularly as la Brabançonne evokes no feelings of heroism in the hearts of those who were not brought up with it. The result of this digression has the title 'Berceuse héroïque'. . . . It was all I was able to achieve, having been physically affected by the proximity of hostility, not to mention my own sense of inferiority in military matters, since I have never handled a rifle. . . .")

[24]Debussy, *Lettres de Claude Debussy à son éditeur,* p. 129. "Pendant que je vous écris, des petits soldats s'exercent, qui sur le clairon, qui sur le tambour . . . Ces sonneries, ces rythmes rappellent irresistiblement les meilleurs themes des deux 'Richard'! Si vous avez le gout des moralités, vous pouvez en tirer une de ce rapprochement."

harmonics on a perfect fourth at rehearsal number $\boxed{4}$ in combination with the divisi second violins tremolando "sur la touche"; parallel chords in the solo oboe, bassoons, and three solo violas; a rising octave figure repeated in each measure of the divided first violins—all familiar textural, intervallic, rhythmic, and orchestral ideas from the *Ballades*.

The early war years were "vile times" for Debussy, as he told his close friend Robert Godet, and nearly sterile except for a few brief compositions, most of them minor and inconsequential, undertaken for pecuniary reasons—Debussy's customary financial desperation—or as a *divertissement*. The compositions begun and completed between 1913 and the summer of 1915 indicate just how deeply and adversely Debussy was affected by the outbreak of war. He completed *Khamma*, a short ballet begun (reluctantly) in 1911–12, and composed the piano score for the children's ballet *La Boite à joujoux*—he did no more than sketch an orchestral score until 1917. The "Marche héroïque" too was a *pièce d'occasion*, more important for what it represents than what it is; only the *Trois Poèmes de Stéphane Mallarmé* from 1913 are truly significant musically, and they are remarkable for the spareness and delicacy of the piano accompaniments. Debussy had always tended toward understatement, always explored how close "presque rien" could come to "rien," to silence itself, but at this terrible time of creative sterility and profound depression, the innate tendency toward understatement became, in historical hindsight, even more exaggerated, a reaction to war and all it engendered—not just the infernal uproar of chaos and carnage itself or the bombast of patriotic fervor, but the artistic savagery that preceded the war, the decibel level and the assault on the senses embodied in works like *Le Sacre du printemps*. With the melancholy fastidiousness that is so characteristic of him, Debussy became—when he could "speak" at all—the arbiter of elegant and poignant softness shading to nothingness.

The *diminuendo* of the years from 1913 through the spring of 1915 is twofold: the refined and precise definition of sounds pared down to silence and the silence of pieces uncomposed. A ballet commissioned for London early in 1914 was to be entitled *Le Palais de silence,* and the only result was just that—silence. The work was postponed until the end of the war, and as it happened, forever. The inability to do more than "guard a fence" for his country or to compose—"I am not referring," he says, referring to it nevertheless, both stoically and poignantly, "to the past two months in which I haven't written a note or touched a piano"[25]—horrified Debussy, whose life was bounded by wars with Germany: the Franco-Prussian War in his youth and the First World War, which was at a crisis for the French when Debussy died in March 1918. In a letter written to Godet on New Year's Day 1915, Debussy wrote, "You are probably the only man who understands that

[25]Ibid., p. 24. Letter from Angers on 21 September 1914.

silence does not mean oblivion. Indeed, these vile times serve to show that tact is a rare and a refreshing flower." If that is one side of silence, the other is his despairing comment in the same letter, "For months I no longer knew what music was."[26]

Debussy emerged from silence in the summer of 1915—the latter part of that year was one of the most productive of his entire life. The suite for piano four-hands, "En blanc et noir," was completed during the summer and followed by the twelve etudes for piano and two of the three last sonatas, those for cello and piano, and for flute, viola, and harp. The date of the Messager manuscript is June 1915, contemporaneous with work on the suite "En blanc et noir," both of them manifestations of Debussy's fascination with Villon, since the second piece in the set—Debussy's favorite—was inspired by Villon's famous "Ballade contre les ennemis de France," a poem with an obvious and powerful appeal to the "musicien français" in wartime. Thus the resurgence of creativity is bound up in its beginnings with Villon, and in the emendations Debussy responds to war with the classicizing restraint and the "chiseling" of details that characterize his last extraordinary works. As the cannons rolled over Europe, annihilating forever the world as Debussy had known it, he became more quiet and refined, insistent in his fashion upon a quality of civilization that was vanishing from sight and sound.

PART II

The emendations in the Messager score have to do entirely with subtle details of instrumentation and dynamics. In most instances, Debussy indicated the presence of a correction or change by a + mark either just preceding the altered passage, in the margin before or after the printed stave, or both. Anything he wished deleted, he crossed out in neat parallel slanting lines, with no cross-hatching; where the measure or passage is too crowded to permit crossing out the unwanted pitches and signs and adding the revisions in such a way that they might be easily legible, Debussy erased the printed score—the paper is thin, rough, almost worn through at these places—and wrote in the desired changes in the familiar red ink. The whole is a model of orderliness and neatness; there is not a single ambiguous or confusing instance in the entire forty-four page score, with emendations on twenty-seven pages and a misprint corrected on one page.

Looking through the emended score, there is clearly a pattern traceable in the revisions. Almost all of them have to do with subtleties of orchestral texture: in particular, Debussy lightens the sound at the ends of phrases or at the end of an entire song (the first *Ballade*), clarifies the dynamic

[26] Debussy, *Lettres à deux amis*, p. 142.

86

indications—making explicit what was only implicit before—and redresses the orchestral balance with revised doublings so that a particular motive or figure is emphasized more strongly than before and another, simultaneous motive less so. There is, however, far more subtraction than addition evident in Debussy's emendations, and the cumulative effect is that of a slightly "leaner" sound, both more transparent and more colorful, the transparency obtained in a variety of ways: punctuating a previously legato passage with rests in a way that "aerates" the phrase, re-voicing chords, and removing accompanimental figures and doublings that he now found to be superfluous. Only once does Debussy add—not new music, but another repetitive measure to a figure already present, and that is in the third *Ballade*, by far the "busiest" and most bustling orchestral accompaniment of the three (the greatest degree of change and alteration between the original version for voice and piano and the orchestral score of 1911 is also in the third and last *Ballade*). The score does not become longer or shorter by a single measure, and the changes only very rarely affect fundamental matters of harmony and melodic line: Debussy's concern was obviously with polish, refinement, clarity, and nuance, nothing else.

Claude Debussy, 1909. From an "Album de photographies dans l'intimité de personnages illustrés, 1860–1920." Gernsheim Collection, *HRC Photography Collection.*

I. BALLADE *de Villon à s'amye*

1. p. 4, mm. 11–12: In the first and second horn parts Debussy no longer wants the octave doubling that appears in the 1911 edition, so he deletes the topmost part for the first horn and substitutes the D a tritone higher, thus altering the distribution of pitches in the added-note harmony.

2. p. 5: The motive for the first and second bassoons playing in unison, mm. 16–17, the third and fourth measures after rehearsal number 2 , is deleted, thereby casting a greater emphasis on the first horn figure, no longer doubled by the bassoons.

3. At almost the same place, mm. 17–18, the fourth and fifth measures after 2 , Debussy indicates that the lower of the two divisi cello parts, rather than a sustained, soft, low E, should be played as a pizzicato quarter note followed by a half-note rest.

4. p. 6, m. 20, the second measure after ⟨3⟩ in the first clarinet part: At the outcry "Haro, haro, le grand et le mineur!" the second note of each figure with the rhythmic pattern  that pervades much of the song has been vigorously erased and altered from a succession of ascending whole steps to descending major thirds which double the oboe part. The half-step and whole-step motives that also compose this chord progression at one of the climactic moments in the song are already amply doubled, and this figure in the first clarinets and oboes constitutes the topmost voice in these emphatic harmonies.

Debussy had earlier used a similar figure in his setting of "La Grotte" or "Auprès de cette grotte sombre" from *Le Promenoir des deux amants* by the early Baroque poet Tristan l'Hermite (1601–1655). This rhythmic pattern and descending seconds, used at the beginning of both "La Grotte" and the first *Ballade,* with somewhat the same connotation, suggest a melancholy atmosphere emanating from love that ended badly or in tragedy, that of Narcissus's self-love in "La Grotte" and Françoys's more bitter complaint.

5. p. 6, m. 19, rehearsal number ⟨3⟩ : In the cellos, now no longer divisi but playing in unison, Debussy adds the word "arco" just beneath the key signature. Only the two low E's in the preceding two measures are changed to pizzicati pitches.

6. p. 8, mm. 29–30, the third and second measures before ⟨5⟩ : Debussy makes some marked changes in the divisi second violin parts. It is only at this one point that Debussy concentrates the orchestration in the strings; for much of this ballade song, the wind instruments predominate over the strings. However, at the words "Ung temps viendra, qui fera desseicher,/ Jaulnir, flestrir, vostre espanie fleur," the accompaniment is for the combined divisi strings and flute, with the obvious ironic intent of emphasizing with

Romantic sonorities the sweetness and beauty in full bloom even as he anticipates its decay, its withering, yellowing, and aging. The second violin parts are indicated for soloists rather than for the entire section, and the harmonies are re-voiced for a higher, lighter, notably more transparent, sound.

7. p. 9, m. 36, four measures after ⑤ : Just above the divided viola parts, Debussy adds the words "En dehors." At the words "Vieil je seray," he evidently wants the orchestral sound to be as minimal and as distant-sounding as possible. However, there is also possibly a subtle question of balance. The divisi bowed violas and cellos begin this passage, followed by the first violins playing "sur le chevalet," or on the bridge—a special sound effect—and the divisi second violins with only the single pianissimo pizzicato interval of a fourth. If the lower strings at the start of this passage, a very muted and delicate one, are not to overpower the upper strings at their entrance, the precautionary note "En dehors" might well have seemed necessary.

8. p. 9, m. 36, the fifth measure after ⑤ : At the words "vous, laide et sans couleur," Debussy adds crescendo markings for the figures in the clarinets as the motives in the strings become softer.

9. p. 11, m. 43, three measures before ⑧ : The horn and bassoon parts are reinforced by the third horn, which now doubles the first horn part, while the fourth horn part and bassoon parts are slightly rewritten. The eighth-note rest in the bassoons at the end of the emended passage permits the upwards motion of the forte motive in the horns to "sound through" more clearly.

90

10. p. 12, m. 47, at the end of the first measure after 8 : Debussy writes the word "più" before the already existing "p" markings at the start of m. 48 in the flutes, oboes, first violins, and celli. For the first and second clarinets, he writes "più p," as there was no former "p" indication. The C# in the bassoons is sustained even longer and the direction "più p ⸺ " added, but he does not bother to cross out the existing rests that earlier followed the quarter-note C# in the 1911 score.

11. Just before the direction "En retenant" in m. 48, the next-to-last measure of the song, Debussy calls for mutes ("Sourdines") in all of the string parts except for the double basses, which are silent until the two bass soloists "sur la touche" sound the last note of the piece.

12. At the direction "En retenant," Debussy adds a decrescendo marking to the indication "p doux et soutenu" already given for the first and second flutes. For the final flute sonority, Debussy deletes the fermata in order to make his new rhythmic specifications more precise, and the same is true of the low F# in the first bassoon part. Only the double-bass soloists now have a fermata marking. Debussy obviously wanted to ensure that this was the last and only sound that one hears at the end, and so he pares down the muted final passage even more. The part for the fourth horn, doubling the second horn part in the next-to-last measure, is eliminated.

II. BALLADE *que Villon feit à la requeste de sa mère pour prier Nostre-Dame.*

Most of the more substantive changes that Debussy made in the second *Ballade* have to do with the woodwind and the brass parts; only twice does one find emendations in the strings. In fact, this song, the accompaniment orchestrated for three flutes, two oboes, English horn, two clarinets, three bassoons, four horns, harp, and strings, is especially notable for Debussy's prominent use of solo winds and horns, particularly at the beginning of the first and third stanzas of this varied strophic form.

1. p. 13, mm. 3–4 in the two separate oboe parts: For the first oboe, Debussy indicates that the phrase marked with a slur and beginning with the A in the middle of the third measure should end with the eighth-note A at the start of m. 4. He deletes the descending scalewise pitches G F E that follow in the 1911 score and adds the appropriate rests, not bothering to cross out the eighth-note rest after the phrase as printed. The simultaneous phrase in the second oboe part is similarly changed so that it begins and ends with the melodic line in the first oboe, unlike the printed score where the last note of the phrase in the second oboe is sustained. This emendation means that only the first flute and first bassoon play the descending scalewise conclusion of the line. Once again, Debussy "thins out" the texture, particularly at the ends of phrases. This also means that the sustained octave E's that sound when the singer enters with the words "Dame du ciel" are lessened by the omission of the oboe, leaving the first bassoon and flute as the only wind instruments with the pedal note.

2. pp. 15–16, m. 9, the second measure after rehearsal number ⑨ : The flute parts in mm. 9–10 are eliminated. That deleted flute figure, doubled in thirds, is one of the most characteristic Debussyan motives, an ascending major second, repeated literally in a two-bar (1 + 1) unit, which is in itself then repeated sequentially a step higher. The second two-bar segment, the sequential repetition, is not deleted but made lighter: the slurred half-note figures become a succession of quarter notes with a rest after each one. The same alteration also appears in mm. 9–10 in the parts for the second and fourth horns and in mm. 11–12 in the first clarinet part.

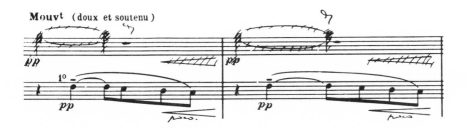

3. p. 15, mm. 9–10: In the 1911 edition, there are crescendo markings in the second half of the measure for the oboe and bassoon parts. Debussy in 1915 adds the indication "poco" to ensure that this will be no more than a slight crescendo.

4. p. 16, m. 14, the second measure after 10 : Debussy deletes the two-note motive F# E for the two bassoons playing à deux (they had been separated and playing in parallel fifths for the previous measure-and-a-half). Now, only the violas and the lower of the two divided cello parts play in unison the pitches F# E below middle C, without the lower, thicker doubling an octave below.

5. p. 17, m. 15, the third measure after 10 : The two flutes formerly each had a separate pitch, C# doubled at the octave. Debussy deletes the topmost C# in the first flute, also the slur markings and accents. However, the harp and first horn parts, which are similar, retain both the slurs and the accent markings.

6. p. 17, m. 16, the fourth measure after 10 : At the words "Je n'en suis menteresse," Debussy changes the spacing of the successive C major and B^b major chords, such that the higher parallel fifths G C and F B^b in the two bassoons become the lower parallel fourths C G and B^b F, while the fourth horn part is also changed. The violas were originally divided into two parts, a doubling at the octave; in the 1915 emendations, Debussy removes the topmost cello part and shifts that pitch to the violas, which are now triply divided. Finally, he adds a "p" marking to the double bass part, which makes its first appearance in the second *Ballade* here. In the next measure (m. 17), the abbreviation "Div." for the violas, which had formerly been directed to play double-stops in m. 16, is no longer necessary, given the triple division of the viola section in the emended orchestration, and so is crossed out.

7. p. 18, m. 21, the second measure after 11 : In the solo first bassoon line, Debussy adds a long decrescendo throughout the measure to the end of the phrase, just as in the first horn part beneath it. In the next measure (m. 22), he adds another decrescendo marking beneath the motive that appears in the last half of the measure in the second clarinet, duplicating the

decrescendo in the first flute. Again, the intent is clearly to make the dynamics both softer and more precise.

8. p. 18, m. 23: Debussy adds the indication "pp" to the harp part, the octave-doubled harmonic fifths A D.

9. The horn part for p. 19, m. 25, the second measure after [12] , reads as follows in the 1911 score:

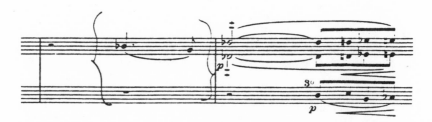

In 1915, Debussy erased the bracketed figure and changed it as follows, an echo of a motive immediately preceding it in the divided violas:

10. p. 19, m. 26, three measures after [12] : Debussy changes the second pitch in the first clarinet part so that it now doubles the second oboe part.

11. p. 23, m. 41, the first two measures of [15] : The third horn, the only one of the four horns playing at this point, formerly had a sustained, accented half note in the last half of the measure, repeated in the familiar Debussyan 1 + 1 bar pattern. This is changed to a two-note descending

motive, doubling the oboes, English horn, and divisi tremolando cellos with the same figure. The rhythmic pattern in the second bassoon part is also changed.

Perhaps these changes are a way of further emphasizing the words "haulte Deesse" on the pitches C B^b in the vocal line.

III. BALLADE *des femmes de Paris.*

There are fewer changes in the third *Ballade* than in either of the preceding two songs, quite striking in light of the fact that the third *Ballade* is longer, 122 measures compared to 47 measures for the second *Ballade* and 49 for the first (of course, it is marked "Alerte et gai," much quicker than the first *Ballade*, "Triste et lent," or the second, "Tres modéré"). Most of the emendations have to do with the dynamic markings, again, with indications for softer and more precisely notated dynamics; for example, the exact duration of a decrescendo. Debussy also changes the attack in a number of brief string passages, which lightens and varies the texture. The resulting alternation between bowed and pizzicato phrases enhances the chattering, bustling sound of the accompaniment.

1. p. 26, m. 13, two bars after 16 : Debussy writes in three added pitches in the first bassoon part, also a "p" marking and a quarter-note rest (the additions are bracketed in the example).

The indication "léger" in the last half of the measure is also an emendation.

2. p. 27, m. 16, five bars after ⟦16⟧ : At the ascending scalewise run in the bassoon part, Debussy crosses out the indication "a 2" and writes above "1°"—this is now a solo passage for the first bassoon.

3. p. 27, m. 18, two bars before ⟦17⟧ : Debussy alters the rhythmic disposition of the sustained low C# in the third bassoon part:

This allows the pizzicato in the divisi cellos to emerge more clearly. The low C# had formerly been tied to an eighth-note A at the beginning of the next measure, and that pitch is now deleted, along with the subsequent rests, and replaced by a whole-note rest.

4. p. 30, m. 34, the fourth measure after ⟦19⟧ : Debussy adds a decrescendo marking in the last half of the measure at the triplet sixteenth-note figures in the first violins, violas, and cellos. He already has a "dim." marking at the beginning of that measure, so the additional decrescendo signs are presumably intended to ensure that the dynamics continue to become softer throughout the measure.

5. p. 30, m. 35, the fifth measure after ⟦19⟧ : Debussy adds the underlined direction "*Meno mosso,*" written once above the entire wind/brass section and again above the voice/strings section, in order to emphasize the change from the sff ending of the first refrain, "Il n'est bon bec que de Paris," to the softer, lighter passage in measures 35–42 ("De beau parler tiennent chayeres").

6. p. 30, m. 38, five bars before ⟦20⟧ : Debussy adds decrescendo markings that extend throughout the measure both above and below the divisi cello parts.

7. p. 31, mm. 39–42: Debussy makes several small changes in this passage. He deletes the third bassoon part in mm. 39–40 (the two sustained pitches E and C#), adds the indication "3°" at the end of m. 40 to restore the third bassoon for the next measure, writes in the direction "p" beside the F# in the third bassoon in m. 41, and adds a small decrescendo marking beneath the F# in the first bassoon part in m. 41 that had been carried over from the previous measure. There are also several small changes in the lower string parts in those same bars, mm. 39–40, such as the addition of two "p"

markings in m. 39, one for each of the cello parts. In m. 40, the double-basses originally had nothing at all; now they play a staccato quarter-note C#. The basses are now clearly intended to replace the deleted sustained third bassoon notes with a lighter touch and texture.

8. At rehearsal number [20] , with the change of key signature, the "Rubato" becomes "Rubato molto," written twice above the winds/brass and voice/strings. In m. 43, the triplet eighth-note figures in the viola are now marked to be played pizzicato, like the double-stops in the second violins and the first cello part.

9. p. 32, m. 47, six bars before [21] : The violas are once again bowed and a "p" sign added.

10. p. 33, m. 51, two bars before [21] : Debussy writes "*Tutti* pizz." above the cello part and then, two measures later, crosses out the now-superfluous pizzicato indication.

11. p. 33, m. 53: At rehearsal [21] in the second violin part, the edition includes a redundant "p" sign at the beginning of the measure, which is now crossed out.

12. p. 33, m. 55, two bars after [21] : Debussy adds a "p" marking beneath the divisi first violin parts.

13. p. 34, m. 57, four bars before [22] : Debussy adds a pizzicato indication for the single accented staccato B^b pitch in the cellos. For all of the minuscule changes to pages 33 and 34, Debussy does not bother to write the usual + signs in the margins or within the score.

14. p. 36, m. 72, at rehearsal [23] : The composer indicates mutes for the two trumpet parts, doubled in thirds. This passage lasts for four measures, after which the trumpets fall silent until [24] at m. 82; two bars before, at m. 80, Debussy asks that the players remove their mutes for the trumpet melody that follows.

15. p. 37, m. 76, six bars before $\boxed{24}$: The word "expressif" is added just after the indication "sul G" for the first violin part, which doubles the vocal line at this point.

16. p. 39, m. 96, rehearsal $\boxed{26}$: The lower of the two violin parts is directed to play pizzicato.

This continues until m. 99 at the change of key signature; there, the alternating E's at different octave registers are bowed.

17. p. 41, m. 104: Debussy adds a decrescendo extending throughout the entire measure for the first and second horn parts.

18. p. 41, m. 105: The dynamics for the third and fourth horn parts are changed from "p" to "pp."

19. p. 42, m. 107, two bars before $\boxed{27}$: The direction "dim." is added for the violas. A diminuendo was originally printed for the other string parts and was apparently omitted from the viola line only by an oversight, corrected here.

20. p. 42, m. 108, one bar before $\boxed{27}$: The composer adds the marking "p ———— ," the decrescendo again extending throughout the measure, for the English horn, the first and second horns, the violas, cellos, and basses.

21. p. 42, mm. 109 and 111, at rehearsal $\boxed{27}$ and two bars after: The word "léger" is written in, first beneath the solo bassoon part and then at the solo oboe line that enters in echo of the previous bassoon phrase.

22. At the end of the third *Ballade*, Debussy has the horns and trumpets begin their sixteenth-note figuration a measure earlier than indicated in the printed score. Instead of a measure of rest for those instruments, we find the following:

Also, above the winds/brass and voice/strings in mm. 119–121, the composer writes "Cédez - - - //mouvt." for the final repetition of the words "bec que de Paris."

Debussy's emendations of the *Trois Ballades* in 1915 consist entirely of subtleties of orchestration and dynamics, with no changes that affect the vocal line, the structure, the harmonies, or the rhythmic patterns in any of the three songs. Rather, it is the *sound* that is slightly but significantly altered in the direction of greater lightness and transparency, this in a score already remarkable for its translucency. Furthermore, there are fewer and fewer emendations as one proceeds through the presentation copy for Messager: those in the first *Ballade* have to do more or less equally with the wind and brass parts, the strings, and dynamic markings, whereas the emendations in the second *Ballade* mostly affect the wind parts, and those in the third *Ballade*, with only a few notable exceptions near the beginning and the end of the song, are virtually all a matter of dynamics.

Sir William Walton, ca. 1952. From the program for the 8 July 1952 performance of *Façade* at the Royal Festival Hall in London. *HRC Collections*.

"Façade" and the Music of Sir William Walton

BY STEWART R. CRAGGS

Among the diverse and significant holdings of musical material at the Humanities Research Center is the largest collection outside the United Kingdom of William Walton's musical settings of Edith Sitwell's poems, which Walton entitled *Façade*.[1] The various settings for *Façade* occupied Walton for most of his creative life, the main gestatory period of evolution stretching from 1921 to 1928. William Walton (1902–1983) was only nineteen years of age in 1921, and though still in the process of forging his own musical language, was already under the influence of the Sitwell family, which was determined to save its young protégé from entering either the Royal College of Music or the Royal Academy of Music. Osbert Sitwell saw the nurturing of Walton's creativity as part of his own struggle with the English cultural Establishment, a struggle which was somewhat of an obsession with him. The Sitwells brought Walton into brief contact with Ernest Ansermet, who was in London as conductor of the Russian Ballet when it first performed Manuel de Falla's *Tricorne* at the Alhambra Theatre on 22 July 1919, and with Edward Dent and Ferruccio Busoni. The Sitwells enabled Walton to attend concerts of contemporary music and thereby were able, as Osbert Sitwell wrote, "to keep him in touch with the vital works of the age."[2] From this association with the Sitwells came Walton's early interest in such works as *Petrushka*, *Le Sacre du printemps*, and *Daphnis et Chloé*, as well as his lifelong interest in "popular" music.

By 1921–22, Edith Sitwell had moved away from the realism of her earlier verse to become increasingly involved in experimental poetry. Although the content of her work grew more abstract, its words sought to imitate certain popular musical forms. She was absorbed by the "texture" of particular words, with assonances, dissonances, rhythms, and repetitions, which could produce particular effects. Music had always meant a great deal to her, and according to Osbert she was experimenting to obtain "through the medium

---

[1] The other location of such material is Oxford University Press, Walton's publisher, with one or two settings still in private hands.

[2] Osbert Sitwell, *Laughter in the Next Room* (London: Macmillan, 1958), p. 182.

of words the rhythm of dance measures such as waltzes, polkas, foxtrots."[3] This naturally must have interested the young Walton, who later admitted that *Façade* was largely experimental from the outset. As with most experiments, it was subject to the usual crop of second thoughts, revisions, and new ideas, which meant that the work was in effect constructed anew for each performance—numbers were placed in a different order, and as often as not new numbers were composed and old ones were revised or rejected. Edith had already published more than half of the poems which would be included in the first production of *Façade* even before the idea of writing music to accompany them was suggested to Walton. This "entertainment" was performed privately by the two artists on 24 January 1922 at Carlyle Square, Chelsea, Osbert Sitwell's London home, at which time the collaborative work consisted of eighteen items, preceded by a "General salute and prologue." One of two surviving copies of the typewritten program for this performance is now at HRC.

The public premiere of *Façade* was held at the Aeolian Hall in June 1923, and for this performance Walton added six further items to make a total of twenty-four "facets" prefaced by the same "General salute and prologue." HRC possesses a handbill advertising the June 1923 performance—"a new and original musical entertainment in twenty-four facets."[4] Although many critics and members of the public found the proceedings an incomprehensible waste of time, this presentation of *Façade* was a celebrated occasion and has been described variously by recent biographers and literary historians, among them John Pearson:

> The Aeolian Hall (or the A-E-I-O-Ulian Hall, as Noel Coward christened it) is in Bond Street, and the performance that took place there was to become part of the artistic history of the twenties, and central to the whole mythology of the Sitwells. According to the 'official' Sitwell view, as expressed by both Edith and Osbert in their memoirs, it was the nearest that they ever came to actual confrontation with the embattled philistine. A large part of the audience was there to indulge their favourite English sport of 'artist-baiting' and were so incensed at their contact with original artists in the flesh that they became infuriated as *Façade* continued and 'manifested their contempt and rage', first by hissing, and finally by

[3] Sitwell, p. 197.

[4] The late Ambrose Gauntlett, cellist at the Aeolian Hall performance in 1923, was able to assist me in reconstructing the program from notes written in a diary at the time: 1: Gardener Janus Catches a Naiad, En famille (allegro), Mariner Man; 2: Trio for Two Cats and Trombone, Lullaby for Jumbo, Ass Face; 3: Small Talk, By the Lake, Said King Pompey—or—Tango (?); 4: A Man from the Far Countree, Herodiade's Flea—or—Foxtrot (?), Tarantella (?); 5: Daphne, Through Gilded Trellises, Sir Beelzebub; 6: Valse, Jodelling Song, Hornpipe (repeated by public demand); 7: March, Something Lies Beyond, The Last Gallop; 8: Aubade, The Owl.

threatening to attack poor Edith, who had to wait until the hostile crowd dispersed. 'She was', she used to claim, 'nearly lynched by the inevitable old woman, symbol of the enemy, who had waited, umbrella raised, to smite her.'

Next day the popular papers took up the battle and continued to insult the Sitwells in their sacred role of artists. All Osbert's wartime hatred of the yellow press revived when he read one item in a gossip column under the headline 'Drivel They Paid to Hear', and in another, an interview with the fireman at the Aeolian Hall who was quoted as saying, quite reasonably in the circumstances, 'that never in twenty years' experience of recitals at that hall had he known anything like it'. 'For several weeks subsequently,' wrote Osbert, 'we were obliged to go about London feeling as if we had committed a murder'—and from then on the battle of the Aeolian Hall appeared to epitomise all that was obscurantist, vulgar and ill-natured in the way society at large reacted to the artist.[5]

Why did *Façade* elicit such a reaction? Hugh Ottaway observes:

> *Façade* was a sophisticated shot and, despite protestations to the contrary, one suspects that the boos and hisses which greeted the first *public* performance gave real satisfaction to the Sitwells. That it was also a brilliant shot was due very largely to Walton's music; it is the music which has survived.
>
> *Façade* brought out Walton's resourcefulness, his ability to seize on an opportunity and his flair for instrumental colour. Behind the stylish bravado there is much ingenuity and a quality of workmanship which has far more bearing on the music's popularity than the 'innocent' listener is likely to suppose. Add to these Walton's genuine feeling for the idiom he has satirized and one gains an insight into his powers as an entertainer.[6]

To this line of thinking Michael Kennedy has added that

> It is misleading to regard *Façade* only as a 'false start', frivolous and unrepresentative. It is unique and unrepeatable, as Walton wisely realised, but it contains the essence of him—even to the 'conservatism' which has earned him so much disrepute in advanced circles lately, for what is one to say of an *enfant terrible* who was so obviously poking fun, witty and elegant fun, at the modish Parisian-type up-to-dateness in which he had been immersed up to the neck?

[5] John Pearson, *Façades* (London: Macmillan, 1978), p. 183.
[6] Hugh Ottaway, *Walton* (Kent: Novello & Co., 1977), pp. 8–9.

103

Musically the 'rhythmical snap', the tango-like languor, the genius for a pregnant melodic phrase are all present. Yet most remarkable of all—in retrospect—is the work's poetic vein of nostalgia which is not something that has been added by the passing of years. For all that *Façade* is rightly called an 'entertainment', . . . beneath and through [it] there runs an awareness of true romance.[7]

In composing the music for *Façade,* the only modern work Walton ever mentioned as an influence was Stravinsky's *L'Histoire du soldat,* which was first performed in Switzerland in 1918 and was subsequently conducted by Ansermet in London in July 1920 as a suite made up of a Viennese waltz, a ragtime serenade, an Argentinian tango, and a Bach-like chorale. By 1925, Walton had found his true voice when he completed his overture *Portsmouth Point,* which was chosen the following year by the jury of the International Society for Contemporary Music (ISCM) for the festival in Zurich. However, much had happened to Walton in the intervening period between the performance of *Façade* and his composition of the overture, the most important being his meeting (probably in 1923) with Constant Lambert.

When Walton returned to *Façade* in 1926, he rejected the "General salute and prologue" and nine items from the 1923 performance, adding fourteen new settings to make a total of twenty-six. This version of the work was performed on 27 April 1926 in the New Chenil Galleries, Chelsea. Direct evidence of Lambert's connection with *Façade* is the inclusion, at the April performance, of a new item, "Four in the Morning," of which Lambert composed the first eleven bars. Other additions at Chelsea were "Country Dance," "Scotch Rhapsody," "Polka," "Old Sir Faulk," and "Tango" (listed as "I Do Like To Be Beside the Seaside"). It was not until another 1926 performance, on 29 June, that "Tarantella," the "March," and "Mazurka" were first included. Lambert made his debut as reciter at this performance, when still two months short of his twenty-first birthday. At the end of that year Walton put together the *First Orchestral Suite,* consisting of five numbers: "Polka," "Valse," "Swiss Jodelling Song," "Tango-Pasodoble," and "Tarantella."[8] Perhaps Walton wisely realized the uniqueness of the music, and by this move extended its appeal to wider audiences and made it more acceptable.

And how do Sitwell's verses blend with Walton's musical concepts? The successful combination of the two arts is best observed in "Valse," no. 2 of the first suite, where the rhythm of the dance-music makes sense of the poem by

---

[7] Michael Kennedy, "William Walton: A Critical Appreciation," in Stewart R. Craggs, *William Walton: A Thematic Catalogue of His Musical Works* (Oxford: Oxford University Press, 1977), pp. 13–14.

[8] A ballet was choreographed to these five dance numbers by Gunther Hess in 1929.

The Sitwells: Edith (standing), Osbert, and Sacheverell. Ink and watercolor by Cecil Beaton, n.d. 29 x 21.5 cm. Reproduced by permission. *HRC Iconography Collection.*

unifying the scattered images of Sitwell's word picture. The poem begins:

> Daisy and Lily
> Lazy and silly
> Walked by the shore of the wan grassy sea.

The poems are spoken in level tones and strict time so as to depersonalize the voice as much as possible, the megaphone and the concealment of the reciter being further devices to achieve the same purpose. The "Polka" contains one of the sharpest of parodies—the old music-hall song, "See Me Dance the Polka," is played loudly by trumpet and trombone. In the version with recitation, the opening words are La-la-la-lo, La-la-lo-la, La (which reinforce the rhythm of the side drum) and the verse declaimed:

> See me dance the Polka
> Said Mr Wag like a bear.

The absence of words in the orchestral suite emphasizes the wit of the music. "Swiss Jodelling Song" is a genial parody with a dig at Rossini's overture to *William Tell*. The heavy Landler rhythm and sentimentality are surely more Austrian than Swiss: the title in the original entertainment is simply "Jodelling Song." A knowingly languid tango rhythm accompanies a skit on "I Do Like To Be Beside the Seaside" in the "Tango-Pasodoble." The manner is witty and polished, perhaps like that of the young composer. The most extended item, and on the whole the most fully scored, is the brilliant "Tarantella Sevillana," in which Rossini is accurately parodied. It is also written in the tarantella idiom which Walton returned to more than once in his long career.

At this point *Façade* included a significant number of dance movements—a foxtrot, waltz, polka, march, and tarantella. This was perhaps a mirror of the times—a creation of the Jazz Age—and an indication of Walton's continuing interest in jazz and "popular" music. By 1923–24, Vladimir Dukelsky, a composer friend of Walton's who had written the ballet *Zephyr et Flore* for Diaghilev, introduced Walton to Gershwin:

> He took me one day to see George Gershwin, who at the time was living in a flat in Pall Mall. I had been an admirer of his brilliant and captivating tunes. He was in the middle of writing his *Piano Concerto in F*, and I was hypnotised by his fabulous piano playing and his melodic gift.[9]

---

[9] Walton in an interview with John Warrack, entitled "My Life in Music," *The Sunday Telegraph* (25 March 1962): 8.

At the time Walton met Gershwin, he was already well steeped in jazz. Angus Morrison recalls from their association in the early 1920s that he and Walton would get together and do jazz improvisations.

> When I was living in Oakley Street, a friend lent me a second piano for a few months. During that time, WW would sometimes come round from Carlyle Square and we would improvise and devise jazz tunes on the two pianos—foxtrots, blues etc. None of them were ever written down to my knowledge—and when the piano departed, the sessions came to an end.[10]

Walton's background in jazz and his admiration for Gershwin's music led to his writing a mysterious and ambitious *Fantasia Concertante for Two Pianos, Jazz Band and Orchestra*, which has long since disappeared, perhaps because at the time it was too popular in style. Presumably this was the work to which Walton referred in a letter to his mother, a month before *Façade* was performed in the Aeolian Hall: "I have to see what can be done with my concerto with these Savoy people, though I am afraid that there is only a remote chance of anything satisfactory coming of it."[11] The jazz band referred to in the title of the *Fantasia*, if it was indeed completed by 1921, must have been the Savoy Havana Band, billed in that year by the American band leader Bert Ralton as the "New York Havana Band" at the Savoy Hotel. In 1920 Debroy Somers (1890–1952) had been appointed as arranger and adviser to the Savoy Havana Band but only conducted it on isolated occasions. However, Somers proved such a success as an arranger that in 1923, after Ralton and most of the original band had departed on tour, he was asked to form a large band (large by the standards of 1923), eleven pieces strong, to be known as the Savoy Orpheans. Somers's band made its first broadcast on 3 October 1923 and during the ensuing years engaged in a number of public appearances, the first being on the London Hippodrome stage in 1923. It was during his sojourn with the Orpheans that Somers conceived the idea of a potpourri of nationalistic and seasonal music, arranged in the now familiar quick-step rhythmic renderings known as the Savoy American, Scottish, English, and Christmas Medleys. Richmond Temple, a director of the Savoy Hotel, introduced Walton to Debroy Somer, and as Constant Lambert wrote in 1926,

> Walton's next phase, though it puzzled some of his friends, was not really surprising. Small wonder that, surfeited with the intellectuality of Schoenberg, he should turn with a sigh of relief towards

[10] Letter to the present writer, dated 4 September 1976.
[11] Kennedy, p. 16. Letter dated 4 May 1923.

107

Constant Lambert. Sanguine crayon drawing by Ivan Opffer, ca. 1936. 56.5 x 37 cm. *HRC Iconography Collection*.

Gershwin. For more than a year he did nothing but study jazz, writing and scoring foxtrots for the Savoy Orpheans Band and working at a monumentally planned concerto for two pianofortes, jazz band and orchestra. Although the concerto was finished and about to be performed, Walton suddenly abandoned the jazz style in a fit of disgust, rightly realising that the virtues of ragtime, its pungent timbres and intriguing syncopation, are more than handicapped by the deadly monotony of the four-square phrases, the inevitable harmonic clichés stolen from Debussy and Delius, the trite nostalgia of the whole atmosphere.[12]

Of the particular arrangements for Debroy Somers, Walton later reported that "In the early days I did do some arrangements for that dance band . . . and tried to write those sort of tunes, but I wasn't slick enough, somehow."[13] Apparently the band never played his compositions, except at rehearsals, since they were more occupied with their own work. As to the fate of the *Fantasia Concertante*, William de Mornys, who was the director of the Dance Bands at the Savoy, remembers

William Walton coming to the Savoy Orpheans rehearsals about 1923 and having meetings with Somers. What happened to the *Fantasia?* But about that time, George Gershwin came to London and he gave a first of the *Rhapsody in Blue*. At the Savoy it had a snob success. On the concert platform at the Queen's Hall, it had no success and worse on the provincial tours. There was no interest then with that type of music and I feared for the *Fantasia*.[14]

Like Walton, Constant Lambert was also committed to jazz at the beginning of his career; he was completely captivated by Florence Mills, who first appeared in London in a Cochran revue in May 1923, and by Will Vodery's "Plantation Orchestra." The impact of Florence Mills's personality on the young Lambert was so great that it appears to have set a pattern which recurred throughout his life. In turn, Lambert's influence was vital to opening up Walton's interest in the popular music of the time. Walton had already provided clever parodies of various jazz and popular styles in *Façade*, but in the twenties some of Walton's most vivid experiences

[12] *Boston Evening Transcript* (27 November 1926): 5. According to Lambert, writing in *The Dominant* for February 1928, Oxford University Press was to publish the *Fantasia Concertante*.
[13] J.W. Lambert, "Imp and Sceptre: Conversation with Sir William Walton," *The Sunday Times* (25 March 1962): 39.
[14] Letter to the present writer, dated 9 February 1976.

consisted of after-concert dashes from Queen's Hall down to the Hippodrome for Paul Whiteman and his band, or to the London Pavilion to hear Florence Mills (on whose death Lambert wrote an elegy for solo piano), or some other newly discovered popular singer. The continuing influence of Lambert can be found in Walton's film scores from the Second World War, several of which were to contain popular numbers, such as the famous foxtrot in *Next of Kin,* written in 1941. A waltz, which first appeared in the ballet *The First Shoot* (1936), turned up as radio music in *Went the Day Well?* (1942), again as a waltz in the dream sequence of *Three Sisters* (1970), and finally in *The First Shoot* again, rearranged for brass band in 1981.

Between 1926 and 1928, two further works appeared from Walton's pen—*Siesta,* the prototype Walton *andante tranquillo;* and the sadly neglected *Sinfonia Concertante* for orchestra with piano obbligato. The former is a work which shows the lyrical, romantic side of Walton's nature, the latter originally destined to be a ballet for Diaghilev, who had attended the revival of *Façade* at the Chenil Galleries. The ballet idea had to be dropped at Diaghilev's insistence, but the music was far too good to jettison. The slow movement in particular had to be salvaged, for in it appears, for the first time in a mature expression, the composer's streak of deeply romantic feeling, hitherto buried under brilliant dialogue, though soon to emerge, ever more fully developed, in Walton's *Concerto for Viola and Orchestra* of 1929.

During the morning of 14 September 1928 *Façade* was again performed, this time at the ISCM festival in Siena, where Lambert recited and Walton conducted twenty-two items. The version of *Façade* performed at Siena was yet another revised and extended version of the original entertainment of 1923. By this time, many of the more abstract items had been removed (some later to reemerge in *Façade 2*), those of more popular and instant appeal being retained. It may have been a deliberate ploy by the composer, who had matured and perhaps realized the work's growing popularity and potential. What has become the best-known number, "Popular Song"—a poem written for Lambert—was first included in this program. "Black Mrs Behemoth" was another of Edith Sitwell's newcomers. At the first morning performance there was some hostility among the Italians to "Tarantella," presumably because the audience objected to an overtly Spanish musical number being included in the program. When it was repeated, however, the number was well received. It was at this performance that the clarinet player, Walter Lear, played his instrument with the mouthpiece upside down! No particular musical reason has ever been provided. The following year, the Decca Record Company issued two 78 RPM recordings containing items from the 1928 program, read by Edith Sitwell and Constant Lambert, and conducted by the composer. Some of the items were included in a reissue by Oxford University Press in 1972 when a deluxe version of the score was published to mark Walton's seventieth birthday.

In 1931 a ballet by Sir Frederick Ashton, choreographed for the Camargo Society (the forerunner of the Royal Ballet), consisted of seven divertissements from *Façade:* "Scotch Rhapsody," "Jodelling Song," "Polka," "Valse," "Popular Song," "Tango-Pasodoble," and "Tarantella Sevillana." An extra number, "Country Dance," was added in 1935 when the Vic-Wells first performed the ballet, and two more, "Noche Espagnole" and "Foxtrot," in 1940. It is believed that the items added to the original *First Suite* for the Camargo Society and later for the Vic-Wells—"Fanfare," "Scotch Rhapsody," and "Popular Song"—were scored by Constant Lambert. Unfortunately, since Lambert's score, if it ever existed, has long since disappeared, it is not possible to compare his orchestration with Walton's, which was scored and published in 1938 when he made his *Second Orchestral Suite.*

The *Second Orchestral Suite* consisted of the "Fanfare," "Scotch Rhapsody," "Country Dance," "Noche Espagnole," "Popular Song," and "Old Sir Faulk." "Scotch Rhapsody" contains a gentle, stylistic parody, with the woodwind instruments taking the lead, and the suggestion is of a Scottish Highland reel. Its neat and polished workmanship (e.g., the side drum player is instructed to play on the wood) typifies one important aspect of *Façade.* In the original "Country Dance," only flute, clarinet, and cello play, and this delicacy is carefully preserved when transferred to full orchestra. There is no parody here, only a reminder of the Ravelian finesse which appears in so many of Walton's works. The music for "Noche Espagnole" accompanies the poem called "Long Steel Grass" in the original version, which bears the song title "Trio for Two Cats and a Trombone," though none of these instruments actually appear in the score. Various suggestions are contained in Edith Sitwell's poem, which begins:

> Long steel grass—
> The white soldiers pass
> The light is braying like an ass.

The poem could be described as a Spanish fantasy. Walton catches the mood exactly, and the result is not so much a parody as a serious exercise in an exotic style. "Popular Song," appropriately, is one of the best-known items. Marked "Grazioso," the mood is gently satirical, and the kind of song tune that is parodied is very much of the '20s—corny and banal. The final item, "Old Sir Faulk," is a brilliant piece of imitation jazz, elaborately scored for orchestra, which goes so far as to borrow the percussion and the saxophone of the typical dance band.

Walton was anxious that his music should achieve greater public acclaim and realized that, by arranging certain items for full orchestra, audiences would come to know these pieces through the concert hall rather than by hearing *Façade* in its original form, performances of which were very rare indeed. Both broadcasting and the gramophone were in their infancy, so concerts were the only adequate way of widening *Façade*'s appeal. Walton always maintained that all the different versions made *Façade* "work for its living"—it provided its composer with a regular financial emolument.

The twenty-one items of the definitive version were performed on 29 May 1942 in London, but not in what we now regard as the published order. The following is the 1942 performance order as given in the program:

1: "Hornpipe," "En famille," "Mariner Man"
2: "Trio for Two Cats and a Trombone," "Through Gilded Trellises," "Tango: 'I Do Like To Be Beside the Seaside'"
3: "Scotch Rhapsody," "Lullaby for Jumbo," "Foxtrot: 'Old Sir Faulk'"
4: "By the Lake," "A Man from a Far Countree," "Country Dance"
5: "Jodelling Song," "Black Mrs Behemoth," "Popular Song"
6: "Polka," "Valse," "Tarantella"
7: "Four in the Morning," "Something Lies Beyond the Scene," "Sir Beelzebub"

For this performance—Lambert was again reciter—no full score was extant and the work had to be reconstructed from the parts. A curtain was specially designed for the performance by John Piper and painted by Aleck Johnson.

Walton took back the score in 1947–48 and made various amendments. At that time, he probably decided on the present order, and when Oxford University Press published the score in 1951, it was dedicated to Lambert, who had suggested the arrangement of the poems into seven groups of three as a parody of Schoenberg's "three times seven" in *Pierrot Lunaire*, which also uses "speech-song." The 1951 "definitive" order as found in the printed score is as follows, with "Fanfare" as preface:

Group I: I. Hornpipe, II. En famille, III. Mariner Man; Group II: IV. Long Steel Grass, V. Through Gilded Trellises, VI. Tango-Pasodoble; Group III: VII. Lullaby for Jumbo, VIII. Black Mrs Behemoth, IX. Tarantella; Group IV: X. A Man from a Far Countree, XI. By the Lake, XII. Country Dance; Group V: XIII. Polka, XIV. Four in the Morning, XV. Something Lies Beyond the Scene; Group VI: XVI. Valse, XVII. Jodelling Song, XVIII. Scotch Rhapsody; Group VII: XIX. Popular Song, XX. Fox-Trot "Old Sir Faulk," XXI. Sir Beelzebub.

The history of *Façade* did not end here, for after much persuasion from Lina Lalandi (a friend who had commissioned the *Jubilate Deo* in 1972) and from his own wife, Walton allowed eight previously unpublished items ("Daphne," "Herodiade's Flea," "The Last Gallop," "The Octogenarian," "March," "The White Owl," "Aubade," and "Said King Pompey") to be recited by Richard Baker, with the English Bach Festival Ensemble, conducted by Sir Charles Mackerras, in the Plaisterers' Hall, London, on 25 March 1977, as part of the Walton seventy-fifth birthday celebrations. However, none of these eight items were included in the 1951 published score.

This 1977 performance (with a repeat in the Queen Elizabeth Hall) was entitled *Façade "Revived,"* and undoubtedly reawakened Walton's interest in the music. The result was *Façade 2: A Further Entertainment,* which was first performed at the Aldeburgh Festival in June 1979 and which should not be confused with the *Second Suite for Orchestra.* Walton dispensed with the "Fanfare," substituting a brief flourish for trumpet and percussion. Three numbers from the 1977 performances—"Daphne," "The Last Gallop," and "The White Owl"—were rejected and replaced by "Gardener Janus," "Water Party," and "Madame Mouse Trots," the total still remaining at eight items. Critics agreed, and Walton confirmed, that these numbers were never rejected for musical shortcomings but rather because they were too difficult to perform, or too difficult for listeners to understand. Some of the items seem quite "avant-garde," with spare, "modern" textures, especially "Madame Mouse Trots" and "Aubade." A separate score and recording were issued by Oxford University Press in 1980.

From the beginning, *Façade* revealed several facets of Walton's highly personal, unmistakable style which were to appear time and time again in later works. There was first of all his sense of fun and wit, which became something altogether deeper (apparent in *The First Shoot* of 1936, and his one-act opera of 1967, *The Bear)* and which matched the second facet, his strongly lyrical instinct which reached its climax in the full-length three-act opera of 1954, *Troilus and Cressida.* There was also the *gewöhnlich,* or "vulgar" facet—much of *Façade* intentionally so—which appears in that splendid night club scene in the film *Next of Kin* (1941); perhaps slightly in the *Johannesburg Festival Overture* (1956); in the last movement of the *Partita* (1958), with its "vulgar" trumpet tune; and in the waltz which accompanies shots of "Gay Berlin" in the film *The Battle of Britain* (1969). There are, of course, other works which contain echoes of *Façade* and which the inquiring and knowledgeable student of Walton's art will delight in pinpointing.

A. *Façade Entertainment*

None of the *Façade* manuscripts are signed or dated and the dedication, "To Constant Lambert," was only added by Walton to the definitive version when it was published by Oxford University Press in July 1951, one month before Lambert's premature death.

No. III*: "Mariner Man"

One of two versions, the other at Oxford University Press in London.

Holograph in blue ink. 4 pp., n.d.

First performed in January 1922 as no. 18 in the program. Edith Sitwell's poem, from *Clowns' Houses*, was first published on 9 June 1918.

No. IV: "Long Steel Grass" (also called "Trio for Two Cats and a Trombone")

The musical accompaniment was later used by Walton as the basis for "Noche Espagnole," no. 4 in the *Second Orchestral Suite*.

Holograph in black and red ink, with pencil notes in another hand. 6 pp., n.d.

First performed in January 1922 as no. 12 in the program. Edith Sitwell's poem was first published in the *Saturday Westminster Gazette*, 3 September 1921.

No. VII: "Lullaby for Jumbo"

Holograph in black and red ink, with pencil notes in another hand. 4 pp., n.d.

First performed in January 1922 as no. 8 in the program. Edith Sitwell's poem was first published in the program for this performance.

---

*Roman numerals indicate numbering of the definitive version.

No. VIII: "Black Mrs Behemoth"

Holograph in black and red ink, with pencil notes in another hand. 2 pp., n.d.

First performed in September 1928 as no. 3c in the program at the Rozzi Theatre in Siena, Italy. Edith Sitwell's poem, from *Troy Park*, was first published on 12 March 1925.

No. XII: "Country Dance"

Holograph in black ink with pencil notes in another hand. 4 pp., n.d.

First performed on 27 April 1926 as Group C (no. 3) in the program. Edith Sitwell's poem, from *Bucolic Comedies*, was first published on 24 April 1923.

No. XIII: "Polka"

One of two versions, the other amongst the Thomas Balston papers in the Washington State University Library, Pullman. There is also a draft version in the British Library in London (Egerton MS 3771).

Holograph in black ink, with pencil notes in another hand, and some holograph notes. 4 pp., n.d.

First performed in April 1926 as Group G (no. 2) in the program. Edith Sitwell's poem was first published in the June 1926 program.

No. XIV: "Four in the Morning"

Constant Lambert wrote the first eleven bars, and Walton continued from there.

Holograph in black ink. 4 pp., n.d.

First performed in April 1926 as Group H (no. 2) in the program. Edith Sitwell's poem was first published in *Vogue* 64, no. 12 for late December 1924.

No. XVIII: "Scotch Rhapsody"

Holograph in black ink. 4 pp., n.d.

Edith Sitwell's poem was first published in the *Legion Book*, 1929.

No. XIX: "Popular Song"

> In *The Guardian* for 29 February 1972, Walton told Edward Greenfield that he wrote the tune when he was back home in Oldham, and "it was very difficult indeed to get it just right."
>
> Holograph in black and red ink. 7 pp., n.d.
>
> First performed in September 1928 as no. 2c ("Canto popolare") in the program at the Rozzi Theatre in Siena, Italy. Edith Sitwell's poem, from *Popular Song*, was first published in September 1928.

No. XX: "Old Sir Faulk"

> One of two versions, the other in private hands.
>
> Holograph in pencil. 12 pp., n.d.
>
> First performed in April 1926 as Group E (no. 2) in the program. Edith Sitwell's poem "Fox Trot," from *Bucolic Comedies*, was first published on 24 April 1923.

No. XXI: "Sir Beelzebub"

> Holograph in pencil. 8 pp., n.d.
>
> First performed in January 1922 as no. 13 in the program. Edith Sitwell's poem was first published in the program for this performance.

B. *Façade 2*

"The Last Gallop"

Holograph in black ink. 6 pp., n.d.

First performed probably in June 1923 at the Aeolian Hall, London (the program for this performance remains undiscovered). Revived in March 1977, but later rejected.

"March"

Holograph in black ink. 2 pp., n.d.

First performed probably in June 1923. Revived in March 1977 and included as no. 3 in *Façade 2* (1979).

"Said King Pompey"

Holograph in black ink, with some pencil notes in author's hand. 4 pp., n.d.

First performed in January 1922 as no. 6 in the program. Edith Sitwell's poem was first published in the program for this performance. Revived in March 1977 and included as no. 8 in *Façade 2* (1979).

C. Façade—First Orchestral Suite

Walton prepared and orchestrated the first suite from *Façade* in late 1926, for performance as an interlude between acts of Lord Berners's ballet *The Triumph of Neptune,* which premiered on 3 December of that year, and which Walton and Constant Lambert helped Berners to orchestrate. There are five numbers:

"Polka"—key change from F to E major

"Valse"

"Swiss Jodelling Song" (lento)

"Tango-Pasodoble" (lento)—key change from F to E flat major

"Tarantella-Sevillana"—key change from E flat major to E major; considerably lengthened and with a new tune in 3/4 time

Holograph in pencil, with several passages gone over in heavier pencil, and one passage in black ink. This superimposing was done by Walton himself since the score was probably used by him for conducting and became too faint for easy reading. There are one or two additions to the manuscript (mostly names of instruments) which are in the hand of Constant Lambert, who also conducted from this score. 62 pp., n.d.

The subtitle for "Swiss Jodelling Song" is "The Waiter's Lament," and "Tango-Pasodoble" is subtitled "I Do Like To Be Beside the Seaside." Walton is said not to have realized that the composer of the music-hall song, J. A. Glover-Kind, was still alive and that the copyright for this piece he had parodied in the "Tango" was still in force. When he learned this, Walton took all necessary steps to ensure that it was not withdrawn from the suite, since he regarded it as one of the best numbers.

Ezra Pound. Painting by Wyndham Lewis in the Tate Gallery, London. Copyright © Estate of
Mrs. G.A. Wyndham Lewis, by permission.

"Townsman" and Music: Ezra Pound's Letters to Ronald Duncan

BY ARCHIE HENDERSON

Ronald Duncan (1914–1982), a British poet and playwright of distinction, numbered among his friends Benjamin Britten, T.S. Eliot, and Ezra Pound.[1] Duncan's friendship with Pound began as early as 1935, when he developed an enthusiasm for Pound's poetry and began writing to the poet. In the course of their correspondence, Pound urged the young Duncan to start a poetry magazine. In 1937, Duncan visited Pound in Rapallo, and together they laid out their strategy for the *Townsman:*

> We . . . planned a new onslaught against the Philistines which was to do for the thirties what *Blast* had achieved twenty years before, Pound scribbling out lists of people whom he thought I should meet, know, and perhaps persuade to contribute to the magazine. . . . My plans for the quarterly magazine which I called *Townsman* took shape: there was constant correspondence with Rapallo.[2]

Most of Pound's correspondence with the editors of the *Townsman*—Duncan and, for a short time, Montgomery Butchart—is preserved in the Humanities Research Center, The University of Texas at Austin.[3]

Pound's interest in the new magazine was not simply to establish contact with a younger generation of writers; he was also looking for a magazine that would, in his words, "contain particularly notable E/P that cant be moved thru ordinary commerce."[4] Perhaps more than anything else (even his

---

[1] See, in particular, Ronald Duncan's first two volumes of autobiography, *All Men Are Islands: An Autobiography* (London: Rupert Hart-Davis, 1964) and *How To Make Enemies* (London: Rupert Hart-Davis, 1968).

[2] Duncan, *All Men Are Islands,* pp. 160 and 174.

[3] Except where noted, all letters cited are from the Humanities Research Center collections. Other letters from Pound to Duncan in the *Townsman* years (1938–39) are found at Columbia University. Excerpts from the letters at Columbia are published with permission of the Rare Book and Manuscript Library, Columbia University.

[4] Letter from Pound to Duncan, 2 December 1937. Permission has been granted to quote from the unpublished writings of Ezra Pound. Copyright © 1984 by the Trustees of the Ezra Pound Literary Property Trust.

pronouncements on economics), Pound's writings on music had been deemed uncommercial. His essay on "great bass" (1928), incorporating a novel theory of music, was never published in a magazine; his translation of Boris de Schloezer's book on Stravinsky, serialized in the *Dial* in 1928 and 1929, was offered as a book to British and American publishers in 1937, but was refused.[5] Furthermore, Pound's first opera, *Le Testament de Villon* (1920–22), had received a partial performance in Paris in 1926, but not the exposure that Pound felt was long overdue.

Although he was "not a musician" and "served no musical apprenticeship," Duncan shared Pound's fascination with music,[6] and in 1937 he agreed that Pound should assist him in editing the *Townsman*'s music section. By that time, Pound's own musical apprenticeship was complete; simply on the basis of his musical activities in the 1930s, Pound was well qualified to write on music for the *Townsman*. In October 1931, for example, Pound's opera *Le Testament* was broadcast by the BBC. In the same month, he wrote his *Ghuidonis Sonata* (for solo violin), part of which he incorporated in his second opera, *Cavalcanti* (1932–33).[7] From 1933 to 1938 he organized a notable series of concerts in Rapallo, featuring ancient as well as contemporary music. By 1936, Pound, along with the violinist Olga Rudge and the German-born pianist and composer Gerhart Münch, began to take part in the early stages of the Vivaldi revival.[8]

Pound contributed essays on music to each of the *Townsman*'s first four issues (January, April, July, and October 1938). Two of these essays ("Muzik, as Mistaught" and "Musicians; God Help 'Em") contain Pound's somewhat unconventional lessons for the student of musical composition, lessons which are simple but, in Pound's view, all too neglected by the musical conservatories:

> In the creation of music: FIRST, melody. . . . When [students'] hunger for melody and their melodic hate (as well as love) is sufficiently keen, then they may get round to noticing bar length, to disliking accordion bars which stretch and contract unintentionally.

[5] On "great bass" see Pound, *Literary Essays of Ezra Pound* (New York: New Directions, 1968), p. 86. On *Igor Stravinsky*, see Donald Gallup and Archie Henderson, "Additions and Corrections to the Revised Edition of the Pound Bibliography," *Paideuma* 12, no. 1 (spring 1983): 130.

[6] Ronald Duncan, "Words and Music," *Townsman* 1, no. 4 (October 1938): 10–11.

[7] Although the sonata was apparently written before *Cavalcanti*, the title of the sonata (Ghuidonis, from Guido?) suggests that Pound had the opera in mind all along. In a letter to Tibor and Alice Serly (October 1939), Pound described the *Ghuidonis Sonata* as "that sonata on my opera basis" (*Selected Letters 1907–1941* [New York: New Directions, 1971], p. 327).

[8] For more details, see Ezra Pound, *Ezra Pound and Music*, ed. R. Murray Schafer (New York: New Directions, 1977). On Pound and Vivaldi, see also Stephen Adams, "Pound, Olga Rudge, and the 'Risveglio Vivaldiano'," *Paideuma* 4, no. 1 (spring 1975): 111–18.

. . . [Then] the pew-PILL is taught that a composition has a main form and articulations, that is a root, a main structure, and details. To remember ONE main fact and not a hundred separate notes. . . .[9]

In these lessons, Pound contrasts "HOW music ought to be taught" with "the folly of conservatory sins."[10] Pound's underlying point seems to be that composers who are badly taught cannot properly fit music to poetry and that poets, by studying musical scores, could improve their own craft.

Pound's other two essays on music provided lessons of a different sort altogether, less hortatory and more explanatory. Each of these essays was written to accompany, and comment on, the reproduction of a short musical score. For the first issue of the *Townsman,* Pound asked Olga Rudge to recopy a score by Gerhart Münch—his version of Francesco da Milano's arrangement of *La Canzone de li Ucelli,* by Clément Janequin.[11] Pound's essay "Janequin, Francesco da Milano" was written for the Münch-Janequin music, and similarly in the second issue Pound paired his essay "Villon and Comment" with the five-page score (in Olga Rudge's hand) of his own aria "La Heaulmière" from his opera *Le Testament de Villon.* This pairing of music and commentary had been one of Pound's critical methods for over twenty years. Between 1912 and 1918, for example, Pound had tried to publish a book on the troubadour poet and musician Arnaut Daniel, in which Walter Morse Rummel's reconstruction of troubadour music was to accompany Pound's text. A decade later, Pound's unfinished draft of *The Probable Music of Beowulf* (1928), a book commissioned by Nancy Cunard, left blank spaces for the insertion of Hebridean music.[12] In these proposed books, music and text were designed to reinforce one another; neither could stand alone. In the *Townsman* examples, however, the lesson of the commentary was already self-evident in the music.

These two *Townsman* essays, while important, were clearly subordinate to the music that they discussed. As Pound explained to Duncan, "The note on Janequin is not use-able *without* the reprod of the music."[13] Pound suggested that the two pages of the Münch-Janequin music "be p. 16 and 17. detachable without damage to rest of mag. = if you use one clip . . . to hold all 32 p."[14] In proposing the detachable pages, Pound had in mind that

[9] Pound, *Ezra Pound and Music,* pp. 437–38.

[10] Letter from Pound to Duncan, 4 March 1938.

[11] A transcription in Münch's hand appears in Canto LXXV of *The Cantos of Ezra Pound* (New York: New Directions, 1948), pp. 28–29 of The Pisan Cantos.

[12] See Donald Gallup, *Ezra Pound: A Bibliography* (Charlottesville: University Press of Virginia, 1983), pp. 446–47 and 450–52.

[13] Letter from Pound to Duncan, 9 July 1937.

[14] Postcard from Pound to Duncan, 7 March 1937. The Münch transcription was actually published on pp. 19–20 of the first issue of the *Townsman.*

Janequin's music could be more widely distributed; and there is no reason to doubt that Pound hoped for an equal circulation of his own aria. He made no similar proposal for the distribution of his prose commentaries. Nevertheless, Pound's prose is useful for getting at the particular lessons which he saw in the reproduced scores. In his writings, Pound made it clear that music can do a better job than prose of teaching the poet about poetry and poetic technique, and that instrumental as well as vocal music has something to say to the practicing poet. For example, a study of instrumental music, such as of Münch's arrangement, makes the poet more sensitive to verbal melody: "For the student of verbal melody, the fiddle is the modern instrument. And the violin sonata or reduced concerto is his most fecund field of experiment."[15] As for vocal music, the setting of a poetic text compensates for the inadequacy of poetic translation: "I personally have been reduced to setting [Catullus and Villon] to music as I cannot translate them."[16] The setting of poetry, moreover, is a kind of commentary on poetry. As he said of his scholarly edition of *Guido Cavalcanti Rime* (1932), "It is I think arguable whether, even there, such attention would have been wisely spent *had I not* later set a good deal of him [Cavalcanti] to music."[17] This is what Pound labeled "criticism via music, meaning definitely the setting of a poet's words," citing as examples his own operas, "*Le Testament* [with] Villon's words, and . . . *Cavalcanti,* [with] Guido's and Sordello's."[18] The music of *Le Testament* is in those terms and "to that extent a comment on, or an elucidation of, the form of the words and possibly of their meaning, or, if you like, of the emotive contents."[19] As a form of criticism, Pound's two operas were "more important than [his] written criticism."[20]

Music's lessons for the poet are implicit in the two musical excerpts that Pound chose for the *Townsman.* The excerpt of vocal music by Pound, his long aria from *Le Testament*[21]—the "fireworks" of the opera—is sung by La Heaulmière, the eighty-year-old whore who laments the loss of her youthful beauty.[22] Certainly the aria, as well as the opera as a whole, is Pound's way of translating and commenting on Villon's French text "via music." In a broader

[15] Ezra Pound, "Another Chance," *Poetry* 52, no. 6 (September 1938): 345.

[16] Ezra Pound, *ABC of Reading* (New York: New Directions, 1960), pp. 104–105. Pound's setting of Catullus 61 has not been located.

[17] Pound, *Literary Essays,* p. 85.

[18] Ibid., p. 74.

[19] Ezra Pound, *Guide to Kulchur* (New York: New Directions, 1970), p. 366.

[20] Ezra Pound, "Useful Critter" [letter], *Time* 21, no. 18 (1 May 1933): 2; reprinted in *Time* 122, no. 15 (5 October 1983): 9, 12.

[21] Pound's second choice of an aria for possible publication was "Si Jayme et sers," also from *Le Testament* (letter from Pound to Duncan, 18 July 1937).

[22] See Robert Hughes's record jacket notes to *Le Testament de Villon* (Fantasy 12001, 1972).

Paroles de
Villon

Musique d'Ezra Pound

Exécutants

Yves Tinayre
(Tenor)

Robert Maitland
(Basse)

Olga Rudge
(Violon)

Jean Dervaux
(Trombone tenor)

Edouard Dumoulin
(Trombone basse)

Paul Tinayre
(Clavecin, cornet de dessus)

Salle Pleyel

29 Juin 1926

Cover of program for 29 June 1926 performance of Ezra Pound's Villon settings. *HRC Collections.*

sense, however, the aria praises "the art of fitting words well with music."[23] This art is "motz el son / relation of word and tune / Voice and Violin together."[24] *Motz el son* was the Provençal term for the union of word and music. When words and notes fit together, "the emotion of the music" has a "connection with the emotion of the words."[25] As Pound explained, "I don't mean just the general flop or wobble of the emotion of a given poem. I mean that the music definitely fitted the consonants and vowels, and in particular it fitted the vowel sequence that stands in the words."[26] This is the art which "has not greatly shone in [England] since . . . the era of Lawes and Tho. Campion," but which Pound made an effort to revive in his own settings of Villon, Cavalcanti, Sordello, and Catullus.[27] When *motz el son* is lacking in a culture, the consequences for the health of the society are grave. As Pound put it, "When a given hormone defects, it will defect throughout the whole system."[28] Given the importance that Pound assigned to a revival of *motz el son*, it should come as no surprise that he considered his setting of Villon's "La Heaulmière" to be "as serious as a Canto."[29] He had waited sixteen years to publish this aria, and, he told Duncan, "I don't begrudge us FIVE pages" for printing it.[30] Duncan, for his part, became interested enough in Pound's opera to try, ten or fifteen years later, to arrange for its performance or broadcast, neither of which was ever realized.

The excerpt of instrumental music that Pound included in the *Townsman* was Münch's transcription of Francesco da Milano's *La Canzone de li Ucelli*, which in turn was a lute version of Janequin's *Chant des oiseaux*. *La Canzone*, in Münch's transcription, was first performed in Rapallo on 10 October 1933 and repeated on many occasions.[31] The performance version was for violin and piano; for the purposes of the *Townsman*, however, Pound decided that the violin part would suffice. Not only did he want to save space in the magazine, but he also knew that "the POINT of the Janequin-Münch is MADE in Violin part."[32] In order to make the two pages of music better fit the proportions of the *Townsman*'s page and to increase their legibility, Pound asked Olga Rudge to recopy the violin part.[33] For the Rapallo

---

[23] Pound, *Literary Essays*, p. 112.
[24] Letter from Pound to Duncan, 17 July 1937.
[25] Pound, *Ezra Pound and Music*, p. 85.
[26] Ibid., p. 395.
[27] Ibid., p. 100.
[28] Pound, *Guide to Kulchur*, p. 60.
[29] Letter from Pound to Duncan, 17 July 1937.
[30] Ibid., 20 December 1937.
[31] Münch's manuscript is dated 21 September 1933. The score for solo violin consists of three sections; at the Rapallo concert of 10 October 1933, only the first two sections (in a version for violin and piano) were performed. See Pound, *Ezra Pound and Music*, p. 340.
[32] Letter from Pound to Duncan, 17 July 1937.
[33] Ibid., 9 July 1937.

concerts, Pound often required such transcriptions; that is, arrangements of musical compositions for a medium other than that for which they were originally composed. In most cases, the Rapallo arrangements were for fewer instruments. Pound came to the defense of this sometimes maligned practice: "The reductions of concerti for piano and fiddle, or for smaller groups of instruments, have their rights. It is sheer superstition, and academic superstition at that, to condemn them unheard."[34] Among these rights was the right to experiment: "Any and every experiment and attempt to display old music is justified *as experiment.*"[35] More practical considerations also justified the use of transcriptions. Chamber music in general was most appropriate for a town hall of the size of Rapallo's; the concert organizers, to expand their repertoire of ancient and modern music, needed large-scale compositions to be rewritten for fewer instruments. Available talent and funds were limited, so the number of capable performers was inherently small: "We have not an unlimited number of executants having sensibility such as that possessed by Olga Rudge and by Münch himself."[36] Finally, fewer performers meant "small groups of modern and available instruments."[37]

The Münch-Janequin music, whether transcribed for solo violin or violin and piano, evokes a long tradition originating in Provençal poetry. The essence of the music was perhaps first found in the words of the troubadour Arnaut Daniel, whose art "is not literature but the art of fitting words well with music, wellnigh a lost art."[38] In this art between literature and music, Arnaut Daniel showed himself "very cunning in his imitation of birds, as in the poem *Autet* [*e bas*], where he stops in the middle of his singing, crying: 'Cadahus, en son us,' as a bird cries."[39] A similar attention to sound—"the sole matter wherein music can be 'literally' representative"—recurred in the work of later composers:

> The best smith, as Dante called **Arnaut Daniel,** made the birds sing IN HIS WORDS; I don't mean that he merely referred to birds singing. . . .
> The music of these songs has been lost, but the tradition comes up again, over three centuries later.
> Clément Janequin wrote a chorus, with sounds for the singers of the different parts of the chorus. These sounds would have no literary or poetic value if you took the music away, but when

[34] Pound, *Guide to Kulchur*, p. 252.
[35] Ibid., 251.
[36] Ibid., p. 252.
[37] Pound, "Another Chance," p. 345.
[38] Pound, *Literary Essays*, p. 112.
[39] Ibid., p. 109.

Francesco da Milano reduced it for the lute, the birds were still in the music. And when Münch transcribed it for modern instruments the birds were still there. They ARE still there in the violin part. That is why the monument outlasts the bronze casting.[40]

For Pound, the transmission—through Arnaut Daniel, Janequin, Milano, and Münch—of the "birds in the music" symbolized the continuity of tradition through time and across cultures. The same kind of continuity linked Arnaut Daniel and Rummel, for example, or *Beowulf* and the Hebridean music.

The Münch-Janequin music, then, like Pound's aria, celebrates the vitality of *motz el son*. Like Pound's aria, it is also an example of music as criticism. Munch's transcription, in fact, exemplifies the "ideogramic method" of criticism, which, as Pound explained to Duncan, "applies throughout the arts."[41] "The ideogramic method consists of presenting one facet and then another until at some point one gets off the dead and desensitized surface of the reader's mind, onto a part that will register."[42] Because "we do NOT know the past in chronological sequence," it is better to construct an ideogramic "history of an art" by isolating "the quality or the direction of a given time's sensibility."[43] The Münch transcription is such an ideogram, and its facets are the various compositions, from Arnaut Daniel to Münch, with "birds in the music." By definition, each facet is slightly different from the others: "There was something [in Münch's version] I did not hear when I heard the song done by chorus."[44] Yet taken together, the compositions isolate the quality of medieval sensibility—"fine demarcation"—that so appealed to Pound:

> Let us say that medieval thought (or *paideuma*) was at its best in an endeavour to find the *precise word* for each of its ideas, and that this love of exactitude created some very fine architecture, and that when it got into song (or, if you like, when it came out of song) it produced a very exact fitting of the melody to the shape of the words.[45]

Pound wrote of Münch's transcription that "The bed rock in any art is composed of such solids. You could construct music again from a few dozen

[40]Pound, *Guide to Kulchur*, p. 152; *ABC of Reading*, pp. 53–54.
[41]Letter from Pound to Duncan, 9 July 1937.
[42]Pound, *Guide to Kulchur*, p. 51.
[43]Ibid., p. 60.
[44]Pound, *Ezra Pound and Music*, p. 435.
[45]Pound, *Guide to Kulchur*, p. 60; Pound, *Ezra Pound and Music*, p. 395.

such proofs of invention."[46] In light of Pound's statement, the importance of this music to him can hardly be overstated.

In the 1930s, Pound's appreciation of Francesco da Milano's *La Canzone de li Ucelli* coincided with his new interest in instrumental music, particularly that of Antonio Vivaldi. Beginning in 1936, Pound and Olga Rudge undertook an intense study of Vivaldi, who was relatively unknown at the time. When the Rapallo concerts were reorganized in 1936, they took the form of study sessions devoted to Vivaldi. Both Pound and Münch spent months transcribing Vivaldi concerti from microfilms that they had obtained from European libraries. As Pound later recalled to Duncan, "My work [on Vivaldi] was dechiff[f]rage & reduction—getting a few concerti in form so that with 2 fiddles & pyanny or piano & fiddle one cd. execute. & see all the notes Viv. had put into the composition."[47] Through several years of transcribing Vivaldi concerti, Pound never lost his enthusiasm for the composer's works: "Am transcribin' another Vivaldi (No. 5 on my l'il list)," he wrote Duncan in 1938. "Vurry nice mind, Mr Vivaldi."[48] Two years later, Pound reported that he "did the best Vivaldi concerto I have found since I did the Eco . . . started another good one today."[49] Pound's interest in Vivaldi was not due simply to the masterful qualities of the music. In the almost universal neglect accorded to Vivaldi's music, Pound saw a symbol of the decline of musical Europe: "With 309 concerti of Vivaldi unplayed, lying in Turin as I write this, it is as useless as it wd. be idiotic to write of musical culture in Europe."[50] Pound did his part to remedy this neglect; by March 1937, Münch's transcriptions of Vivaldi were being performed in Rapallo. Largely because of Münch's efforts, the concerts were successful: "The Rapallo music is more than justified when Münch's Janequin is followed by his reduction of Vivaldi's Sol minore Concerto."[51]

Pound's ambition was to bring Vivaldi's music to a much wider public than simply the concert audience in Rapallo.[52] To this end, he asked Duncan to publish part of a Vivaldi concerto which had appeared in the January 1938 issue of *Broletto*, and for which Pound had obtained the blocks.[53] Although it

---

[46] Pound, *Ezra Pound and Music*, p. 435.

[47] Letter from Pound to Duncan, 18 March (?), New York, but written from Washington, D.C.

[48] Letter from Pound to Duncan, 20 August 1938.

[49] Ibid., 1 March 1940.

[50] Pound, *Guide to Kulchur*, p. 237.

[51] Ibid., p. 251.

[52] According to Dorothy Pound, the Rapallo audience never numbered more than about eighty. See Pound, *Ezra Pound and Music*, p. 325.

[53] *Broletto*, published in Como, Italy, was edited by Carlo Peroni, with the assistance (in 1938) of Ezra Pound. Perhaps the Vivaldi score reproduced in *Broletto* was the source of Vivaldi's "slow movement for oboe" which was published at about the same time in *Il Mare*, the Rapallo newspaper. Pound described this movement as "probably only single page of Viv's music that is . . . complete and useful in itself" (letter from Pound to Duncan, 4 March 1938).

"AMICI DEL TIGULLIO„

RAPALLO - Gran Sala del MUNICIPIO

NUOVO
QUARTETTO
UNGHERESE

VEGH

HALMOS

KOROMZAY

PALOTAI

GIOVEDI' 4 MARZO
ORE 21
CONCERTO EXTRA
Programma da determinare
Probabilmente :
MOZART - BOCCHERINI ed un
compositore d'oggi.

VENERDI 5 MARZO
ORE 21

BARTOK : Quartetto II, op. 17 -
Moderato, allegro molto ca-
priccioso, lento.

HAYDN : Quartetto G-moll op. 20
N. 3 - Allegro con spirito, mi-
nuetto, poco adagio, finale.

BARTOK : Quartetto V - Allegro,
adagio molto, scherzo alla bul-
garese, andante, finale.

OLGA RUDGE - GERHART MÜNCH

GIOVEDI' 18 MARZO
ORE 21

PERGOLESE - Tre Sonate - Vio-
lino e pianoforte - J. Mate-
lart (1559) Fantasia - Cesare
Negri Milanese, Pass' e mezzo
- Giovanni Picchi (1620) Pa-
dovana (pianoforte).
J. S. BACH - Sonata in Sol mag-
giore - Violino e pianoforte.
STRAVINSKY - Serenata e Rag.
Music.

LUNEDI' 29 MARZO
ORE 21

VIVALDI - Concerto.
FR. BACH - Elaborazione di un
concerto di Vivaldi.
J. S. BACH - Concerto in La minore - Violino.
CHOPIN - Polacca - Fantasia (Op.
61) - Scherzo - No. III, Do
diese minore.

GIOVEDI' 1 APRILE
ORE 21

VIVALDI-MUNCH - Concerto.
J. S. BACH - Sonata e fuga - Pia-
noforte e violino.
HONEGGER - Sonata per violino
e pianoforte.
BARTOK - Sonata per pianoforte
- Allegro, barbaro.

IL "MARE„ DI RAPALLO
ILLUSTRA L'ATTIVITÀ DEGLI
"AMICI DEL TIGULLIO„

Program for a Rapallo concert featuring Olga Rudge and Gerhart Münch. *HRC Collections.*

may very well have been performed in Rapallo, the Vivaldi music was never published in the *Townsman*, which did, however, print music by Jenkins and Mozart.[54] For the distribution of Vivaldi's works, as well as those of other composers before 1800, a long-term solution was called for. Vivaldi's unpublished works existed in such number that recopying them would be too time-consuming, and photographing them too expensive. Scholarly editions were less accurate than original manuscripts and therefore unsatisfactory. With the development of microphotography in the late 1930s, however, Pound saw a solution to the problems of availability, expense, and accuracy that had plagued music studies.

"Microphotography" was a technique for printing music in reduced facsimile of the original manuscript. The music could be printed directly from a microfilm of the manuscript rather than from a more expensive photograph. Using this technique, *Broletto* had economically published the Vivaldi concerto "in small half-tones taken from 'microfoto' Leica films—an enormous saving over the old system where half-tones were made from full size photos."[55] Microphotography would not render scholarly editions obsolete, but unless *some* microphotographed manuscripts were included, Pound felt that new editions would be inadequate. "Microphoto strips in the margin in no way exclude the necessity of proper engraved or photo-engraved editions, critical editions, repristinations, fittings of the stuff to modern convenience."[56] At the same time, "NO edition of old inedited music is valid or contemporary unless it be accompanied by the photographic verification now COMMERCIALLY possible by reason of the grainless film and new modes of photoprinting."[57] For the same goal of "paleographic verification," Pound had included forty plates of manuscripts in his edition of *Guido Cavalcanti Rime*, predating the commercial use of microphotography.[58]

By 1938, Pound approached commercial publishers, including Faber, with the idea of reproducing music by the microphotographic method; but Faber, at least, was not interested.[59] Pound offered an explanation:

> The stagnation in music publishing is due, in part, to the decades wherein music has been a separate interest, not an integral part of the most active intellectual life. With the reintegration of the arts

[54] The Jenkins and Mozart excerpts were published in the January and April 1939 issues, respectively.

[55] Ezra Pound, "Notes on Micro Photography," *Globe* 2, no. 5 (April–May 1938): 29.

[56] Pound, *Guide to Kulchur*, p. 151.

[57] Pound, *Ezra Pound and Music*, p. 443.

[58] Letter from Pound to Duncan, 12 December 1937.

[59] Ibid., 29 March 1938.

there should be a considerable stirring up of the reading of music, even among those of us who don't perform it even in private.[60]

Lacking a publisher, Pound turned to publicizing the microphotographic method himself. Since an "UTTERLY NEW phase in music scholarship" was beginning, the most appropriate place to publicize it was the first issue of a new magazine.[61] The *Townsman*, as Pound put it, "DEMANDS use (and NOW) of microphot processes for music."[62] Pound asked Olga Rudge to write the publicity article; after Pound's revisions, the article was published in the first number of the *Townsman* as "Music and a Process." This was the first of several news articles that Rudge was to write for the *Townsman*.[63]

Other musical interests shared by Pound and Duncan did not result in *Townsman* articles but played an important part in their joint activities, correspondence, and conversation. Duncan's own musical enthusiasms, for example, included music for the Noh drama and the music of Stravinsky and Britten. For Pound's visit to London in late 1938, Duncan arranged a private performance of one of Pound's Noh translations:

> During the next week or two Pound and I tried to find some method of staging one of his Noh plays for our own private pleasure. I managed to persuade Ashley Dukes to lend us the Mercury Theatre. Britten produced a musician who could play gongs, and Henry Boys, who had composed some music for Michel St Denis at the Studio Theatre, suggested a dancer [Suria Magito].[64]

During the same visit, Duncan apparently took Pound to the first Queen's Hall performance of Stravinsky's *Jeu de Cartes*.[65] By the time of this concert, Pound had long since exhausted his anti-Stravinsky and pro-Antheil rhetoric. "Among composers whose work I have heard," said Pound in 1935, "Stravinsky is the only living musician from whom I can learn my own job."[66] Duncan, likewise an admirer of the composer's work, was angered "when a Mr Wilfrid Mellers had sneered at Stravinsky."[67] This was an allusion to Mellers's article "Tight-Ropes to Parnassus," in which Mellers had described Stravinsky as a "genuine, vital, but minor and escapist talent" whose "vitality

[60] Pound, "Another Chance," p. 346.
[61] Letter from Pound to Duncan, 5 July 1937.
[62] Letter from Pound to Montgomery Butchart, 12 December 1937.
[63] Olga Rudge was the editor of several Vivaldi facsimiles that were published in the late 1940s. See Pound, *Ezra Pound and Music*, p. 330.
[64] Duncan, *All Men Are Islands*, p. 198.
[65] Duncan, *How To Make Enemies*, p. 278.
[66] Pound, *Ezra Pound and Music*, p. 508.
[67] Duncan, *All Men Are Islands*, p. 194.

TOWNSMAN

Editor : Ronald Duncan.   Associate : Montgomery Butchart.

Volume One	January 1938	Number One

CONTENTS

TOWNSMAN : A Quarterly Review.
Per copy 2s. 6d.; per year 10s., post free.
Contributions : Manuscripts invited.
Advertisement : Informative only; rates on application.
Editorial : 37 Museum Street, London, W.C.1
Publishing : 40 Great Russell Street, London, W.C.1

Contents page of the *Townsman* 1, no. 1 (January 1938). The issue was spiral bound. *HRC Collections*.

seems completely to have atrophied."[68] Pound, siding with Duncan, wrote to him that "Strawinsky [*sic*] [is] the only modern musician that gtly/ matters. . . . Yr/ obs[ervation] / re Mellers is correct."[69]

Duncan and Pound went as far as to invite Stravinsky to London and Rapallo, respectively, to conduct concerts of his music. In one volume of his autobiography, Duncan recounted the unfortunate circumstances surrounding his invitation:

> I asked [Stravinsky] if he would consider the idea of coming over to London to conduct the first performance of *Jeu de Cartes* for the memorial concert the Peace Pledge Union was arranging for Dick Sheppard.[70] Stravinsky immediately agreed. . . . The next day I wrote to the Royal Philharmonic Society and told them the great news that Stravinsky himself was prepared to come to London to conduct the first performance of *Jeu de Cartes, Symphony of Psalms* and a new work especially written for the occasion. Two days later I received a reply from the Secretary of the Orchestra to say they were not interested.[71]

The Orchestra, it turned out, was unwilling to take the financial risk. Duncan also approached Ralph Hawkes (of Boosey and Hawkes, Stravinsky's publisher in London) about sponsoring the proposed concert. Duncan was outraged to hear Hawkes's answer: "'Stravinsky hasn't written anything interesting since *Firebird.'*"[72] Though Pound was critical of what he called Stravinsky's "DumBarton Oaks" (1937–38), he wrote a letter of invitation to Stravinsky, which he asked Duncan to forward.[73] In the letter, Pound

[68] Wilfrid Mellers, "Tight-Ropes to Parnassus," *Scrutiny* 5, no. 2 (September 1936): 152. Mellers wrote: "With the series of facetious exercises for unusual combinations Stravinsky's vitality seems completely to have atrophied." Curiously, Mellers was to use almost identical language in describing Britten as "a genuine if rather facile talent" whose strength had been "dessicated in a series of facetious exercises." See Wilfrid Mellers, "Edmund Rubbra and Symphonic Form," *Scrutiny* 8, no. 1 (June 1939): 69–70.

[69] Letter from Pound to Duncan, 15 April 1937.

[70] In separate accounts, Duncan described both the 1938 London concert and his 1939 proposal to the Royal Philharmonic Society as featuring the "first performance [in London] of *Jeu de Cartes.*"

[71] Duncan, *All Men Are Islands*, p. 195. Duncan first described the incident in *Townsman* 2, no. 7 (August 1939): 13–14. In the *Townsman* article, Duncan reprinted the actual letter from the Royal Philharmonic Society, which is dated eight days after Duncan's letter to the Society.

[72] Ronald Duncan, "Merit Is Always Recognised," *Lying Truths: A Critical Scrutiny of Current Beliefs and Conventions*, ed. Ronald Duncan and Miranda Weston-Smith (Oxford: Pergamon Press, 1979), p. 13.

[73] Letter from Pound to Duncan, 10 January 1939. The letter to Stravinsky, dated 17 January 1939 (and addressed to Duncan), was apparently enclosed with the letter of 10 January. Both letters are at Columbia. See Pound, *Selected Letters*, pp. 320–21.

mentioned that as far as he was concerned, the Rapallo town hall was "at their disposal, pere et fils [Igor and Soulima Stravinsky], for anything they care to do."[74] Pound made this offer to a man he had never met.[75]

Duncan, who was to write some libretti for Benjamin Britten in the 1940s, hoped to include some of Britten's music in the *Townsman*. Though his effort was unsuccessful, Duncan announced wishfully, "THE SECOND NUMBER OF TOWNSMAN will contain . . . music by Benjamin Britten and/or Ezra Pound's *Villon* and/or Olga Rudge's Thematic Catalogue [of Vivaldi]."[76] Although Pound had not heard any of Britten's music, in 1938 he showed an interest in helping to arrange an Italian performance of Britten's new composition:

> After the 16th. [of September] Brit/ cd/ send his Suite to O[lga]. R[udge]. . . . // IF she liked it and IF the Princess [Edmond de] Polignac is in Venice / she wd/ prob/ play it for &/or with the Pcs [Princess] // wich iz good fer rizink talent.[77]

Pound and Duncan shared other interests in music, such as a fondness for English Renaissance composers—Dowland, Bird, Purcell, Jenkins, Young. In 1938 Pound mentioned to Duncan that there was Jenkins "and the rest of English inedited music to DO."[78] Forty years later, Duncan complained that the music was yet to be done: "Jenkins, and a dozen more Elizabethan thrushes, where are they? At the taxidermist's?"[79] Also, in conversations in Rapallo and London, Pound and Duncan may have "spent some time trying to define melody," as Duncan reported to Murray Schafer.[80] While they did not discuss melody at any length in their correspondence, Pound did write to Duncan that "wot I am after is the FORM of the KOMposishun, wich means mostly the LINE, i.e. melody / and other melodies or lines COMposed."[81]

---

[74]Letter from Pound to Duncan, 17 January 1939 (at Columbia); Pound, *Selected Letters*, p. 320.

[75]See Pound, *Selected Letters*, p. 208, and letter from Pound to Duncan. n.d., but written from Washington, D.C.

[76]Duncan, [announcement], *Townsman* 1, no. 1 (January 1938): [33]. Olga Rudge's thematic catalogue was not published in the *Townsman*.

[77]Letters from Pound to Duncan, 17 June, New York, but written from Washington, D.C. (at Texas) and 13 September 1938 (at Columbia). On Princesse Polignac's patronage of the arts, see Michael de Cossart, *The Food of Love: Princesse Edmond de Polignac (1865–1943) and Her Salon* (London: H. Hamilton, 1978).

[78]Letter from Pound to Duncan, 21 September 1938.

[79]Duncan, "Merit Is Always Recognised," p. 14.

[80]Pound, *Ezra Pound and Music*, p. 434.

[81]Letter from Pound to Duncan, 13 September 1938 (at Columbia).

Ronald Duncan, n.d. Photograph by Nicholas Elder. *HRC Photography Collection.*

They certainly would have talked about the relation of Pound's poetry to music. In an early issue of the *Townsman*, Duncan formulated his esthetic about the interrelation of the two arts:

> Songs became squawking when the composers set to please the concert singers. The tradition to and from Bayreuth is mere vocal gymnastics, virtuosity, effect. . . . I require to hear the words distinctly. The music can go with and against but should add to. I believe that a good verse can make a better song than a bad verse whoever sets it.[82]

In Duncan's terms, Pound's poetry follows not in the Wagnerian tradition, but in the tradition of the troubadours:

> Pound's technical achievement has been to give song back its masculine rhythms and make it move again with its own muscles. Pound's lyrics can be accompanied in the same way as the Troubadours improvised a bass; but the melody is in the verse itself. . . . Neither Elgar, Brahms, Delius nor Schumann could have accompanied a Pound lyric—which requires the free melodic line of Purcell, Jenkins, Vivaldi or Lawes.[83]

After January 1939, Pound wrote less frequently to Duncan and his role as music editor effectively ceased, although his contributions appeared in the *Townsman* until March 1941. The ending of Pound's association with the *Townsman* had many causes: the Second World War, the disruption of the mails, Pound's absorption in economic policy and political broadcasts, and the changing interests of Duncan himself. Beginning in 1939, Duncan ran an experimental, self-supporting agricultural community in England.[84] Even after the community was abandoned in 1942, Duncan continued to write a column on "Husbandry Notes" for the *New English Weekly*. The final issues of the *Townsman* were devoted almost exclusively to agricultural subjects, and the magazine (the *Scythe*, as it was then called) ended publication in the summer of 1945. After the war, when Pound and Duncan resumed their correspondence, Pound recalled the early *Townsman* years with fondness. On at least one occasion, Pound expressed the wish that the *Townsman* as he remembered it could be revived.[85]

[82]Duncan, "Words and Music," *Townsman* 1, no. 4 (October 1938): 10–11.

[83]Ronald Duncan, "Poet's Poet," *An Examination of Ezra Pound*, ed. Peter Russell (Norfolk, CT: New Directions, 1950), pp. 160–61. Duncan's draft of this essay is at Texas.

[84]See Duncan, *Journal of a Husbandman* (London: Faber and Faber, 1944).

[85]Many of these post-war letters are at Texas.

Ross Russell with musicians in the C.P. MacGregor Studios, Hollywood, on 19 February 1947.
From left to right: Charlie Parker, Ross Russell, Hal Doc West (behind Russell), Earl Coleman,
and Shifty Henry. *HRC Collections*.

From Bird to Schoenberg:
The Ross Russell Collection

BY RICHARD LAWN

"Who *is* Ross Russell?" This was a question asked frequently by library and Music Department personnel of The University of Texas at Austin during a period of nearly five years of casual correspondence and negotiations with Russell concerning his archive. The correspondence was initiated by Russell himself in the fall of 1976 and culminated in January 1981 with the purchase of Russell's lifelong collection of materials, which is now housed at the Humanities Research Center and in branches of the University's General Libraries. Who was, or is, Ross Russell, and why did he contact The University of Texas, are still questions in the minds of those not closely associated with the study of the jazz community and its culture.

Ross Russell is described briefly in *Contemporary Authors* (Gale Research, 1967) as an ex-Merchant Marine, golf pro and course owner, raceway publicity director, record shop proprietor, jazz journalist, photographer, part-time lecturer at the University of California at San Diego, pulp novelist focusing primarily on hipsters, crime, and sex, and most importantly as far as HRC's interest was concerned, founder of Dial Records and author of *Jazz Style in Kansas City and the Southwest* (University of California Press, 1971) and *Bird Lives: The High Life and Hard Times of Charlie "Yardbird" Parker* (Charterhouse, 1973). Russell's initial contact letter, addressed only to "acquisitions department," eventually reached the desk of Carolyn Bucknall, Assistant Director for Collection Development in the University's General Libraries, in August 1976.[1] In the letter, Russell suggested that he was preparing to "dispose of [his] library of jazz books," collected over a period of forty years and containing many out-of-print and first edition items. He described his collection of books, periodicals, booklets, programs, record catalogues, and memorabilia as "one of the finest and most complete collections in private hands in the country." His letter went on to describe himself as "author of 3 well-known books and over 100 articles on jazz and a well-known jazz scholar and teacher." Actually this was a rather modest and

---

[1] Letter from Ross Russell, 10 August 1976. All quoted correspondence is from the Ross Russell Collection in the Humanities Research Center and is published with permission.

brief biography, but unfortunately Russell was not as "well known" as he imagined, except to a small coterie of jazz scholars. Bucknall wisely channeled Russell's initial correspondence to Delmer Rogers, Associate Professor of Music Theory, and Glen Daum, Assistant Professor and then director of the University's Jazz Ensemble, requesting their evaluation and comment. Both professors raised enthusiastic eyebrows at even the faint prospect of the acquisition of the Russell collection and confirmed his stature as a jazz historian and author of high esteem. Rogers and Daum strongly urged that the University's library personnel carry on their dialogue with Russell, and Bucknall responded to Russell's initial inquiry by requesting an itemized inventory of his books and periodicals.

Russell indicated that two eastern universities, including the University of Pittsburgh, and one western school had also shown preliminary interest; however, he felt that "UT might be the best place for it."[2] The specific names of the other universities have never been disclosed, nor have his reasons for being so interested in The University of Texas. One possible explanation could be the University's location in the Southwest and its proximity to Charlie Parker's beginnings in Kansas City. Another possibility could be the University's growing reputation as a research center in the many areas covered by Russell's career.

The University responded to Russell's initial queries by showing mild interest in the previously described materials but a new and greater interest in materials relating to three of his most highly acclaimed books: *The Sound* (Dutton, 1961), a jazz novel; *Jazz Style in Kansas City and the Southwest;* and *Bird Lives,* the definitive biography of jazz saxophonist Charlie Parker. However, negotiations were stalled between the fall of 1976 and late 1979 but were resumed in 1980. Why the delay? Russell explained to Bucknall in his September 1980 letter that

> litigation involving the last book *Bird Lives* made it impossible to make a commitment on related research material.[3] Since 1976 the litigation has been brought to a conclusion and I am now sole owner of the copyright and rights to all related materials. Like materials for the *Jazz Style* book [are] on hand, including many rare photographs. At this time I am preparing to retire and possibly emigrate and would like to dispose of both the book collection and the research material.[4]

Russell went on to explain in the letter that from 1949 to 1951 Dial Records

[2] Ibid., 19 November 1976.

[3] A libel suit was instigated by Robert Reisner and his widow accusing Russell of plagiarizing Reisner's book *Bird: The Legend of Charlie Parker.*

[4] Letter from Ross Russell, 5 September 1980.

had expanded its scope and interests to include contemporary classical music as well as jazz and that because of his company's various business dealings the collection also contained letters and holographs from Ernst Krenek and Rudolph Kolisch, and seventeen letters from Arnold Schoenberg. He described the latter as being "typed by [Schoenberg] and signed" and that they "concern various arrangements and suggestions for recording various of his works." These letters added the extra fuel to rekindle the fires of interest at the University. This information not only interested Bucknall but also attracted the attention of Olga Buth, Fine Arts librarian, who passed this most recent correspondence and the entire Russell file to the present writer. As director of Jazz Studies in UT's Department of Music, I set about trying to trace Russell's whereabouts through the last correspondence between the collector and the University. Knowing that such a jazz resource was of inestimable value, I made a series of phone calls to what proved to have been Russell's temporary California residences mentioned in his letters from 10 August 1976 through September 1980, but all attempts to locate the collector resulted in dead ends. I feared that Russell had already emigrated and that the collection had been lost to us. At last, however, I was able to reach Russell's wife by phone, and none too soon. She was still in California but informed me that indeed Russell had already left the country to set up their new retirement home in Warm Bath, South Africa, and that she would join him there in a matter of days. This was the bad news; the good news was that the collection had not yet been sold. Only one other university remained in the competition, but it was apparently interested only in portions of the collection, and Mrs. Russell indicated that her husband would like to see his collection kept intact. Since they were leaving the country and were forced to depart with this cumbersome issue still unresolved, they felt compelled to turn the sale of the collection over to a specialist, antiquarian Laurence McGilvery. Mrs. Russell also indicated that the size and value of the collection had more than doubled since her husband's initial query letter in 1976, and she was very direct in expressing the need for expediency on behalf of the University if the collection was to be acquired in its entirety. The Russells were obviously interested in settling their affairs in the United States and making a clean break with their past.

At this point I promptly contacted Decherd Turner, director of the Humanities Research Center, who also shared a genuine interest in the Russell collection. It was now late December 1980 and close to semester break, during which time it would be difficult to accomplish any negotiations. As luck would have it, the director, through his many years of handling archival negotiations, was acquainted with McGilvery and knew him to be a respected and trustworthy antiquarian. After speaking with McGilvery, Turner was convinced that the collection would be a valuable addition to the HRC's holdings. Serious negotiations between McGilvery and the director occurred just a few days before Christmas 1980. Turner was particularly interested in the Schoenberg letters and made an offer for the entire collection that McGilvery accepted before the day was out. During the five-year period of these Russell negotiations, no one at the University ever spoke directly with the mysterious collector himself.

Ross Russell's collection was shipped from California shortly after the first of the year (1981) and proved to be well worth the University's effort. (To insure their safety, the Schoenberg letters were hand delivered to the HRC's director in San Francisco on 29 January 1981.) Bucknall, Buth, Professors Rogers and Daum, and the HRC's director were all rewarded for their parts in the acquisition of the Russell collection when on its receipt they discovered a collection much larger than any one had imagined. McGilvery had provided a box-by-box inventory of fifteen legal-sized boxes of correspondence, research materials, manuscripts, photographs, and miscellaneous papers. The collection had also grown to include approximately 3,500 LP and 78 RPM discs; reel-to-reel and cassette tapes; 265 books, which deal primarily with jazz and jazz-related topics; some 400 periodicals, including complete or nearly complete runs of *Down Beat, Jazz Review, Cleff, Record Changer,* and *Jazz Record;* approximately 200 miscellaneous booklets, pamphlets, programs, and record catalogues; and other memorabilia. The recordings were an unforeseen bonus, particularly since the acquisition of jazz recordings had not been a top priority at the University in past years and many of the Russell discs are classics which add significantly to the collections in the University's Fine Arts Library.

Collection Catalogue and Locations

Little has been written about Ross Russell, yet his personal correspondence offers a great deal of insight into his many roles, struggles, and relationships with others, especially those close to the music business. Russell's own life, spent investigating the lives and labors of others, presents a fascinating biographical specimen in itself. Evidence reveals Russell to have been a conscientious collector absorbed for over forty years with filing every note, letter, and scrap of paper, seemingly anticipating from the first that some day his efforts would be respected and rewarded. The fruits of his labors were eventually harvested, and yet they seem insignificant when weighed against his years of costly disciplelike devotion to Black music, which is still looked upon by many as the "black sheep" of American art forms.

Although Russell did save everything, his methods of organization leave something to be desired. Laurence McGilvery discovered Russell's haphazard filing systems while spending many Christmas vacation hours poring

I am very satisfied that you agreed not to publish
works of other composers on records with my music.
I have only these reasons:I do want to depend on not
the attractiveness of other peoples music,nor suffer
from their failure to be attractive.And,having waited
so long for being recorded,I would not give up half an
inch from the space which can serve my music tecome
known.Do not forget what happend to me:All my works
at Universal Edidition are o u t of print.So I
need the sound of re ords more than any other composer.
I have written myself already to Leibowitx.He is
certainly a good friend of mine.But there is one
serious misunderstanding:He believes in the s c h oo l
of atonality,but I believe only in the music.Webern
and Berg are to me great composers,I would almost
say: i n s p i t e of their belonging to the method
of composing with twelve tones.

If you have already made up with Koldofski about the
Trio and do not want to change it,then I would be very
happy if the Kolischs would record the Strinqartetes.
I think they have them reqdy.And I believe Alco will
have to give up.I have written   them today,that I
would not wait longer than to January 17.If he cannot
issue the records to this time I would consider the
contract void.Will it not be the best if you contact
him?I am sure he hasnot the money to finish the job.

I see with great pleasure that to you publishing of
these records is done"in a spirit of enthusiasm
and good will". If, as I hope, you are also a capable
busynessman, this capacity will blend very well with
your artistic beliefs. I am also convinced that the
views on your commercial success are excellentb, because of your enthusiasm and because of your belief
in the future.

I am looking forward to receiving the test pressing
of the Ode.

I will send you occasionally a number of photos,
which I will select according to your wishes.
Please remind me on that from time to time.

Your plan to issue records of: the Suite Op. 29,
the Woodwind Quintet, the Herzgewächse and even some
orchestra works, pleases me immensely.

I would like now to receive soon a contract, because
my lawyer always asks for it.

Thank you very much for your telegram. I enjoyed
your good opinion and enthusiasm for the piece, and
I hope the record will emenate the same effect and pro-
voke the same emotion in the listener.

I hope I have answered all your questions and problems
and paved the way to a conclusion.

Happy New Year, and cordial greetings,

Most sincerely yours,

Arnold Schoenberg

Pages 2 and 3 of a letter from Arnold Schoenberg to Ross Russell, dated 3 January 1950, in which Schoenberg thanks Russell and Dial Records for producing the composer's music. Used by permission of Belmont Music Publishers, Los Angeles, California 90049. *HRC Collections.*

through the collector's paper-and-pen existence prior to the collection's disposition to the University. Although McGilvery did an excellent once-over job of organizing the Russell papers, he did recommend further sorting and refiling, a task which has not yet been completed. Of the 3,500 recordings which arrived in Austin with no catalogue, approximately 1,500 jazz and jazz-related LPs and 78 RPM recordings have now been catalogued through assistance received from the University's Research Institute. Along with the discs, a detailed card file for these recordings exists in the special collections area of the Fine Arts Library. As project director, I also maintain a more detailed card file in the University's Department of Music.

The Russell Collection contains the most complete assemblage of recordings by Bebop saxophonist Charlie Parker in the world. Since many of the discs are long out of print, each is being transferred to tape for student and general public use. The collection includes many Dial Records test pressings of jazz recordings by such masters as Charlie Parker, Kenny Durham, Dexter Gordon, and Red Rodney, as well as recordings of works by Schoenberg and other classical composers. The Collection Deposits Library (CDL) houses most of the 2,000 unsorted and uncatalogued classical recordings which arrived along with the Russell archive. Approximately 265 books and 400 periodicals are housed and catalogued in the Fine Arts Library, and a special Russell Collection card file has been established. The Humanities Research Center holds the Russell archival materials: correspondence, manuscripts, unpublished works, photographs, and all paper items related to the author-collector's legal defense.

Items of Special Interest

Ross Russell's years of correspondence show him to have been unusually persistent in keeping in touch with friends via mail. To quote Laurence McGilvery: "much of the personal correspondence deals with jazz or writing or both [with the exception of wartime letters home to his mother] and many of Ross Russell's jazz or business associates are also close personal friends."[5] His correspondence files date back to the 1940s when he was serving in Europe as a member of the Merchant Marine. Of special interest to jazz scholars are letters in the correspondence files, some personal and others in interview format, from fellow jazz historians throughout the United States and Europe. These correspondents include Martin Williams (now of the Smithsonian and Rutgers Institutes), Whitney Balliett (of *New Yorker* magazine), Max Harrison (jazz journalist), Charles Delauney (editor of *Jazz Hot,* Paris), Rudi Blesh (jazz author), Leonard Feather (noted jazz author

[5] Letter from Laurence McGilvery, 1981.

and critic), Ralph Gleason (journalist), André Hodeir (seminal French jazz author), Gunther Schuller (noted composer, author, conductor, performer, and educator), Nat Hentoff (author), Marshall Stearns (author), and Ira Gitler (author and jazz recording producer). Correspondence and interviews are with such jazz artists as John Lewis, Cootie Williams, Sonny Criss, Bud Freeman, Don Lanphere, Hampton Hawes, Fats Navarro, Jesse Price, Jay McShann, Gene Ramey, Kenny Clarke, Charlie Parker, Chan Richardson Parker Woods (Charlie Parker's last wife, now married to contemporary saxophone great Phil Woods), and Red Rodney. The Rodney letters are most revealing and relate to other files and notes for an uncompleted book Russell planned to coauthor with this trumpeter who replaced Charlie Parker's sidemen Dizzy Gillespie and Miles Davis.

In addition to jazz record albums, the Fine Arts Library houses tape recordings in cassette and reel-to-reel formats. These recordings represent some of the rarest and most interesting items in the Russell Collection. Taped interviews with Jesse Price, Jay McShann, Fats Navarro, and most importantly, Charlie Parker himself in a backstage dressing room, are awe-inspiring. Though Parker was one of the most sought-after recording artists of his time, he was rarely captured on film or in a relaxed interview situation when he wasn't disguising his real character behind a protective shell. He frequently assumed a role which would fit the expectations of a particular situation; however, the Russell tapes reveal an unassuming, personal side of Parker seldom revealed in public. Parker discusses candidly his relationship with his father, mother, and son, and talks in great detail about his early musical training and experiences. Other miscellaneous Russell tapes derive from lectures for college courses in Modern Jazz, Jazz in Kansas City, and The Blues taught by Russell at the University of California at San Diego. Accompanying lecture notes for these tapes may be found in the HRC's Russell files.

Charles Christopher Parker, nicknamed "Yardbird" or simply "Bird," was the self-styled genius of the modern jazz movement in the 1940s and 1950s known as Bebop. Since his death in 1955 at the age of thirty-four, Parker has been the musical model and guru of aspiring young jazz musicians, many of whom have fostered a near cultlike worship of the man and his music. Parker's artistry, his self-destructive, unorthodox life style, and his disdain for business affairs touched and changed the lives of many and certainly that of Ross Russell, author of one of the several Parker biographies. Russell's Dial Records label was the first to press Bird as a soloist and group leader after his exodus in the early 1940s from Jay McShann's Kansas City band. Materials relating to contractual arrangements, royalties, mechanical rights, reviews, and promotion of Dial recordings illuminate Russell's relationship with Parker, as well as with other artists in the Dial catalogue, including Arnold Schoenberg. The Schoenberg file, located in the HRC, offers months

This contract made the 26th day of February 1946 at Hollywood California between Charley Parker and DIAL RECORD COMPANY 5946 Hollywood Blvd Hollywood California provides the following covenants:

1. That the undersigned Charley Parker agrees to record exclusively under his own name only for DIAL RECORDS for a period of one year from date.

2. That DIAL RECORDS agrees to make at least twelve ten-inch sides with Charley Parker as featured artist or band leader during the above period of one year.

FOR
DIAL RECORDS
Ross Russell

Charlie Parker

"RECEIVED"

MAR 26 1946

Ross Russell's handwritten recording contract with Charlie Parker, 26 February 1946. *HRC Collections.*

of correspondence between Russell and the well-known twentieth-century composer. These letters provide the reader with a complete picture of their relationship and negotiations, which gradually soured. Though their relationship eventually became strained, Russell's Dial Records did press several Schoenberg works, including the famous *String Quartets* and *Verklärte Nacht*. The letters reveal a demanding and misunderstood artist who in his later years yearned for the recognition he so deserved but was not attaining from either the music industry or the public. A letter dated 13 January 1950 attacks the Golschmann recording of *Verklärte Nacht*, which through poor interpretation completely misrepresented Schoenberg's musical intentions. The letter later provides an accurate description of the composer's intended interpretation of this important work.

Financially and personally the record business and its occasional sordid and bizarre dealings with artists left Russell disenchanted. As a result, Russell's Dial Records was gradually laid to rest. Master tapes were sold or leased to other, more well-established companies which began to reissue in particular the Parker sides so wildly sought after by Bebop enthusiasts. More recently Spotlight Records, under the leadership of Tony Williams, another Russell correspondent, began a special limited-edition reissue series. Williams has contacted the HRC on several occasions in search of original materials which might be of use to this reissue series.

With the death of Parker and Dial Records, Russell apparently concentrated his efforts on writing, though never abandoning his interests in jazz and its creators. Two legal-sized boxes offer for scholarly pursuits a vast file of research materials, interviews, drafts, notes, chronologies, discographies, promotion materials, letters, photographs, holographs, reviews, litigation instigated by Robert Reisner, contracts, and screenplay versions of the Charterhouse publication, *Bird Lives*, as well as some unpublished material. Similar files contain documentation leading to Russell's two other important publications, *The Sound* and *Jazz Style in Kansas City and the Southwest*. Due to the lengthy court battle which ensued shortly after the release of *Bird Lives*, Russell dropped his plans to base a major film on this biography of Charlie Parker. Recently, Richard Pryor has announced his intention to release a movie based on the life of Bird, and reportedly Pryor has sought out Russell's old friend Red Rodney as musical director and is himself attempting to gain weight in order to play the part of the jazz musician. At this date it is not known who has been chosen as script writer, but anyone interested in basing a film on Parker's life and work would certainly want to consult the University's Ross Russell Collection.

Countless pages in the HRC's archival holdings represent Russell's years of research that culminated in published jazz articles, unpublished articles, notes for potential publications, book ideas and outlines, unfinished articles, and a series of unpublished novels, many in nearly completed form. Several of these manuscripts ("Red Azalea," "Goodbye to Bohemia," "The God That Failed," "The Girl Who Liked Muscles," "Good Samaritans," "My Collar Got Dirty," "Call Girl," "The Gold Plated Melody," and "The Disc Jockey") are completed as far as ten chapters and 30,000 words. Like the works of many other artists, Russell's unfinished projects may far outnumber those he completed. Yet the uncompleted works can now offer a stimulus not only to the jazz historian and performer but to the literary scholar as well.

The lengthy, insulting, and costly litigation surrounding Reisner's *Bird: The Legend of Charlie Parker* and Russell's *Bird Lives* left a bitter taste with Russell, and no wonder. He had been out a small fortune defending his name and reputation and in fact was forced to spend nearly every penny realized in royalties from the book in his own defense. In this same general time period, Russell had received an advance and green light from another publisher encouraging his completion of an in-depth biography of Raymond Chandler. Russell completed nearly fourteen chapters through many devoted hours of preliminary research, all of which is contained in the HRC's Russell archive. But apparently the Chandler estate, much like Parker's, had become something of a legal entanglement, posing what Russell considered a potential repeat of his Parker publication fiasco. Still a bit gun-shy, he went back to his publisher and requested an insurance policy protecting him from any legal action resulting from the publication of the Chandler biography. The publisher refused and Russell promptly dropped the entire, potentially volatile, project and began organizing his affairs for his departure from the United States. Many details of the Chandler project are sketchy and the above information was gleaned largely during a phone interview with Laurence McGilvery, who oddly enough has never met nor even spoken with Ross Russell, even though he handled the sale of what could be considered forty years of the collector-author's life.

Russell described his jazz book collection as "one of the 3 or 4 world's finest collections," which may not be a gross exaggeration.[6] Olga Buth and I have evaluated the book collection prior to its shelving by the Fine Arts Library staff to ascertain the value and importance of each of the more than 265 items. Rare, irreplaceable books and discographies are closed-shelf items limited to in-library use, as are books with personal inscriptions and notes to and by Ross Russell. One of the most fascinating books in the collection, which can broaden the historian's perspective on the history of jazz, is a 1926 Sears edition (no relation to Sears Roebuck) of *Jazz* by Paul Whiteman, the orchestra leader who later hired the legendary jazz cornetist Bix Beiderbecke. Naturally this book, along with first editions and other volumes long out of print, is also limited to in-library use.

One can hardly pursue a career in journalism and record production without becoming at least mildly involved in photography, and as a journalist

[6] Letter from Ross Russell, 5 September 1980.

146

Ross Russell was no exception. The HRC archive includes copies of all the photographs reprinted in Russell's two historically important jazz studies, although most of the photographs corresponding to *Bird Lives* and *Jazz Style in Kansas City* were borrowed by Russell and used with the permission of owners such as Duncan Scheidt. The Russell Collection does contain many other prints, proof sheets, and contact sheets produced from photographs by Russell, along with photographic essays of the 1968, 1970, 1971, and 1974 Monterey Jazz Festivals, as well as the 1968 Newport Jazz Festival, the 1967 Dixieland Festival at Disneyland, and the 1969 Jazz by the Bay Festivals. The Russell files include candid photographs of the Modern Jazz Quartet, Louis Bellson, Sonny Criss, Duke Ellington, Dizzy Gillespie, John Handy, Hampton Hawes, Harold Land, Don Lanphere, Tony Ortega, Jessie Price, Archie Shepp, and Randy Weston, in addition to many as yet unsorted and unidentified shots.

Many of the holograph manuscripts concerned primarily with Russell's Parker research have been published. Recently several have appeared in a new large-format pictorial biography of Charlie Parker compiled by Chan Richardson Parker Woods and Francis Paudras. This book, entitled *To Bird With Love*, was produced in a limited-edition publication in France and may be viewed in the special collections area of the Fine Arts Library. Although many of the Russell holographs have appeared in print with his permission, there still remain a number of intriguing items as yet unseen by the public.

Ross Russell has led a varied and productive life which was often devoted to the study of others. As a result, the fifteen boxes of materials comprising the Russell Collection provide us with not only clear insights into the life and times of Ross Russell but also into those of countless friends and associates who are potential literary subjects. After many hours spent in exploring Russell's own past, as well as his research into biographical subjects, I myself am far from unearthing even a fraction of the beckoning secrets of his archive. The wealth of the Russell Collection should stand for years to come as a continuing resource for music scholars, casual listeners, and avid readers. Its purchase was timely and an important step in the dedicated development of the University's archival holdings. The acquisition of the collection also affirmed the University's serious commitment to jazz scholarship, an area which has gone nearly unnoticed on many campuses throughout the country. There is little doubt that the collection has already provided further impetus to the Music Department's growing support for jazz studies and commercial music, a program that has begun to gain recognition from journals such as *Down Beat* and from music educators throughout the nation. The Ross Russell Collection will also serve as a vital resource in the areas of literature, photography, film, biography, and cultural history.

Paul Bowles working with musicians, n.d. Photograph by David Linton. *HRC Photography Collection.*

Paul Bowles: Lost and Found

By Bennett Lerner

In Tangier, Morocco, late one afternoon in the summer of 1982, I knocked on the apartment door of expatriate writer-composer Paul Bowles. I had read one of his novels but had never heard any of his music, although, as a pianist with a special interest in contemporary American music, I was aware that he had written many songs. Now, two years later, that picture has changed considerably, for I have read all of Bowles's books, have made a record of twelve Bowles piano pieces, and plan to learn more of his works and to perform them in future concerts.

My curiosity about Paul Bowles was originally sparked by the enthusiasm of my composer friends Aaron Copland and Phillip Ramey. Bowles himself is a friend and former student of Copland, and Bowles's novels and stories are practically the only fiction Copland, who prefers biography and *belles-lettres*, reads with interest. Ramey, also an admirer of Bowles, had met him in New York with Copland during the author's last visit to the United States in 1969. The two often discussed Bowles and his work in my presence, and when Phillip and I decided to take a trip to North Africa, my first thought was, "In that case, let's visit Paul Bowles in Tangier."

Bowles is unusual in that he has pursued two very different careers in the arts. Until the late 1940s, he was primarily a composer—a student not only of Copland but of Virgil Thomson—and had gained a reputation for chamber works, operas, and songs. (The latter are still widely considered among the best of American art songs; a collection of forty was published recently by Soundings Press.[1]) Bowles was also active in the theatre, writing incidental music for plays by Tennessee Williams (*The Glass Menagerie*, with Bowles's score, was revived on Broadway during the 1983–84 season), Lillian Hellman, Arthur Koestler, William Saroyan, and Bowles's wife, Jane Bowles (*In the Summer House*), among others. There were more than twenty such theatre scores (many unfortunately lost by careless producers), and Bowles still occasionally provides music for plays staged at the American School in Tangier. In the 1930s and 1940s his music was commissioned and performed

---

[1] Paul Bowles, *Selected Songs*. Preface by Virgil Thomson, with a note on Paul Bowles by Peggy Glanville-Hicks. Santa Fe, NM: Soundings Press, 1984.

by distinguished artists such as Leonard Bernstein, Gold and Fizdale, Lukas Foss, and Maro Ajemian, and much of it was published and recorded.

In 1949, at about the time he settled in Morocco, Bowles published his first novel, *The Sheltering Sky*, about Western travelers in the Sahara desert brutalized by their encounter with a primitive culture. This and three subsequent novels, numerous short stories and poems, two travel books, and the recent *Points in Time* (1982), an impressionistic history of Morocco, have enjoyed a good deal of success and high critical acclaim. Bowles is often referred to as a writer's writer.

While there have been books on Bowles's literary works, relatively little commentary exists on his music. In their books, even Copland and Thomson mention Bowles only in passing. Until the Soundings Press publication, Bowles's music had been almost entirely out of print, and until my recent recording of Bowles's piano music, only two songs were available on record.[2]

My knock at Bowles's door was answered by Mohammed Mrabet, a Moroccan storyteller discovered by Bowles, whose tales the American has transcribed, translated, and seen published (as he has done for several others, virtually creating a school of Moroccan writers). Mrabet led the way into a small, rather dark living room with cushions on the floor, Arab-style. Although isolated, with no telephone, Bowles nevertheless has often been visited by literary friends who have found themselves in his part of the world— people like Allen Ginsberg, William Burroughs, Truman Capote, and the late Tennessee Williams—but he sees relatively few musicians. Thus, when Phillip Ramey and I arrived bringing greetings from Copland and Thomson, the occasion was for him hardly an everyday one. He greeted us cordially. Thin, white-haired, his eyes serene but watchful, his demeanor self-effacing yet given to sudden flashes of cutting wit, Bowles was not quite what I imagined the author of the violent *Sheltering Sky* would be.

At first, our conversation was of old friends in New York. Then it began to focus on his books, and ultimately, his music. A recurrent motif with Bowles was the fact that a good deal of his unpublished music had been lost ("But wherever are the scores? I've got nothing."). I asked him if there were any piano works he had never heard played, and he offered to look in his files. When I returned the next day, he had found a brief piece entitled *Orosí*. (*Orosí* is a valley in Costa Rica that Bowles once found "idyllic.") He was apologetic about there being just one piece, but he said he would look further. (Those scores which survive in his collection are only loosely organized.) Taking *Orosí* to Bowles's electric organ (he calls it his *organcito* or "little organ"; he has no piano, perhaps because of the climate), I read through the piece and was charmed by the music, even on the inadequate

    [2] "Once A Lady Was Here" and "Song of an Old Woman," Donald Gramm, baritone; Donald Hassard, piano. New World Records, NW-243, 1977.

Paul Bowles looking on while Bennett Lerner plays the *organcito* in Bowles's Tangier apartment, 1982. Photograph by Phillip Ramey, courtesy of Bennett Lerner and Phillip Ramey.

instrument. *Orosí*, a miniature in lilting Latin American folk style, suggestive of marimbas, made me aware for the first time of the curious dichotomy in Bowles's creative life: on the one hand, his grim, even brutal literature; on the other, his witty, graceful music. Bowles has since written to me that when engaged in fiction he feels "the door to the subconscious" is open and, consequently, hostility is liable to emerge when writing about other people. Music, however, is "about music—a closed cosmos that exists only in musical terms." He considers these two parts of his mind as more or less separate, a division not to be tampered with: "Let the machine alone as long as it functions."[3]

In February 1983 I was privileged to give the world premiere of *Orosí* in New York. Hearing of this, an enterprising company, Etcetera Records of Amsterdam, expressed an interest in Bowles, suggesting that if I could find more of his piano music a recording was possible. Trips to the music stores turned up nothing except the fact that almost all of Bowles's music had gone out of print, and the only score available from the circulating division of the New York Public Library was the *Six Preludes* for piano of 1934–45. (It should be noted that several of Bowles's scores are available for study in that library's research division, as are many recordings of his music from the 1930s and 1940s.) A friend happened to have a copy of the 1947 *Sonatina* for piano, but a principal Bowles publisher that I contacted did not even possess file copies of printed works.

In the meantime, I had been reading Bowles's books with fascination, and also the very individual writings of his late wife, Jane. It was in *A Little Original Sin*, the 1981 biography of Jane Bowles by Millicent Dillon, that I found a reference to the sale of Paul Bowles's papers to the Humanities Research Center at The University of Texas at Austin.[4] I wrote to the HRC and promptly received a three-page list of Bowles's musical works, both published and unpublished, in the collection, including songs, chamber music, orchestral music, and piano music. I ordered photocopies and found just the material I needed. Bowles wrote that he was pleased I had located scores I liked at the HRC.

Recently I performed and recorded Bowles's *Six Preludes* and also six of his pieces in Latin American style for the Etcetera label.[5] Unpublished scores of *Orosí* and *Tierra Mojada* came from Bowles directly. When he sent me *Tierra Mojada*, "dragged out of hiding," he professed himself unsure of

---

[3] Letter to author, 8 August 1983.

[4] Millicent Dillon, *A Little Original Sin: The Life and Work of Jane Bowles* (New York: Holt, Rinehart and Winston, 1981), p. 349.

[5] *American Piano Music*, Bennett Lerner, piano. Music of Copland, Thomson, Bowles, Barber, Bernstein, and Ramey. Amsterdam, The Netherlands: Etcetera Records, ETC 1019, Cassette XTC 1019, 1984. Available through Qualiton Imports, New York.

its musical value, as he had never heard it.[6] The scores of the other Latin American pieces (*Huapangos* nos. 1 and 2, *El Bejuco*, and *La Cuelga*) came from the HRC collection. In a recent letter Bowles wrote that he is "naturally very eager to hear the pieces" and "delighted to think that there will be a new recording available after so many years."[7]

Throughout my involvement with Bowles's music, I had two questions: Why was it so neglected, and how had his scores found their way to Texas? My answer to the first question is hypothetical. For the most part, Bowles's musical works are brief. As a result, they are difficult to program in concert, unless several are grouped together in a set. Bowles's piano pieces were usually published separately, and single pieces can easily go unnoticed. Further, his work is most often light in tone and such music has been to a great degree out of favor in the concert world since about 1950.

As for the second question, how Bowles's music ended up at the HRC, the answer seems to be that it was due to a combination of goodwill, misunderstanding, and luck. The fact is, Bowles was never careful about his manuscripts; for instance, the score of his "Negro opera," *Denmark Vesey*, was lost in the New York subway. While he was traveling in such places as Bali, Costa Rica, or the Rif mountains of Morocco, his scores and papers were left with various friends. One of them was Libby Holman, the famous torch singer, for whom Bowles wrote an opera based on García Lorca's *Yerma*. The materials at Libby Holman's were sold to the HRC in 1969 through Andreas Brown of New York City's Gotham Book Mart. When I interviewed Brown in the summer of 1983, he stated that he had made the arrangement to raise money for Bowles and that he and Bowles had gone to Holman's apartment to look for his effects, with Bowles wondering, "Are they still there?" They were, stored on shelves and piled in closets. Brown remembered subsequently packing and crating, without any cataloguing or sorting, and shipping everything to Texas. According to research librarians at the Center, the Bowles music materials came to HRC primarily in June 1969 from Andreas Brown.

Bowles suggested in a letter to me that he had intended that Texas should have only letters and autographed books, not music.[8] If so, the scores may have gone by mistake. A mistake perhaps, but a felicitous one, for otherwise most, if not all, of Bowles's scores would probably be lost. As Bowles himself

---

[6] Letter to author, 9 May 1983. *Tierra Mojada* was originally entitled *Iquitos* and is in the HRC collection under this title. Bowles felt that the title was one "that needs changing. . . . In 1947, Iquitos wasn't as well-known a place as it is now" (letter to author, 18 December 1982). In another letter, in response to my report that Orosí is now a favorite tourist spot in Costa Rica, Bowles wrote "I was saddened but not surprised to hear that Orosí has become a different place; that's the danger of naming pieces after idyllic spots!" (letter of 22 January 1983).

[7] Letter to author, 14 October 1983.

[8] Ibid, 23 July 1983.

Page from Paul Bowles's original musical score for his opera based on García Lorca's *Yerma*. *HRC Collections.*

wrote, he is uncertain whether "items not at Austin are anywhere."[9] The Humanities Research Center is thus the only source for Bowles's unpublished musical works and, given the difficulty of tracing Bowles's scores in private collections, is also the most accessible source for most of his published works.

Aaron Copland recently observed of Bowles's music, "It is always fresh, never dull, and is full of melodic charm and invention."[10] I can only echo his sentiment and reflect how fortunate it is that, thanks to the Humanities Research Center's collection, this very special music is being held in safekeeping for performers and scholars.

[9] Ibid.
[10] Author's interview with Copland, November 1983.

David O. Selznick playing the piano at home, 1940. *HRC Theatre Arts Collection.*

The Music for David O. Selznick's Production No. 103

By William Penn

From all indications and reports, *Duel in the Sun* (1946), Production No. 103 from Vanguard Films, Inc., was intended as David O. Selznick's triumphant return to the major success he had achieved as the epic filmmaker of *Gone With The Wind* (1939).[1] Selznick firmly believed that one had to spend money in order to make money, and therefore, logically, the more one spent, the greater the profits. However, Selznick was not one to fritter away his hard-earned capital, so having scrutinized a vast number of scripts before deciding to produce *Duel*, he conducted extensive feasibility studies and research before concluding that his conception of a Texas-styled western would be successful with the film-going public and at the box office.[2] Even though the artistic merits of *Duel in the Sun* may remain questionable—it was hardly of the caliber of his renowned classic *Gone With The Wind*—the film did succeed financially, and the key to this success was David O. Selznick's absolute genius at manipulating others and at the promotion and exploitation of a product. The cast of stars that Selznick employed is impressive, but

[1] Between *Gone With The Wind* and *Duel in the Sun*, Selznick International was responsible for four films: *Rebecca* (directed by Alfred Hitchcock, music by Franz Waxman), *Since You Went Away* (directed by John Cromwell, music by Max Steiner), *I'll Be Seeing You* (directed by William Dieterle, music by Daniele Amfitheatrof), and *Spellbound* (directed by Alfred Hitchcock, music by Miklos Rozsa).

[2] In late 1944, Selznick employed Audience Research, Inc. to test-market the conceptual feasibility of *Duel*. The areas of concern ranged from audience response to the title *Duel in the Sun* to whether the "want-to-see market" would support a picture whose selling theme had "emphasis on sexy story of wild passionate girl." (In this essay, all references to Selznick correspondence are from materials in the Selznick Collection at the Humanities Research Center.) Audiences were perhaps the same in the mid '40s as they are today. A report submitted to the Selznick studio on 17 January 1946 reveals that, from a series of nationwide surveys conducted by ARI, seventy-three percent of those interviewed wanted to see a picture whose selling theme had an "emphasis on Western setting and story" (ARI suggests that "this approach *reduced* the average market potential of the picture by three points"); "emphasis on sexy story of wild passionate girl" yielded a seventy-six percent "want-to-see market" (which "did not change the average market potential of the picture"); but the selling theme that would, according to ARI's research, "increase the average potential of the picture by two points" had an "emphasis on spectacular adventure, passionate conflict, with Western setting." The overall market want-to-see was an impressive seventy-eight percent.

so too is the cast of characters behind the scenes who were involved in Production No. 103, for the producer surrounded himself with highly talented and experienced personnel.[3] Among such figures was the composer Dimitri Tiomkin, one of the major contributors to the success of *Duel in the Sun*. The Russian-born Tiomkin's substantial contribution to the film and his relationship with other members of the Selznick team during the mid 1940s are the basis for a fascinating chapter in the saga of Production No. 103.

Dimitri Tiomkin was born on 10 May 1894 in the Ukraine, Russia. From 1912 to 1919 he studied piano and composition at the St. Petersburg (Leningrad) Conservatory of Music—with the renowned composer Alexander Glazounov as director—and was greatly influenced by the late nineteenth-century Slavonic Romanticism of Tchaikovski, et al. Although Tiomkin studied composition at the Conservatory, his primary *raison d'être* was to become a concert pianist. In 1919 he left Russia for Berlin, where he studied with the prestigious composer-pianist-pedagogue, Ferruccio Busoni. There Tiomkin also made his debut with the Berlin Philharmonic Orchestra and established himself as a viable concert pianist. In Berlin he formed a duo-piano team with Michael Kariton, and in 1922 the duo traveled to Paris, where Tiomkin was undoubtedly influenced by French impressionism, "Les Six," Stravinsky, Diaghilev, and the Ballet Russe. In 1925 the duo-piano team accepted an offer to tour America on the vaudeville circuit. An anonymous document in the Selznick Collection at the Humanities Research Center indicates that the "duo-pianists played the Albee circuit and eventually made the Palace." In this same document Tiomkin states that "We making big money, but obliged to play four times, often, in day." The tours introduced Tiomkin to American society and its musical spirit of the mid 1920s, and it was during this period that his concert piano career began to take hold: he made several tours, performed at Carnegie Hall, appeared with major symphony orchestras, and even gave the 1928 European premiere of George Gershwin's *Piano Concerto in F* at the Paris Opera. America also introduced Tiomkin to his wife-to-be, Albertina Rasch, a ballerina, dance director, and choreographer. The couple married in 1927, and Albertina's New York theatrical connections provided Tiomkin with access to many of the leading Broadway personalities, producers, and composers of the day. In 1930 Albertina was offered a position at MGM in Hollywood to supervise

[3] *Duel in the Sun* was directed by King Vidor, with screenplay by David O. Selznick, from Oliver H.P. Garrett's adaptation of the novel by Niven Busch. The principal actors were Jennifer Jones (Pearl Chavez), the "tempestuous half-breed"; Gregory Peck (Lewt McCanles), the rough cowboy "violent as the wind-swept prairie"; Joseph Cotten (Jesse McCanles), the son who rebels against the tyranny of the father; Lionel Barrymore (Senator McCanles), the rich and proud master of a million acres; Lillian Gish (Laura Belle McCanles), the martyred mother of a strange brood; Walter Huston (Sinkiller), the lusty philosopher of the far-flung prairie. Both Jennifer Jones and Lillian Gish received Academy Award nominations for best actress and best supporting actress respectively.

Dimitri Tiomkin, n.d. Photograph by Hurrell, M.G.M. *HRC Theatre Arts Collection.*

musicals and create modern ballet sequences, and she interested MGM in giving her husband a chance to write music for some of the filmed dances. MGM bought its first Tiomkin composition for $3,000—a previously composed ballet piece with the unlikely title of *Mars Ballet*. He wrote several ballet sequences for MGM and was eventually assigned his first original score in 1931: *Resurrection*. Tiomkin's rise to fame, however, was hardly meteoric. At one point there must have been a major conflict in his life—to compose or to concertize. However, as the result of an injury to his right hand in the late 1930s, there remained only one choice: composition. Tiomkin's film scoring career was firmly established in 1937 with his score to Frank Capra's *Lost Horizon,* and subsequently Tiomkin wrote at least one score per year until his semiretirement in 1965. In his lifetime he wrote over 100 feature film scores and in 1952 won two Oscars for *High Noon* (best score and song). His scores for *The High and the Mighty* (1954) and *The Old Man and the Sea* (1958) each won him an Oscar for best score. He received many other prestigious honors and awards, including some twenty Oscar nominations for his music. Dimitri Tiomkin died in London on 12 November 1977.

The masterful score created by Tiomkin for *Duel in the Sun* possesses all the hallmarks of the most legendary Hollywood scores found in the films of the 1930s through the 1950s: essentially wall-to-wall music,[4] ranging in mood from pulsating and impassioned emotionalism to epic western theme, conducted by the composer and performed by a typical Hollywood orchestra of the day: ninety musicians with a sixty-member chorus.[5] Tiomkin's seemingly Herculean task was accomplished by a single composer with the aid of a highly sophisticated and organized music production staff of enviable proportions. Its size ranged from a single rehearsal guitarist (José Barroso) for Gregory Peck, to a staff of orchestrators, copyists, musicians, and recording engineers that, although suggestive of the assembly line approach to music composition, echoed an era of Hollywood richness and opulence and created an artistic environment that is still the envy of the industry today. Indeed, the music departments at the major studios were a world unto themselves; their complex organizational structure will perhaps never again be duplicated and was, at one and the same time, not only totally supported by the Hollywood studio system but dependent upon it as well, thus spawning a curious relationship between art and business. While it is true that these

---

[4] Probably the all-time record for the most music packed into a feature theatrical film was Max Steiner's score for Selznick's *Gone With The Wind*: well over three hours of music for a picture that lasted three hours and forty minutes. The 1956 George Stevens film *Giant* was perhaps Tiomkin's toughest assignment: two hours and twenty minutes of music for a film that ran three hours and thirty minutes.

[5] From a preproduction budget memo to the studio one learns that Tiomkin had "an idea of using human voices for the end of the picture and for the main title, for additional [tone] color and as part of the orchestra." Tiomkin believed "that this sound will help bring a great climax to the picture and a big majesting [*sic*] opening."

departments were required to produce music "by the yard," it is also true that the composer and his staff created for each film an original, tailor-made score performed by a virtuoso orchestra.

The composition of a film score in the golden days of Hollywood was, to be sure, a communal effort. The departments were huge. Among the copyists who worked on *Duel in the Sun* were Frances McDermott, Einar Nelson, Richard W. Petrie, Russ Garcia (who has since established himself as a successful TV and film composer), Francis Magliocco, George E. Miessner, Don Clark, Arthur W. Grier, Peter Brunelli, Allan B. Campbell, Fred Sternberg, George Fields, James G. Porter, W.D. Garlock, Paul Discount, L.W. Ley, Percival Goldenson, Nicolai Bolin, Joseph Oroop, Max Reese, William Schiller, Stephen Pasternacki, and John M. De Rubertis. Manuel Emanuel was the head copyist and librarian. Among the arrangers/orchestrators involved with *Duel* were Joseph Nussbaum, William Ellfeldt, Paul A. Marquardt, H.B. Gilbert, Dave Tamkin, Ed Plumb, William L. Fontaine, James C. Lane, Lucien Cailliet, and George Parrish; the only arranger/orchestrator to receive even minimal credit for work on Production No. 103 was Frank S. Perkins. The list of rehearsal and recording musicians numbered over 100. For the recording session of 16 September 1946 alone, there was a seventy-four-piece orchestra that included sections consisting of twenty-four violins, six french horns, four percussion, and six trumpets.

On 13 December 1945 Tiomkin submitted a "BREAKDOWN OF MUSIC ESTIMATE FOR 'DUEL IN THE SUN'" to Selznick. The composer's estimated costs to complete the score by 9 March 1946 came to $82,000; Tiomkin seemed proud of his estimate because he cites comparative music costs: *Gone With The Wind*, $126,000, and *Since You Went Away*, $115,000.[6] Due to several strikes within the industry and other circumstances, the final score was not only more than six months late but as of 16 November 1946, $211,754.60 had been spent on the music, with the projection of another $41,546.22, resulting in a total budget of $253,300.82. From the music estimate submitted on 13 December one immediately senses that although Tiomkin might have been wrong about the final cost of the music production, he was certainly very seasoned in terms of how the game was played. In his original estimate he qualifies costs with some very precise and experienced comments:

> In making this estimation, I have taken it for granted that my score will run approximately two (2) hours or one hundred twenty (120) minutes. Because of general character and change of mood in "Duel

---

[6] How Tiomkin arrived at this budgetary information is something of a mystery. It seems unlikely that he had access to the film company's financials, and it is equally unlikely that he was quoting figures from the trade papers to, of all people, producer Selznick, since the trades are known for being inaccurate. Perhaps the best explanation would be that in a meeting between Selznick and Tiomkin, the producer provided the figures himself.

In The Sun" requiring chase music, pulsing background and sus-
penceful [*sic*] mood, I have an estimate figure of an approximate two
(2) seconds for one (1) bar of music.

Tiomkin then goes on to describe the number of musicians and the
amount of time it will take to record the score. His comments about the orchestrators are particularly noteworthy:

I will be obliged to pay to the best orchestrator different pay, vary-
ing according to the size of the orchestra and quality requirements
for my music from five dollars ($5.00) to ten dollars ($10.00) a page.
Amount of pages will be approximately between nine-hundred (900)
and one thousand (1000) pages for the complete score based on (2)
seconds for one (1) bar of music or seven and one-half (7½) orchestra
pages for one (1) minute of music.

Tiomkin felt that a chorus of singers was necessary for the film. He got
one. However, as one learns from several memos in the files, the chorus was
not at all popular with the administration. A "DUEL overage report on singers" memo of 10 June 1946 from Selznick to Einar Nelson suggests this nega-
tive feeling about the inclusion of a chorus:

This seems absurdly high to me and I wish you would have a talk
with Tiomkin. For the few places we are using voices it does not
seem to be worth $5000, nor do I see why for the few places we are
going to use it we need so much rehearsal and scoring.[7]

Selznick maintained significant input and control concerning all aspects of
production, and music was no exception. Several of Tiomkin's musical numbers required rewriting and major changes; this was due either to retakes,
changes in the editing of the picture, Selznick's likes and dislikes, or simply
to a desire to leave as many options open as possible. The "Rape Sequence"
in *Duel in the Sun* is a case in point. Selznick's music notes of 4 February
1946 show that he anticipated censorship problems with the scene:

Finish score at fence line—then *no music* until after the first crash
of thunder in the Pearl-Lewt struggle. The Desire Theme should be
introduced here at the point of her surrender . . . as she looks at
him and as her mood changes, and she suddenly feels a desire for
him, creeping it in just as she opens her eyes after he kisses her.
(Throughout the picture, this theme should always play on her passion.) The music can blend into something else on the return of the
cavalcade from the fence line. (CONFIDENTIAL NOTE: There's

[7] The actual budget for the chorus was $4,813. The budget for rehearsals was $3,750.

some possibility of censors cutting Pearl's surrender, so be prepared for two endings musically.)[8]

Some of Selznick's other concerns about the music were expressed elsewhere in these same notes of 4 February:

> This music is very disappointing. It has none of the eerie quality it should have. Overall effect not nearly as good as preview track. Sweeten it with another novachord or two.[9] Try fiddling with in reverberation chambers. Be careful in dubbing[10] that you don't lose Welles,[11] as in this running.

From the same set of music notes we can see that Selznick was not only critical but knowledgeable, and that he knew what he wanted and frequently offered solutions for changes. Selznick's comments concerning the "Bordertown Presidio" sequence are frank and insightful:

> This is very disappointing. Too shrill. All the primitive frenzy is lost in the substitution of the brass band. Don't like the tambourine. Do this in two ways: (1) Sweeten with drum track and reduce the brass band. (2) Repair the preview track. (Merge the two tracks where the tambourines are prominent.)

At times, Selznick would give in. Concerning the "Runaway Sequence," he comments that Tiomkin

> paid no attention whatever to the long verbal discussions on the subject, or to the notes. It has no menace, no suspense—nothing frightening about it. It could be a friendly race. Unfortunately, this will have to do.

For the remake of the "Second Sump Scene," Selznick not only has in-depth comments but is willing to reedit a shot for the sake of the music; he also wants to participate in the musical creation of a dance routine.

> DOS [Selznick] does not like any of the new guitar; does not like the introduction of the Sex Theme into the realistic guitar music; feels the guitar is much too professional; lacks continuity and build. He is

---

[8] There *were* problems, in fact, especially with the Catholic Church and various other religious organizations, and the scene had to be recut after the picture was first released.

[9] "Sweetening" is the procedure of adding music or other sounds to augment an existing track; for instance, adding strings to an already recorded track, or even adding a single instrument to an orchestral track. The novachord is a six-octave electronic, tone-generated keyboard instrument. There is a separate vacuum tube oscillator for each note of the chromatic scale. The instrument also produces fourteen different tonal qualities, including organ, piano, woodwind, and strings. The novachord was a favorite of Hollywood composers and was used in many film scores of the day, including Max Steiner's score for *Gone With The Wind*.

[10] In the film industry, "dubbing" has two meanings: either the actual recording of music for a film or the mixing of the various sound tracks (dialogue, narration, sound effects, and music) into a single, blended track.

[11] Orson Welles was the narrator for the opening Legend sequence of *Duel in the Sun*.

willing to change the last close shot of Lewt if it will help obtain a better musical build. He likes the preview dance track from the start to the point where the piano comes in, and believes this music should be the basis of the new recording. DOS wants to get together with Tiomkin, Stewart,[12] a guitar player and a drummer, and work out a routine for the dance.[13]

A reference to *Gone With The Wind* from Selznick is always worthy of note. From his 16 October 1945 conference with Tiomkin, Selznick suggests that the "'Pearl-Jesse Theme' ought to have the quality of the Ashley theme in 'Gone With The Wind.' It ought to be gentle, sentimental and tender. Shouldn't have any of Pearl in it."

The most famous situation concerning Selznick's reaction to Tiomkin's music was the result of a memo Tiomkin received from Selznick prior to the *Duel* recording session. Selznick wanted to have an idea of the type of music Tiomkin would compose for the various dramatic elements in the film, such as "jealousy," "flirtation," "conflict," and "orgiastic." Tiomkin relates in his autobiography that all the pieces were acceptable except for "orgiastic." After Selznick heard the second rewrite of the orgiastic number, he exclaimed:

> "No, Dimi, it still is not right. It hasn't the unbridled, throbbing urge."
>
> So I had to write it again, this time giving it plenty of throb, with violent palpitations in the orchestra. If this wasn't it, I was going to shoot somebody.
>
> It wasn't. When the orchestra had played through the feverish measures, I saw Selznick leave the auditorium alone.
>
> I was ready for murder. When the summons came, I went to his office. If he said once more that "orgiastic" wasn't satisfactory, I might kill him.
>
> "What is wrong now?" I restrained myself with difficulty.
>
> "Dimi, that is not the way I make love."
>
> With that, my Russian inflections thickened in a shout of rage: "But is the way I make love."
>
> He burst out laughing. That was the end of it.
>
> He agreed I should make musical love in my own way.[14]

Pearl Chavez, played by Jennifer Jones, was billed as the turbulent half-breed "built by the devil . . . to drive men crazy."[15] Selznick was concerned

---

[12] James Stewart was sound director, technical supervisor, and sound engineer for Selznick International from 1945 to 1948.

[13] Music notes from 6 November 1946.

[14] Dimitri Tiomkin and Prosper Buranelli, *Please Don't Hate Me* (Garden City, NY: Doubleday, 1959), pp. 221–22.

[15] From a fall 1945 Sunday tabloid that appeared across the country.

about the Hebraic overtones of a few bars of the Pearl theme, and the closing paragraph of a 6 November 1945 letter from Selznick to Tiomkin reads: "I would like to remind you that I thought the Pearl theme superb except for the first two or three bars which seemed to me to be slightly Hebraic in nature." On the following day, Audray Granville, music production manager, attempted to relieve Selznick's misapprehensions about the few bars in question, as revealed by an excerpt from a memo dated 7 November:

> I believe your feeling that it's being slightly Hebraic is due to the fact that Hebraic, Irish, Russian, Spanish, and Indian music have similar construction.[16] As I mentioned before, Mr. Tiomkin has changed the original treatment of this music which has helped a good deal, and which will be played for your approval.

As noted earlier, Selznick reacted to Tiomkin's music with a characteristically frank estimate of the composer's work. One of Audray Granville's duties was to pass along to Tiomkin such reactions by Selznick as appear in the memo of 6 November 1945:

> I wasn't madly in love with the RIO GRANDE theme which I thought could have more grandeur and sweep and that possibly might have some traditional Texas State music as counterpoint. Generally I thought sections of this theme were too much like ordinary cowboy music. . . .
>
> As to the "desire" theme, my understanding is that Mr. Tiomkin is trying to give us a melodic section of somewhat greater length, and to make the theme somewhat more sultry. This theme too must be treated rather lightly in the earlier places in the picture.

In a 7 November memo to Tiomkin, Granville described Selznick's remarks concerning the theme music for "Pearl," "Rio Grande," "Desire," "Jesse," and "Cowboy." However, Granville held opinions of her own, which she would share with Selznick, as seen in a memo dated 1 April 1946, where she enthusiastically defended Tiomkin's music:

> In your music notes of the 29th, you spoke of an old Mexican folk tune for Pearl's dance in the street. It is my opinion that there is nothing I could find which would have more lightness, charm or gaity [sic] than the present melody which Mr. Tiomkin wrote. This melody is authentic Mexican in style and it is a simple matter to have Mexican lyrics written to it's [sic] tune. . . . I do hope you will retain Mr. Tiomkin's music, as I remember how delightfully it impressed you when you first heard it and I believe that the piano guide track you have heard so often is spoiling it for you.

---

[16] This is a misleading point.

Page 1 (top and bottom halves) from *Duel in the Sun*'s "Squaw's Head Rock Sequence" for reel 15, part 1, orchestrated by Joseph Nussbaum. The orchestration is for eighty-one players. Note the distribution of the instrumentation and that the celli and double basses are divided in three

parts and that double basses 5 and 6 tune their low E string down to an E flat. *HRC Theatre Arts Collection.*

Of the 115 separate pieces of music in the film, eighty-two were originally composed by Tiomkin. Those not composed by him were either in the public domain, done by another composer for use in the picture, or owned outright by Selznick International Pictures: Vanguard Films, Southern Music Property. These non-Tiomkin pieces include the first number of the picture after the overture-medley;[17] the Selznick International Trademark, composed by Alfred Newman, originally made for *The Prisoner of Zenda* (1937), 12 seconds; fifteen separate presentations of Stephen Foster's 1864 song "Beautiful Dreamer" (the theme music for Laura Belle, played by Lillian Gish) for a total of 5 minutes, 34⅔ seconds;[18] "Sometimes I Feel Like a Motherless Child" (anonymous), appearing in the film two times for a total of 9 seconds; and Allie Wrubel's song, commissioned for *Duel in the Sun*, used six times for a total of 1 minute, 27 seconds. Each of the following appears one time: "Tales of the Vienna Woods" (Strauss) for solo piano, 5⅔ seconds; "Column Left Bugle Call" (anonymous), 4⅔ seconds; "First Party Music" (anonymous), 1 minute, 46⅔ seconds; "Cowboy's Dream" (traditional), also for 1 minute, 46⅔ seconds; "Heel & Toe Polka" (anonymous), 51⅓ seconds; "Varsoviana" (anonymous), 2 minutes, 40 seconds; "Rye Waltz" (MacLaughlin), 50⅔ seconds; "Ford Schottische" (anonymous), 25⅓ seconds; and "I've Been Working on the Railroad" (traditional), 7⅓ seconds. The remaining music in the film—all by Tiomkin—totals 1 hour, 12 minutes, and 8 seconds.[19] By today's feature film standards, this represents a substantial body of music; for Tiomkin, *Duel in the Sun* was a typical assignment for the day.

The following is a list of the music contained in the first three reels of the film (there are fifteen reels in all). Unless either "dialogue" or "silence" is indicated, the music is continuous, but on separate reels.[20]

[17] For Hollywood features of the magnitude of *Duel in the Sun*, it was common to have an overture-medley played prior to the start of the actual picture. This, of course, is not done today.

[18] While today it is possible to time cues as close as 1/192 of a second (⅛ of a frame), Hollywood composers of Tiomkin's day timed to the nearest ⅓ of a second, which is the smallest fraction of a second a conductor can catch while conducting and watching a screening of the picture and which is close enough for the music and picture to appear to be in sync. Although click tracks (a type of metronome beat) were available, they were seldom used to achieve exact synchronization of music and picture. It is interesting to note that both Max Steiner and Tiomkin claimed to have independently invented the click track.

[19] As one might surmise, Tiomkin composed much more music for the film, but due to fade outs, cross fades, cuts, rewrites, and the like, this additional music is not included.

[20] When using several pieces of music for a single, extended sequence, composers record each cue separately and then the music mixer dubs the various cues together into one continuous piece of music. This procedure translates into significant savings in terms of studio time and the cost of the musicians. In the industry, this method of recording is known as the "A-B roll" technique.

Reel 1:

Overture-Medley
1. "Round Up"; partial background, instrumental; 28 seconds.
2. "First Sump"; partial background, instrumental; 44 seconds.
3. "Pearl-Lewt Love Theme (part 1)"; partial background, instrumental; 38 seconds.
4. "Pearl-Lewt Love Theme (part 2)"; partial background, instrumental; 14⅔ seconds.
5. Selznick International Trademark; background, instrumental; 12 seconds.
6. Main Title; background, instrumental; 1 minute, 21⅓ seconds.
7. Legend; background, instrumental-vocal; 1 minute, 6⅔ seconds.
8. "El Bolero"; partial visual, instrumental-vocal; 33⅓ seconds.
9. Dialogue (no music); 12 seconds.
10. "Casino Dance"; partial background, instrumental; 3 minutes, 3 seconds.
11. Silence; 2 seconds.

Reel 2:

12. "Pearl's Humiliation"; background, instrumental; 1 minute, 19⅓ seconds.
13. Dialogue; 37 seconds.
14. "Bordertown Jail"; partial background, instrumental; 5⅓ seconds.
15. "Beautiful Dreamer"; background, instrumental; 51⅓ seconds.
16. "Bordertown Jail"; partial background, instrumental; 2 minutes, 26⅔ seconds.

Reel 3:

17. Dialogue (no music); 2 minutes, 17 seconds.
18. "The Buggy Ride"; partial background, instrumental; 8 seconds.
19. "Beautiful Dreamer"; partial background, instrumental; 8 seconds.
20. "The Buggy Ride"; partial background, instrumental; 6 seconds.
21. "Arrival at Spanish Bit"; partial background, instrumental; 12 seconds.
22. "Beautiful Dreamer"; partial background, instrumental; 10⅔ seconds.
23. "Arrival at Spanish Bit"; partial background, instrumental; 1 minute, 32 seconds.
24. "Pearl-Lewt Love Theme"; partial background, instrumental; 31⅓ seconds.
25. "Beautiful Dreamer"; partial visual, instrumental-vocal; 34⅔ seconds.
26. "Laura Belle's Room"; partial background, instrumental; 28 seconds.
27. "Pearl-Lewt Love Theme"; background, instrumental; 25⅓ seconds.
28. "Laura Belle's Room"; partial background, instrumental; 14⅔ seconds.
29. "Beautiful Dreamer"; partial visual, instrumental; 23⅓ seconds.
30. "Tales of the Vienna Woods"; partial visual, instrumental-vocal; 5⅓ seconds.

As with any production of this magnitude, there is always the "hurry up and wait" syndrome. As part of the general "panic," Bernard Herrmann, distinguished composer for several films by Orson Welles and Alfred Hitchcock, was sought out to do some composing for *Duel in the Sun*. In a memo to Selznick from Audray Granville dated 23 March 1945, Granville asked: "Do you think it advisable to write Mr. Hermann [*sic*] in detail regarding the balance of the music involved in production . . . ? We have the Southern waltz to consider, the Negro spiritual . . . and the dances in the Party Sequence." Apparently Herrmann was difficult to contact. In the same memo Granville states that "There is always a time lapse between any communication we make and his answer." On that same day Harriett Flagg, Selznick's studio representative in New York, received a Western Union Telegram from Granville: "MONDAY IS THE VERY LATEST I CAN HEAR FROM MR. HERMANN [sic] AS THIS PARTICULAR SCENE IS BEING HELD UP ON ACCOUNT OF MUSIC NOW." What appears to be the next and final correspondence on the Herrmann subject is dated 16 April 1945, from Granville to Selznick:

> Jennifer Jones does her dance at the Sump to a playback of a record called "Rumba Rhapsody" recorded by Xavier Cugat. She has learned her dance to this record. It was our intention to have Mr. Hermann [sic] write original music, using the same rhythm. Today, we are shooting the scene where Pearl hears Lewt playing and singing o.s. [off screen]. It is supposed to be the same music that is heard at the Sump. If you intend photographing Lewt, it will be necessary for Mr. Hermann [sic] to write this number and set lyrics to it. Please let me know what you wish done about this.

As it turned out, according to marginalia written on the same memo, it was not all that urgent: "Audray: We won't see Lewt playing in this scene, although we will see him in the 'Sump' scene. Therefore no lyrics are necessary; and it will be all right to use the 'Rhumba Rhapsody' so long as we don't see his hands too closely in the Sump scene, permitting us to change the music later."

The contract Tiomkin struck with the studio was lucrative. He usually received a base fee solely for his compositional services, with additional fees for conducting, arranging, and any other services, as well as royalties from music publications and recordings, but he was required to be totally committed to the project and to relinquish all rights, including copyright of his music, to the organization, a practice which was common in the industry and which still exists today, except in the case of a few prestigious composers like John Williams. The pressures and responsibilities of Tiomkin's task were great, but essentially they were commensurate with the composer's rewards. For example, as a base fee for *Duel*, Tiomkin received $7,500 (1946) solely for his compositional services.[21]

The eleven-page, seventeen-article contract, dated 15 October 1945,[22] addressed to Mr. Dimitri Tiomkin, c/o Mr. David Chudnow, 8913 Sunset Boulevard, Hollywood, 46, California, and signed by Richard Hungate for Van-

---

[21] In a memo dated 28 December 1948, he was to receive $17,500 for his *Portrait of Jenny* "score," which was largely based on the music of Debussy.

[22] Because of a union strike, the entire time frame of Tiomkin's contract had to be pushed up several months; but, according to other memos and documents, the 15 October 1945 contract for the film remains in force to this day.

Gregory Peck in a publicity photo from *Duel in the Sun*, 1946. *HRC Theatre Arts Collection.*

guard Films, Inc., indicates that Tiomkin was to be employed and engaged as a "composer and/or as a musical director, or otherwise" and that his service generally consisted of

> writing, composing and revising musical compositions and musical works of all kinds . . . of writing, changing and revising lyrical and/ or literary compositions . . . of supervising the preparation, the recording and the re-recording of the musical score . . . of directing and supervising all work involved in the arranging, orchestrating, performing and recording of such musical score; of rehearsing, conducting and directing musical soloists, orchestras and bands in connection with the recording of [the] musical score; of scoring, synchronizing, recording and re-recording musical and other sounds during the course of production of, and until the completion of production of [the picture]; of preparing and/or scoring the sound track of [the picture] for preview purposes; of giving . . . advisory assistance on all musical matters . . . as [they] may direct; and of performing such other related duties . . . as [they] may assign to [him] from time to time.

The contract continues with a statement regarding the relationship between the employee and the employers:

> Said services shall be rendered, either alone or in collaboration with others, in such a manner as we [Vanguard Films, i.e., Selznick] may direct, under the instructions and control, in accordance with the ideas of, and at the times and places required by our duly authorized representatives, and in a conscientious, artistic and efficient manner, to your best ability, with loyalty to our organization and with regard to a careful, efficient and economical operation of our business activities; it being understood that such activities involve a matter of art and taste to be exercised by us and that your services and the manner of rendition thereof are to be governed entirely by us.

Tiomkin was left with practically no claims to his creative product. The document is liberally laced throughout with general and very specific references to Tiomkin relinquishing "all of the results and proceeds of [his] services hereunder generally (including, but not limited to, all rights throughout the world of production, manufacture, recordation and reproduction by any art or method, including television and/or radio broadcasting, and of copyright, trademark and patent)."[23] In addition, the contract also states that Tiomkin's music must be original (and therefore copyrightable by the Selz-

---

[23] In the contract the word "employed" indicates that it was a "work made for hire." Under the copyright law of the time, the creator gave up all rights, including the right of copyright, to an employer; e.g., to the Selznick organization.

nick organization). For example, a section of article seven of the document states that

> You agree and warrant that all material composed and/or submitted by you hereunder for or to us shall be wholly original with you and shall not infringe upon or violate the right of privacy of, or constitute a libel or slander against or violate any common law rights or any other rights of any person, firm or corporation.

In consideration for relinquishing all rights to his music, Tiomkin received $7,500 as a base fee, an additional $750 per week (on a pro rata basis) for the periods of the second and third terms of the contract,[24] as well as a healthy percentage for music published and record royalties (to be described later). As is standard with most commercial music contracts, the payments were in stages:

(a) the sum of . . . ($1500) upon the execution of this agreement [15 October 1945];

(b) the sum of . . . ($2000) on the first day of recording of the musical score of the material or on January 1, 1946, whichever shall be the earlier. . . .

(c) the sum of . . . ($3000) upon the completion of recording of said musical score or upon March 1, 1946, whichever shall be the earlier. . . .[25]

(d) the sum of . . . ($1000) upon the completion of all services required of you hereunder.

Article sixteen outlines the publishing and record royalties. The thrust behind this section is that even though Tiomkin was relinquishing all rights to his music, he would be compensated by receiving a percentage of revenues from the music.[26] If Tiomkin wrote both music and lyrics (which he did not), the royalties listed below would be doubled; but he would receive roy-

---

[24] From article two: "the second term shall continue for a period of 60 days"; and the third term "continues until the completion of all services required of you by us in connection with the motion picture."

[25] Even though the recording did not start until several months later, Tiomkin received all payments on time. In a 1 March 1946 memo, Billie Edwards (contract office assistant for Vanguard Films) instructed Mr. Beaman (assistant treasurer) to issue a $3,000 check to Tiomkin. Edwards notes that "this third payment of $3000.00 was to be paid to Tiomkin on completion of recording or on March 1, 1946, whichever date is earlier, and March 1, 1946 is the earlier date."

[26] As was standard with the industry in those days, Tiomkin did not expect to receive "points" (a percentage of the box office receipts) or any other generated income from the film, its exploitation, or its sale. This is not necessarily true today and will vary, depending upon how much the composer is receiving "up front," or how established and sought after he or she is. Today, the percentages and royalties are also slightly higher because of (1) changes in the copyright law, (2) inflation, and (3) a change of attitude within the industry, which generally expects to give up part of the box office gross to certain extraordinary talents, including stars and "star" composers.

alties only for original music and not for "translations, arrangements, adaptations, paraphrases or orchestrations of other original compositions."

    (a) 1½¢ upon each and every complete pianoforte copy . . . sold . . . in the United States and paid for;

    (b) 1¢ upon each and every copy of orchestration . . . sold . . . in the United States and paid for;

    (c) 16⅔% of the net amount of all royalties received [by Vanguard Films, Inc.] . . . in the United States for the mechanical reproduction . . . in [the form of] player piano rolls, phonograph records, discs or any other form of mechanical reproduction (other than mechanical recordings used in synchronization with motion pictures, which synchronization rights,[27] and all royalties or other payments to be derived therefrom, are reserved exclusively to us, without any right on your part to participate therein);

    (d) 16⅔% of the net amount of all royalties received [by Vanguard Films, Inc.] . . . [from] the mechanical publication and reproduction rights from any and all sources outside of the United States, other than the synchronization rights referred to in (c) above.

Tiomkin also had another contract dated (revised) 15 March 1947, several months after the film initially opened, concerning the title song from the film. The song, appropriately enough, was titled "Duel in the Sun (A Duel of Two Hearts)" and was sold as "the love theme" from the film. There were two lyricists involved: Stanley Adams (former president of ASCAP [American Society of Composers, Authors and Publishers] from 1953–56 and 1959–80, and director since 1944) and Maxson Judell. The song was excerpted from the "Sump Ecstasy" section of the background musical score. The tune was commercialized; Adams and Judell added lyrics; and it was published by Bourne, Inc. of 799 Seventh Ave., New York. The eight-page contract was between Bourne, Inc., the publisher, and Vanguard Films, Dimitri Tiomkin, Stanley Adams, and Maxson Judell, the "authors." Since Vanguard was the legal owner of the music, it could participate on an equal-share basis with the authors, each party receiving twenty-five percent of the royalties. In accordance with article nine of the contract, the publisher agreed to pay the authors joint royalties as follows:

---

[27] The term "synchronization rights" (or synchronization license) refers to the use of music which is timed to synchronize with, or relate to, visual images. This includes slide shows as well as films. Today, among other licenses, film producers need to acquire a performance license, which grants the producer the right to perform the music with the film. Both synchronization and performance licenses are most commonly acquired by means of negotiation from either the Harry Fox Agency in New York or directly from the copyright owner, who may be the composer, the publisher, or a representative.

174

(a) Five cents (5¢) per copy with respect to regular piano copies or orchestrations sold and paid for in the United States of America and Canada.

(b) ($12.50) if the said composition is included in any dance or other folio published by the Publisher, and the sum of . . . ($12.50) for each monthly license granted to any publisher in the United States of America and Canada of song sheet folios in which the said composition or any part thereof is used, regardless of the number of different folios issued in any such month.

(c) An amount equal to fifty percent (50%) of the net receipts of the Publisher in respect of any licenses issued in the United States of America and Canada authorizing the manufacture of parts of instruments serving to mechanically reproduce the said composition or to use the said composition in synchronization with sound motion pictures or to reproduce it upon so-called electrical transcriptions for broadcasting purposes.

(d) 50% of net for foreign publication, mechanical, synchronization and electrical transcription rights.

Of the authors involved, Maxson Judell was clearly the most difficult character and was apparently quite irritated at the way the studio was treating him. He appeared to be a real pest to the studio, sending daily correspondence and frequently phoning. His complaints were valid and would be of concern to most authors, but the avenues of redress he chose and his persistence made the situation worse. He essentially had three complaints: first, the contract referred to above was not signed on time; second, "The studio fell down pitiably on publicity . . . actually did nothing as to it, and did nothing as to any radio broadcasts of the song";[28] and third, which seemed to be uppermost in his mind, he had "spent $55 on the wires and 'phone calls to New York. . . . Publishers right and left turned down the song (due to the LEGION campaign at the time and the negative inferences of the picture). I got a publisher anyway. To this day I have not been able to get the $55 from the studio."[29] Maxson F. Judell wanted his money; it was a sticking point and seemed a matter of pride. It is curious that the studio, after spending millions of dollars on *Duel*, was reluctant to send Judell the $55.

In a 28 July 1947 postcard to Robert Dann, vice president of Selznick International, Judell expresses the following folksy, yet ominous sentiment:

> While the heat and I are not friends (I like my weather cool and my wimmin hot—is my motto!) I take this moment to drop you this

---

[28] From a 28 August 1947 letter from Maxson F. Judell to Daniel O'Shea, president of Selznick International.

[29] Ibid.

card to ask what was what re: my recent explanation concerning the $55 request and what was your further thought upon consideration.

There remains a very *vigorous* unanimity among men I check with as to the legitimacy of my request, so naturally I will follow through on it.

Daniel O'Shea, president of Selznick International, concerned that Judell would pester Selznick, forwarded one of Judell's complaint letters to Robert Dann and, in a note attached to the letter, wrote: "Please take this guy off my neck—let me know what's what about him, just in case he gets to David. However, I wish you would handle it so he doesn't." From a 5 June 1947 memo from Robert Dann to Ted Wick, director of radio at Vanguard Films, Dann states "Will you please note and return the attached epistle from Judell. These are becoming longer and longer!" An excerpt from a 29 May 1947 letter to Saul Bornstein of Bourne, Inc. from Dann reveals that "Maxson F. Judell continues to make a nuisance of himself and is blaming us because the contracts have not been signed and the advance to Adams and himself received." In a three-page letter dated 28 May 1947 to Ted Wick, Judell writes:

Now: whether you or Mr. Dann, I wish your word as to the contract and advance—also as to the publicity promised.

I'll also be very frank with you: *you know that I do not bluff.*

If I am ignored on these obligation matters and not advised I shall take steps that will insure action. They may concern Mr. O'Shea; they may concern Loyd Wright [attorney for United Artists]; that [*sic*] may concern David Selznick; they may concern the Board of Directors; and a dozen other possibilities.

But as I told Mr. Dann when I first met him—you were there— I'll fight to the last ditch for what is *fair* and *right*.

All this outrage came from a lyricist who was at least partially responsible for composing these lyrics:

Our DUEL IN THE SUN
began just in fun,
could I believe your eyes
would weave a spell like this!
A duel of two hearts
who knows how it starts,
you touched the fire
of love's desire
with just one kiss.
The spark divine
was yours and mine.
The sun beguiled
looked down and smiled.

176

My arms reached for you
and then, dear I know
how dreams were spun
and love had won
our DUEL IN THE SUN.[30]

Before production for *Duel* began, Selznick, in his typically thorough fashion, took steps to exploit the music of the film through sales of sheet music and recordings. He realized that the income generated from royalties could be enormous, but only if the course were carefully charted. In a 22 February 1945 memo from Granville to Selznick we learn something about the profitability of having a "hit" song from a movie, even if not the title song:

> Some songs which were not picture titles, but were great hits, are as follows: "Don't Fence Me In" from "Hollywood Canteen" . . . "As Time Goes By" from "Casablanca." The average sale of a hit song goes between 200,000 and 500,000 copies. Insofar as we will control the publishing rights of this song, we should be able to make a deal with a reputable publisher, wherein we would net a royalty of approximately two cents per copy of sheet music.[31] Songs and records are selling unusually well now. As you can see, the initial cost of the song to us could very well come back four-fold. The importance of the picture, Gregory Peck's singing for the first time, etc. should make this song very much sought after on the part of the publishers.

Selznick wanted to have a successful song from the movie and was sold on the idea that established composer and lyricist Allie Wrubel could write one. On 24 February 1945, Dann wrote to Selznick:

> Wrubel is a Class-A composer (ASCAP), and regularly gets $2500 a song from Walt Disney, RKO and others. We are getting a song for $1500. We paid the same price to Lou Forbes [musical director and head of music department at Selznick International Pictures] and the other two for their song which was not used in "SINCE YOU WENT AWAY." In the Forbes' song, also, we did not have control of the publishing rights, which we do control in the case of Wrubel's song. When we make a deal with any publisher we will be in a position to obtain royalties payable to us with respect to the song, and also to request in advance from the publisher amounts equal to or in excess of the $1500 we will have paid for the song.

[30] The complete chorus lyrics from the song "Duel in the Sun (A Duel of Two Hearts)." Copyright © 1947 by Bourne Co. Copyright renewed. Used by permission of Bourne Co.

[31] If 500,000 copies were to sell at two cents each, their gross would amount to $10,000. It should be noted that Vanguard Film's share of "Gotta Get Me Somebody To Love," Allie Wrubel's song composed for *Duel in the Sun*, was 1¼¢ per copy sold.

177

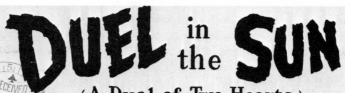

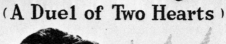

Cover of the sheet music for "Duel in the Sun (A Duel of Two Hearts)," 1947. *HRC Theatre Arts Collection.*

This was a pretty sweet deal for all three parties concerned. The song was "Gotta Get Me Somebody To Love," and Wrubel received $1,500 up front, plus a percentage of royalties.[32] Since Vanguard Films paid Wrubel from an advance it intended to receive from the publisher, the company essentially got a free song for the film and stood to make a profit on top of that. For the "risk" of advancing the "$1,500" to Vanguard, the publisher could expect to reap a fairly substantial return from this not-so-risky investment. All parties would profit from the several recordings that would be issued prior to the film, and the song would also gain exposure in the film itself: it was used six times in the film, twice with Gregory Peck singing excerpts from it, and part of it with Peck whistling.

"Gotta Get Me Somebody To Love," music and lyrics by Allie Wrubel (AS-CAP), was published by Edwin H. Morris & Company, New York, and was recorded by Bing Crosby the week of 3 May 1946. That same week, almost eight months before the picture finally opened at the Egyptian Theatre in Los Angeles, record releases were being planned by Frank Sinatra and Perry Como. The venture was rather successful for everyone involved. The statement of royalties sent by Edwin H. Morris to Vanguard Films reveals that "Gotta Get Me Somebody To Love" yielded $2,148.43 to Vanguard solely from record royalties for the quarter ending 30 June 1947. Below is the breakdown as it appears in the Selznick files:

Rate: 16⅔%

Victor Records	4,046.68
Capitol Records	1,158.81
Decca Records	4,879.83
Columbia Records	1,380.26
Miscellaneous Records	1,425.01
Mech.[33]	
Amount Re'd	12,890.59
Your Share	2,148.43

Success, however, can breed potential disaster: almost a year after the first release of the Bing Crosby recording, a 26 February 1947 "MEMO FOR THE FILE" dictated by Robert Dann reveals that "A man, representing himself to be Walter Donaldson, the composer, telephoned me today and claimed that the music of Allie Wrubel's song GOTTA GET ME SOME-BODY TO LOVE was a direct infringement of the music of Walter Don-aldson's song 'NEVADA' published by the Dorsey brothers, some two years

---

[32] Wrubel wanted a total of $2,500 and ended up getting it.

[33] This refers to "mechanical royalties"; i.e., sales of recordings for three months. This does not include other forms of income that could be derived from the various avenues of exploitation of the same song.

ago. . . ." Two days later, Ted Wick compared both songs. Wick's written reply to Dann states:

> I have played both records of NEVADA and nowhere was I able to find two consecutive bars even remotely connected with GOTTA GET ME SOMEBODY TO LOVE. It's my belief that in order to be called a direct infringement there must be two consecutive bars which are note for note including the tempo [Wick really means "rhythm"] exactly alike. In NEVADA there is a musical progression of which six notes of one bar are the same as in GOTTA GET ME SOMEBODY TO LOVE.

Donaldson may have felt that his rights were infringed upon, but in fact they were not. No lawsuit followed and the matter was dropped.

Much of this is beginning to suggest that *Duel in the Sun* was viewed by its producers as a musical, not a "spectacular adventure, with a passionate conflict and Western setting." There were no fewer than six more songs written, various purely instrumental pieces recorded, and two record albums cut,[34] not to mention several national and regional broadcasts.[35] On 1 November 1946 Vanguard entered into a contract with Frederick Herbert (the pseudonym of Herbert Stahlberg) to compose lyrics for the musical numbers "Orizaba," "Headin' Home," "On the Rio Grande," "Tempting You," and "Falling Star." All the music for these numbers was by Tiomkin, who also collaborated with Alfred Palacios on a song titled "El Bolero"; there was also a separate, purely instrumental version of "Orizaba" and "Varsouviana." In addition, there are three unpublished songs in the Selznick Collection, all titled "Duel in the Sun." One is by Tiomkin and Herbert in a Beguine tempo, another by Nigel Tangye (music and lyrics undated), and a final one by James C. Lane (music and lyrics dated 2 October 1946).

All this composing activity began to brew in late 1945 when Selznick was preoccupied with having a title song for the film. In an 8 December 1945 memo to Ted Wick, Selznick writes: "Even more important . . . is my desire to get a song called DUEL IN THE SUN which can be part of our exploitation campaign." In this same memo he mentions the idea of a prize for the best song based on the film and also his plans for exploitation through re-

[34] A two-sided twelve-inch RCA Black Label recording by Al Goodman and his orchestra and an eight-sided ten-inch RCA Red Seal recording performed by Arthur Fiedler and the Boston "Pops" Orchestra.

[35] One such national broadcast was on 27 May 1947, when Arthur Fiedler conducted "The Orizaba Dance" from *Duel in the Sun*, performed by the Boston Symphony Orchestra. There were also several readapted and unauthorized broadcasts of certain pieces from the *Duel* score, the most notable being the *Duel* music used on the Mutual Network broadcast of *The Cisco Kid*. (See a memo dated 28 May 1948.) Tiomkin was never a member of ASCAP, BMI (Broadcast Music, Inc.), or SESAC (Society of European Stage Authors and Composers), so he did not derive additional (and rather substantial) income from the public performances and broadcasts of his music.

cordings. But at times his efforts to obtain the song led to frustration, as indicated in a memo dated 24 October 1946:

> The main problem . . . is to get a song called DUEL IN THE SUN. A song that would reach the Hit Parade carrying the title of the picture would have the equivalent value of a huge expenditure of advertising. . . .[36] I have been trying to get this song for almost a year and we are no further advanced than we were at the outset.

The prize idea crops up again in a 22 July 1946 memo from Selznick to Paul MacNamara, director of publicity at Vanguard Films: "There are many approaches on exploiting a song called DUEL IN THE SUN including a prize contest tied up with ASCAP and/or with some important radio stations." Selznick thought the prize idea would be a "good publicity stunt." In a 27 November 1946 memo to MacNamara, Selznick states:

> Pearl-Lewt theme would make an absolutely wonderful popular song and dance number. . . . Get it played on a Sunday radio program that introduces new numbers. What would you think of having a contest . . . under which we [Vanguard] would offer an award of perhaps $500 plus a guarantee of publication for the best song submitted under the title of DUEL IN THE SUN the specification being that it must be in the torch field?

There was no further correspondence on the matter. Prior to this, however, there had been an in-house contest that ended 1 October 1945 in which Vanguard employees were asked to submit possible titles for the film. As a memo indicates, "None of the submissions in the recent contest for a new title for DUEL IN THE SUN were considered satisfactory for use on this picture. . . ." A prize of $100 had to be given in accordance with the conditions of the contest, but the records reveal that it was a very tough decision to reach and was practically a toss up between the Mac Johnson and John Mills title of "Flame of Spanish Bit" and Ann Harris's "Untamed." Ultimately Ann Harris won the $100. Other titles of passing interest that were submitted were "The Devil Saw Her First," "Nail Up My Spurs," "The Outlaw Heart," "Duel in the Sand," "Primitive Pearl," "Love To Burn," "Wild Mating," and "Delilah of the Prairie." There were well over 100 submissions. Perhaps it was just as well that the *Duel in the Sun* torch song contest never materialized.

[36] Today there is a new aspect to advertising and promotion: product manufacturers have been known to pay filmmakers considerable sums of money, sometimes into six figures, to have their products significantly exposed in a film and/or associated with a particular film and/or star of that film. Examples range from Jennifer Beals (*Flashdance*) with her can of Diet Pepsi to Sylvester Stallone (*Rocky III*) eating Wheaties. It is estimated that after being "plugged" in *E.T.*, Hershey's Reese's Pieces sales leaped by sixty-five percent. See *Newsweek*, 4 July 1983, p. 46.

Publicity photo for *Duel in the Sun*, 1946. The caption on the back reads "Dallas Beauty Queen and Queen of Aviation and her ladies in waiting posing with 'DUEL in the Sun' aircraft at the Dallas air show. During the day sky writers were busy writing 'DUEL in the Sun' with two airplanes simulating a dog fight. . . ." Photograph by Bill Williams. *HRC Theatre Arts Collection.*

In terms of advertising, publicity, and exploitation of the movie, there was the customary barrage of elaborate marquees, lobby displays, and so forth, but the Selznick organization also launched a major and extensive campaign blitz that was typical of Selznick's genius and commitment to a picture. There were displays in every conceivable type of store front, from florists to bus terminals to cigar shops. Even ice cream parlors beckoned to the public to "TRY OUR 'DUEL IN THE SUN'DAE'." The beauty salons announced a "DUEL HAIR-DO by Clara," and Cynthia Hayden presented the junior miss "'DUEL' hair style." From the cosmetic industry came Chen Yu's "Sun Red" nail polish and lipstick. One could even purchase a "Dual Set!," which was advertised as "An untamed red. Wear it to be wooed and won. Under moon or under sun." The fashion industry produced "sweaters and jerseys inspired by and adapted from 'DUEL IN THE SUN'." Alice Stuart, Inc. of New York manufactured a blouse "faithfully adapted from one of the exotic blouses worn by lovely Jennifer Jones in DUEL IN THE SUN." Clothes were modeled in "windows of prominent stores built around SUN fashions." And there were *Duel* tee shirts, sweatshirts, dresses, shawls, newsboy aprons, and practically any item of clothing that could either display a *Duel in the Sun* sticker or exploit the film. The Stetson hat was very popular as a giveaway to local officials. The "DUEL GIRLS" presented Stetsons to Commissioner Webb of Brooklyn, Mayor Clark of White Plains, President Burke of Queens, and Postmaster Goldman of the Bronx, to name but a few. Haberdasheries coined the slogan "RUGGED MEN OF THE WEST WEAR STETSON HATS." There were *Duel* parades and floats "manned with pretty girls" and others "with dancing girls with cowboys strumming"; stunts were carried out in the Polo Grounds before a big crowd; a twenty-five-cent paperback edition of the book (the hardbound was $2.50) was issued, calling itself "A Lusty Novel of the Southwest"; hundreds of memorabilia items like glass tumblers and stickers appeared on the market; 150 buses in New Jersey carried bumper cards in front and back announcing "Take this bus to see DUEL IN THE SUN at Lowe's Jersey City," while other buses trumpeted "Take the Bee Line Bus Direct to DUEL IN THE SUN now at Lowe's Valencia Theatre." There were also *Duel* streamers on the sides of trucks and any other vehicles that could display signs. After the movie, one could imbibe a "DUEL IN THE SUN cocktail made with white rum, apricot brandy, fresh orange and lime juice: 60¢."

Among the popular *Duel* dance contests, there was one that offered the prize of a "DUEL IN THE SUN Waltz Cup." Arthur Murray even gave *Duel in the Sun* dance lessons. Tiomkin, of course, benefited not only from the dance contests and general ballyhoo, but from extensive advertisement of the various record albums and singles from the movie, including the following from Decca Records: "Now you too can Square Dance, accompanied by THE DUEL IN THE SUN Square Dance Orchestra with calls by Lloyd Shaw on Decca Records. Have fun at home with special SING-ALONG

BOOK including EASY SQUARE DANCE INSTRUCTIONS. Ask for Decca Album No a-524."

The stars of the film put in their appearances at various public places, especially the theatres, and they were called upon for some product testimonials as well. Here are a few examples: "Gregory Peck of DUEL IN THE SUN says 'Rice shot from guns makes a *hearty breakfast*'"; "Joseph Cotten of DUEL IN THE SUN says 'Now! Medical science offers *PROOF POSITIVE!* No other leading cigarette [in reference to Raleigh] is safer to smoke!'" Herbert Marshall and Walter Huston of the *Duel* cast also appeared in the same ad at a later date. The publicity saturation for *Duel in the Sun* was complete and thorough, to say the least.

David O. Selznick's genius at promotion and exploitation benefited everyone around him, and this certainly included the composer, Dimitri Tiomkin. While the base salary for the featured players in Production No. 103 was substantial, so too were the additional incomes and the recognition derived from being associated with a Selznick film. The "small rights" Tiomkin received were hardly "small."[37] If *Duel* had attained the same artistic success as *Gone With The Wind*, perhaps Selznick might have attempted a broadway musical adaptation.[38] Tiomkin's natural flair for showmanship irresistibly inspired Selznick to plan for further exploitation of the film with a five-minute Technicolor short which would promote not only *Duel*, but also the music from the film. It was to be directed by Joseph Von Sternberg at a cost of well over $30,000. The music was to be recorded on Monday, 19 August 1946, on the Goldwyn scoring stage, with a three-day schedule as follows:

> 1 day scoring, 90 musicians for 6 hours
> 2 days shooting, 90 dummy musicians[39] for 8 hours

The essence of the two-page narrated script was: instruments tuning up; narrator introduces composer Tiomkin; Tiomkin walks toward the podium, taps twice, and conducts the orchestra in the overture-medley. As the medley is finished, Tiomkin says "main title" and the music segues to the Selznick In-

---

[37] Small rights are performance rights in nondramatic music; e.g., royalties from recordings, sheet music, radio and television broadcasts, concert performances, and the like.

[38] From the late 1950s through the early 1960s, Selznick attempted to organize and produce a stage musical version of *Gone With The Wind* entitled "Scarlett O'Hara." Some of the proposed song titles for the musical were "Fiddle-Dee-Dee," "The Land Is the Only Thing That Matters Because It's the Only Thing That Lasts," "You Should Be Kissed By Someone Who Knows How," and "I'll Think About That Tomorrow." Selznick negotiated contracts with several composers and lyricists; Tiomkin was to work with lyricist Dorothy Fields, and Leroy Anderson was to work with Ben Hecht. Selznick died in 1965, and other producers ultimately commissioned Harold Rome to write both the music and lyrics; Horton Foote wrote the book. The musical, entitled *Scarlett*, premiered at the Imperial Theatre in Tokyo on 2 January 1970. On 3 May 1972, the adaptation opened at the Theatre Royal, Drury Lane, bearing the original film title, *Gone With The Wind*.

[39] Actors replaced the actual musicians.

ternational Trademark music. Although the trailer was never completed, Selznick's heart and intentions were in the right place.

The producer recognized Tiomkin as a valuable asset to the Selznick organization, and each respected the other's talents. In 1955, when accepting the Oscar for his score of *The High and the Mighty*, Tiomkin gave his most memorable speech: "I like to thank Johannes Brahms, Johann Strauss, Richard Strauss, Richard Wagner . . . Beethoven, Rimsky-Korsakov. . . ."[40] Laughter drowned out the other names on his list. This speech, which haunted Tiomkin for the rest of his life, was made with all good intentions and was meant to be taken seriously; unfortunately, given the tension in the air and the timing of the moment, Tiomkin's acceptance speech was misunderstood. One would like to think, however, that David O. Selznick was one of the indistinguishable names mentioned among the greats.

Dimitri Tiomkin

[40] Tiomkin and Buranelli, *Please Don't Hate Me*, pp. 253–54.

The author would like to thank Dr. Raymond Daum of the HRC staff for his unfailing support and guidance in the preparation of this essay.

The directors and composers for David O. Selznick's theatrical films.
(Television and short films are not included.)

THEATRICAL FILM (year opened)	CREDITED DIRECTOR(S)	CREDITED COMPOSER(S)
Roulette (1924)	S.E.V. Taylor	(silent)
Spoilers of the West (1928)	W.S. Van Dyke	(silent)
Wyoming (1928)	W.S. Van Dyke	(silent)
Forgotten Faces (1928)	Victor Schertzinger	(silent)
Chinatown Nights (1929)	William Wellman	(part talking)
The Man I Love (1929)	William Wellman	Song: Leo Robin and Richard Whiting
The Four Feathers (1929)	Merian C. Cooper	William Frederich Peters
The Dance of Life (1929)	John Cromwell and Edward Sutherland	Songs: Richard Whiting, Leo Robin, and Sam Coslow
Street of Chance (1930)	John Cromwell	(uncredited)
Sarah and Son (1930)	Dorothy Arzner	Nathaniel Finston
Honey (1930)	Wesley Ruggles	Songs: W. Franke Harling and Sam Coslow
The Texan (1930)	John Cromwell	Songs: L. Wolfe Gilbert and Abel Baer
For the Defense (1930)	John Cromwell	(uncredited)
Manslaughter (1930)	George Abbott	(uncredited)
Laughter (1930)	Harry d'Abbadie d'Arrast	Frank Tours
The Lost Squadron (1932)	George Archainbaud	Max Steiner
Symphony of Six Million (1932)	Gregory LaCava	Max Steiner
State's Attorney (1932)	George Archainbaud	(uncredited)
Westward Passage (1932)	Robert Milton	Max Steiner
What Price Hollywood? (1932)	George Cukor	Max Steiner
Roar of the Dragon (1932)	Wesley Ruggles	(uncredited)
Age of Consent (1932)	Gregory LaCava	(uncredited)
Bird of Paradise (1932)	King Vidor	Max Steiner
A Bill of Divorcement (1932)	George Cukor	(uncredited)
The Conquerors (1932)	William Wellman	Max Steiner
Rockabye (1932)	George Cukor	(uncredited)
The Animal Kingdom (1932)	Edward H. Griffith	(uncredited)
The Half-Naked Truth (1932)	Gregory LaCava	Max Steiner
Topaze (1933)	Harry d'Abbadie d'Arrast	Max Steiner
The Great Jasper (1933)	J. Walter Ruben	(uncredited)
Our Betters (1933)	George Cukor	(uncredited)
King Kong (1933)	Ernest B. Schoedsack	Max Steiner
Christopher Strong (1933)	Dorothy Arzner	Max Steiner
Sweepings (1933)	John Cromwell	(uncredited)
The Monkey's Paw (1933)	Wesley Ruggles	(uncredited)
Dinner at Eight (1933)	George Cukor	William Axt
Night Flight (1933)	Clarence Brown	(uncredited)

Meet the Baron (1933)	Walter Lang	Songs: Jimmy McHugh and Dorothy Fields
Dancing Lady (1933)	Robert Z. Leonard	Songs: Burton Lane and Harold Adamson, Richard Rodgers and Lorenz Hart, Jimmy McHugh, Dorothy Fields and Arthur Freed
Viva Villa! (1934)	Jack Conway	Herbert Stothart
Manhattan Melodrama (1934)	W.S. Van Dyke	Song: Richard Rodgers and Lorenz Hart
David Copperfield (1935)	George Cukor	Herbert Stothart
Vanessa: Her Love Story (1935)	William K. Howard	(uncredited)
Reckless (1935)	Victor Fleming	Songs: Jerome Kern and Dorothy Fields
Anna Karenina (1935)	Clarence Brown	Herbert Stothart
A Tale of Two Cities (1935)	Jack Conway	Herbert Stothart
Little Lord Fauntleroy (1936)	John Cromwell	Max Steiner
The Garden of Allah (1936)	Richard Boleslawski	Max Steiner
A Star Is Born (1937)	William Wellman	Max Steiner
The Prisoner of Zenda (1937)	John Cromwell	Alfred Newman
Nothing Sacred (1937)	William Wellman	Oscar Levant
The Adventures of Tom Sawyer (1938)	Norman Taurog	Lou Forbes
The Young in Heart (1938)	Richard Wallace	Franz Waxman
Made For Each Other (1939)	John Cromwell	Lou Forbes
Intermezzo: A Love Story (1939)	Gregory Ratoff	Lou Forbes; Theme Song: Robert Henning and Heinz Provost
Gone With The Wind (1939)	Victor Fleming	Max Steiner
Rebecca (1940)	Alfred Hitchcock	Franz Waxman
Since You Went Away (1944)	John Cromwell	Max Steiner
I'll Be Seeing You (1944)	William Dieterle	Daniele Amfitheatrof; Song: Irving Kahal and Sammy Fain
Spellbound (1945)	Alfred Hitchcock	Miklos Rozsa
Duel in the Sun (1946)	King Vidor	Dimitri Tiomkin
The Paradine Case (1947)	Alfred Hitchcock	Franz Waxman
Portrait of Jennie (1948)	William Dieterle	Dimitri Tiomkin (based on Claude Debussy's music)
The Third Man (1949)	Carol Reed	Anton Karas
The Wild Heart (1950)	Michael Powell, Emeric Pressburger, and Rouben Mamoulian	(uncredited)
Indiscretion Of An American Wife (1954)	Vittorio De Sica	Alessandro Cicognini
A Farewell to Arms (1957)	Charles Vidor	Mario Nascimbene

Tome I. Page 279.

1. *Trich Varlach.* 2. *Xilorgano.* 3. *Grande Guittare Italienne dont les Mendians jouent montés sur des Anes.* 4. *Violons des Negres.* 5. *Violon Turc.* 6. *Trompette marine.*

The tromba marina, or marine trumpet, is a one-stringed instrument being played by the musician at the far right. An illustration from Jean Benjamin de Laborde's *Essai sur la musique*, vol. 1 (Paris: De l'imprimerie de Ph.-D. Pierres, 1780), p. 279. *HRC Collections.*

A Progress Report on the "Trumpet Tablature" at HRC

BY ROBERT B. LYNN

The Humanities Research Center of The University of Texas at Austin lists among its musical holdings a small manuscript book with the call number Pre-1700 MS 104. This source has presented serious problems for researchers who have sought to discover the key to the transcription of its music and the instrument(s) for which it was intended. In the following preliminary study I will offer a possible means of unlocking its unique notation, suggest types of instruments which may or may not have been used, and reveal a glimpse of unsophisticated music-making in early seventeenth-century Italy.

Acquired in 1971 from the firm of Richard Macnutt of Tunbridge Wells, Kent, the manuscript is written on paper, now fragile, and the closely trimmed leaves are lightly stained and loosely bound, with several now detached. Measuring approximately 22 x 10 cm., the oblong leaves are ruled with three five-line "staves," apparently drawn with a rolling staff liner, to which (on fols. 1^r-10^v) are added two more widely spaced lines, drawn by hand. On the staves and lines, two rows of numerals and other signs are written, forming what is called a tablature notation.

A description supplied by the seller refers to the opinion of the late English musicologist Thurston Dart that the manuscript was written in Italy about 1620 and that the music may be intended for two trumpets or possibly two trombe marine (in the singular called tromba marina or marine trumpet). The manuscript has been referred to as a "trumpet tablature," and the apparent contradiction in terms within this title raises several questions: What are the characteristics of tablature notation? Can these characteristics be applied to the technique of the seventeenth-century trumpet or tromba marina? If the tablature is not for one of these instruments, on what type of instrument(s) could it be played? How can the symbols of the notation be translated into pitches, and how would the symbols relate to the playing technique of an instrument? What assistance can we gain from a study of the titles and composers' names indicated in the source? Such questions are only a starting point, but until they are addressed, it will be difficult to pose, much less answer, other meaningful questions regarding the nature of this manuscript.

According to the *Harvard Dictionary of Music*, tablature is the "general name for the various early (15th-17th cent.) systems of notation . . . in which the tones are indicated by letters, figures, or other symbols instead of notes on a staff."[1] A further aspect of tablature is suggested by Friedrich Wilhelm Riedel when he points out that instrumentalists are necessarily concerned with how the fingers are applied to the fingerboard of a stringed instrument, to the holes of a woodwind instrument, or to the keys of a keyboard instrument.[2] As a result of the needs of instrumentalists, tablature notation is often a *Griffschrift*, that is, a notation which symbolizes the actual technique by which the fingers "grip" the instrument in producing different tones. For example, woodwind tablatures may show different patterns of open and blackened circles to indicate open and stopped holes; German tablatures for the organ frequently employ letters corresponding to the actual keys to be depressed; Spanish sources assign a number to each key from bottom to top of the keyboard, matching the numbers 1–7 to the keys f-e; and lute tablatures have different arrangements of numbers or letters to indicate each point in the grid of strings and frets that the performer might "stop" with the fingers of the left hand.[3] Most tablatures involve this correspondence of playing technique and notation, although there is one instance in which a tablature, in the broad sense of a letter or number notation, indicates only indirectly the specific application of the fingers to the instrument. This is found in church music of the late seventeenth and early eighteenth centuries in northern Germany where composers sometimes used organ tablature in writing for stringed instruments. Here a method of notation which began as specific to a particular instrument is later used in a more generalized way.

In dealing with a tablature supposedly for trumpet, a crucial question must be: How were the fingers employed in producing different pitches on the instrument? In fact, the fingers were not used. Until well into the eighteenth century, the trumpet consisted of a brass tube of cylindrical bore with no finger-operated devices such as valves or keys. Pitch was changed by altering the vibrations of the player's lips and by regulating the air pressure. The tones which could be produced on such a "natural" instrument were limited to the harmonics of the tube's fundamental pitch. In the lower register, only fanfare figures were possible, but if the player had mastered higher harmonics, which are progressively closer together, he could play melodies which follow the scale.

[1] Willi Apel, *Harvard Dictionary of Music*, 2d ed. (Cambridge: Belknap Press of Harvard University Press, 1969), p. 829.

[2] Friedrich Wilhelm Riedel, "Notation: C. Instrumentale Notationen. I. Grundsätzliche Bemerkungen," *Die Musik in Geschichte und Gegenwart*, ed. Friedrich Blume (Kassel: Bärenreiter, 1961), vol. 9, col. 1642.

[3] Willi Apel, *The Notation of Polyphonic Music, 900–1600*, 5th ed., rev. (Cambridge: Mediaeval Academy of America, 1953), pp. 211–81. See also Thurston Dart and John Morehen, "Tablature," *The New Grove Dictionary of Music and Musicians*, ed. Stanley Sadie (London: Macmillan, 1980), 18:506–14.

If then our "trumpet tablature" cannot represent graphically the technique of playing the trumpet, might the numbers represent the tones which the instrument could produce, perhaps starting the numbering with some particular harmonic and then proceeding from low to high? The answer to this question must await some further means of decoding the notation. Suffice it to report now that the manuscripts of trumpet music preserved from the seventeenth century use a staff notation in which lines and spaces, controlled by a clef sign, indicate specific pitches.[4] This writer has found no evidence to suggest that the trumpet might have used a tablature notation already established for some other instrument.

The suggestion that this tablature was intended for the tromba marina seems a more reasonable possibility. The instrument, which is not a member of the trumpet family, was commonly used from the fifteenth through the mid-eighteenth centuries and has a single long string which the player bows between the points where he touches (not stops) the string and the nut (that is, the top end of the string). Since the string then vibrates in segments, sounding harmonics of its fundamental pitch, these touching-points might be identified by numbers. However, as with the trumpet, the preserved examples of music for the tromba marina are written with notes on a staff.[5] Again, we must seek another means of evaluating the notation to determine if this might be a unique tromba marina tablature.

Among other stringed instruments that have used a number tablature is the violin known as the viola da braccio. An example of such a tablature, written in Dalmatia about 1625, bears considerable resemblance to the source at HRC.[6] This violin tablature uses the numerals 0–4 written on four lines (not a staff, but a representation of the four strings of the instrument, with the lowest string represented by the highest line). As in the HRC manuscript, there are no rhythmic signs, but there are vertical strokes resembling barlines, which on closer examination suggest caesuras at melodic phrase endings. On comparison, the HRC tablature notation reveals the same numerals 0–4 plus the numeral 6, the figure x, and numerous dots, short lines, and signs resembling either the full character or segments of a sharp. The numeral 5 does not occur at all. The figures are arranged in two rows on each five-line "staff" and on the two lines drawn at the bottom of most pages. At the beginning of the first page and on the final page the up-

[4] Don L. Smithers, *The Music and History of the Baroque Trumpet Before 1721* (Syracuse: Syracuse University Press, 1973), *passim*.

[5] See Cecil Adkins, "Trumpet Marine," *New Grove*, 9:226–29. The fragment of tablature associated with the instrument in an engraving in the series entitled "Grotesque Costumes" by Nicolas de Larmessin (ca. 1700) bears no resemblance to the HRC manuscript or to any of the known sources of tromba marina music. I am grateful to Professor Adkins for discussing with me the possible relationship of this tablature to the tromba marina.

[6] Dragan Plamenac, "An Unknown Violin Tablature of the Early 17th Century," *Papers of the American Musicological Society Annual Meeting* (1941), pp. 144–57.

per row is preceded by the letter *S* and the lower row by *D*. These signs may indicate that the two lines of numbers are played by two instrumentalists, in contrast to the multiple lines in the violin tablature which indicate different strings of the same instrument. The letters may stand for *Sinistra* and *Dextera*—the player on the left and the player on the right. Both lines usually move at the same pace and often employ the same numbers, which suggests two musicians playing together, often in unison. If the numbers do represent frets on a stringed instrument, then were the two lines to be played by one player, they would surely represent strings of different pitches, and the use of the same numbers would create movement in parallel intervals at whatever pitch distance might exist between the strings. However, the continuous presence of the two lines would require a continuous double-stopping technique unlikely in bowed string-playing of this period. Thus we find evidence that the tablature was written for a pair of instruments, although we are not much closer to identifying the instruments or to being able to transcribe the number notation.

Cataloguing the contents of the manuscript supplies a partial solution to this puzzle. In the following table the titles and miscellaneous inscriptions are transcribed.

Folio	Title	Inscriptions
1^r	Litania	Chirie christe Pater miserere Fili miserere Spiritus miserere Sancta Trinitas Miserere Sancta Maria Ora————[text above lines of tablature] libro————simone [?]———— [text at bottom of page]
1^v	Ruggiero	
	Ruggiero	
2^r	Ruggiero	
	Ruggiero in tripula	
2^v	Ruggiero a lorfidia	
	Sopra lo stesso Ruggiero	
3^r	Sopra l'istesso Ruggiero	
3^v	Partite pa. lo stesso contrapunto di Ruggiero	
4^r	Sopra lo stesso contrapunto di Ruggiero	
4^v	Sopra lo stesso	
5^r	Ruggiero dell Abbate	
5^v	Tuono misto Magnificat	
	Miserere del Dentice	
	Pastorale	
	Tormillo	

192

6ʳ	-unico figlio	
6ᵛ	Sopra lo stesso	
	Pastorale	
	Tormillo	seqor—Zapognell
7ʳ	Sampognelle della stessa Pastorale	
	Zampognelle	
7ᵛ	Zampognelle	
8ʳ	Bona nova	
	Ceraselle	
8ᵛ	Gagliarda	fo. 15
	Gagliarda per abballare	
	Gagliarda	
9ʳ	Gagliarda per abballare di 20⁷ Contrapunto	
	Gagliarda Franzese detta la signoria	
9ᵛ	sopra l'istessa	21
	Fedele	
10ʳ	fedele	
	fedele	
10ᵛ	fedele	23 [top of page]
	fedele	24 [bottom of page]
11ʳ	Fedele	24 [top of page]
		25 [left of 2d system]
11ᵛ	fedele	[2]6 [left of 1st system]
	Fedele	27 [left of 3d system]
12ʳ	[F]edele p 6 mollo⁸	a: Qui vitam sine termino
		Nob[is] donet in Patria.⁹
		[written upside-down, across
		bottom of page]
12ᵛ	[untitled example combining staff notation and tablature]	

This is an odd mixture of sacred and secular material. The sacred repertory includes the partially texted Litany, the Miserere by Dentice (derived from a setting of the penitential Psalm, no. 51), and the Magnificat, which is the Canticle of Mary from Luke 1:46–55. These liturgical pieces are contrasted with dances (the Gagliarda), with pieces of rustic association such as the Pastorale and Zampognelle (the name of a type of bagpipe), and with settings of

[7] The numbers 20–27 may represent part of an original numbering of the pieces in the manuscript. The smaller numbers must have been lost when the pages were trimmed. Counting backwards we find a few more than nineteen items, which suggests that certain of the earlier titles were grouped together as single works.

[8] The notation "p 6 mollo" may indicate "per hexachordum mollo," i.e., employing the "soft hexachord," f g a b♭ c d.

[9] A quotation from verse 6 of the hymn "Verbum supernum prodiens." Sometimes verses 5 and 6 are performed separately as the hymn "O Salutaris hostia." See *The Liber Usualis* (Tournai: Desclée & Co., 1950), pp. 940–42, 1854–55.

the Ruggiero and the Fedele, which were popular patterns for improvisation or variation by musicians of the early seventeenth century.

Returning to the problem of transcription, we may discover a key to the nature of the instruments called for in the settings of the Ruggiero. If we supply a bass line (one of several variants actually used), we may try out possible interpretations of the figures in the tablature lines as counterpoints to that bass.[10] Let us take as a sample the first composition on fol. 1ᵛ (see Figure 1) and try equating the tablature numbers with diatonic scale-step numbers, beginning with 1 as g (see Example 1). This procedure is arbitrary but is chosen after considerable trial and error to produce a reasonable musical solution. The moving in and out of unison, a texture called heterophony, is often associated with improvised music of an unsophisticated origin. With the rhythmic values I have supplied, the phrase lengths of the bass match well with the vertical lines of the tablature notation, which then, as in the violin tablature, mark musical caesuras. The parallel fifths between the upper voices and the bass in m. 5 would hardly have been permissible in a sophisticated vocal style. Not surprisingly, there is little documentation of the sort of informal music-making which took place away from the courts or in the large religious establishments. However, there was a type of vocal composition (called the villanella) popular in the beginning of the seventeenth century, utilized by leading composers of madrigals, which used parallel fifths in an apparent parody of what must have been a folk idiom.

My decision to place the sixth scale degree below the first scale degree creates a much smoother melodic contour. Although the numeral 0 does not fit into this scale-step scheme, the fifth scale degree does fit in both instances where the 0 occurs. As in the Italian lute or violin tablatures, 0 may indicate an open string, here possibly d¹, the lower fifth degree of the scale.

On the last page of the tablature there is a line of music written in staff notation to which are added two lines of numbers (see Figure 2). Here we would seem to have a Rosetta stone by which the tablature can be deciphered, or at least by which a tentative solution can be tested. The melody on the staff uses the soprano clef (middle-c on the lowest line) to define the lines and spaces. A possible transcription of the entire example, using the scheme employed in the first Ruggiero, and defining the new symbol 0̲ as a lower g, follows as Example 2.

Thus far the musical results are defensible. However, at the conclusion of the second Ruggiero on fol. 1ᵛ (see Figure 1), the scale-step hypothesis is threatened by the final combination of numbers: 4 in the upper line and 3 in the lower. If these final figures represent the third and fourth degrees of a diatonic scale beginning on g, the tones c and b would result—a dissonance impossible as a final sonority (Example 3). The upper fifth scale degree is an

[10] See John M. Ward, "Ruggiero," *Die Musik in Geschichte und Gegenwart*, ed. Friedrich Blume (Kassel: Bärenreiter, 1963), vol. 11, cols. 1086–88.

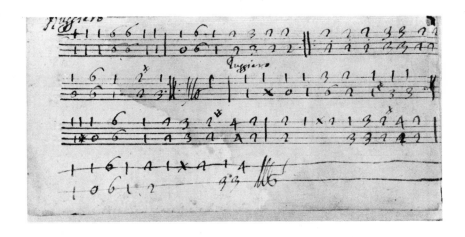

Fig. 1

Ex. 1

Fig. 2

Ex. 2

Ex. 3

unused tone which would harmonize in the final chord, but the question of why the figure 4 should represent the fifth degree is perplexing, as is the question of why the figure 5 is never used. One possibility is that a gapped pentatonic scale (that is, a five-tone scale lacking certain pitches of the major or minor scales) is the point of departure for the notational system. Such scales underlie folk music of varied traditions. If there is no c in this scale which begins on g, d would be the fourth scale degree, but in such a scale the sixth degree would be f#, not e (the tone I have assigned to the numeral 6).

In the second Ruggiero we also find the symbol x, which in certain Italian lute tablatures indicates that a tone is sustained.[11] Here that does not seem to be the case. The presence of a greater quantity of symbols within each phrase (as compared to the first Ruggiero) shows that there must be some shorter (not longer) note values. Comparing the figures of the two pieces, it is clear that the second version is a variant of the first. By comparison we can determine which are the structural pitches (to be placed against the supplemented bass notes) and which are ornamenting notes. If the symbol x is not a rhythmic alteration, it may indicate a pitch. The seventh scale degree (leading tone) is still unrepresented and fits well into the context of this example. Assuming that the notational system was first applied to a gapped pentatonic scale, a letter rather than a numeral might be appropriate for the leading tone, which would fill in one of the gaps in the basic scale.

[11] Geoffrey Chew, "Notation III, 5: Alphabetical, Numerical and Solmization Notations," *New Grove*, 13:406.

There is one composition in the HRC tablature, identified by title and composer, which may be used to check the reliability of the many suppositions in which I have indulged thus far. It is the "Miserere del Dentice" found on fol. 5ᵛ (see Figure 3), which I have been able to compare with a transcription of the version published in Dentice's *Lamentationi* (1593), hereafter referred to as *Dentice*,[12] and with an embellished version published in Francesco Severi's *Salmi Passaggiati* (1615), hereafter referred to as *Severi*.[13]

In Example 4 we see a transcription of *Dentice*, in Example 5 of *Severi*, and in Example 6 a transcription of the tablature according to our putative scheme, without the addition of rhythmic values. Comparison of *Dentice* and *Severi* with the tablature is at first glance disappointing. However, there is a way to link the tablature with the published versions if, as in the case of the Ruggieros, we consider the tablature to be a supplement to the underlying musical structure. If one version is transposed (a common practice), the tablature parts can serve as inner voices between the bass and treble of the published versions. To fit with the pitch of the tablature as determined by the "key" on its last page, *Dentice* must be transposed up a step, and *Severi*

Fig. 3

[12] Fabrizio Dentice, *Lamentationi . . . aggiuntori li responsori, antiphone, Benedictus, & Miserere* (Milan, 1593).

[13] Françesco Severi, *Salmi Passaggiati per Tutte le Voci nella maniera che si cantano in Roma sopra i Falsi Bordoni di tutti i tuoni ecclesiastici da cantarse nei Vespri della Domenica e delli giorni festive di tutto l'Anno con alcuni versi de Miserere sopra il falso bordone del Dentice composti da Francesco Severi Perugino Cantore nella Capp. di N. S. Papa Paolo V. Libro Primo* (Rome: Nicolo Borboni, 1615). See Francesco Severi, *Psalmi Passaggiati (1615)*, ed. Murray Bradshaw, *Recent Researches in the Music of the Baroque Era*, vol. 38 (Madison, WI: A-R Editions, 1981). Bradshaw's edition is the source for my Example 5.

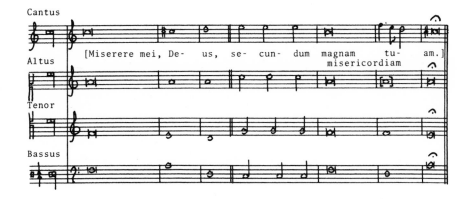

Ex. 4

Ex. 5

Ex. 6

Ex. 7

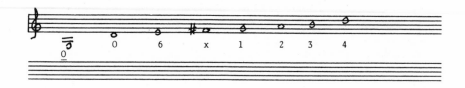

Ex. 8

Ex. 9

transposed up a perfect fifth (see Example 7, which joins the Cantus and Bassus voices of *Dentice* [transposed] with the tablature). The resulting harmony is reasonable, except for the final chord, where the figure 2 adds a dissonant seventh. Having otherwise achieved so much of a reasonable result, I suggest that the 2 may be a slip of the pen. If the figure were 3, the tone would be consonant. The seventh found in m. 2 is surprising, but perhaps possible in an ingenuous style.

In Example 8 I have summarized the equivalent symbols and pitches. From this example we can consider if there is a rational scheme, and what instruments, or types of instruments, could have played the tones we have established. I see no simple scheme here. If the solution is correct, one must suppose that it evolved in a series of stages (involving manuscripts now lost) as a means of reminding performers of music with which they were already familiar (hence the lack of rhythmic signs), and that it was worked out in isolation from the larger musical centers where logically consistent tablature systems were well known. The first stage, as I have suggested above, might have been figures 1–4 representing four basic tones within a pentatonic framework. Later, when the pentatonic basis was expanded, signs were added for the lower sixth scale degree and a special sign x for the leading-tone, with 0 and 0̲ possibly representing open strings, the lower of which could be used as a drone (or sustained pitch), and the upper of which might be played open or stopped. Most of the playing of melodies would have been done on the highest string, for which the figure 1 may have represented the open string. At least for the Ruggiero settings, the "Miserere del Dentice," and the "key" on fol. 12ᵛ, the fourth scale degree (c) is not used.

It is possible that there are differences in the interpretation of the lines for *Dextera* and *Sinistra*, as certain symbols occur only in one line or the other—specifically 2# only in the upper line and 0̲ 2˙ and 6# only in the lower line. The dots and figures resembling sharps may indicate ornaments or fingering. Other settings of the Ruggiero in this tablature raise the possibility that the player of the upper line may have had a choice of octave placement for the tones b and d (indicated by the numerals 3 and 4).

If my decoding is correct, the tablature may be a *Griffschrift*—a notation showing the actual application of the fingers to the instrument, but in an arbitrary and inconsistent manner. In the tablature, open strings and certain touching- or stopping-points may be identified by specific signs. The manuscript is written for two instruments, possibly one with two strings and another with three, which performed with a bass instrument whose part was not notated, or with various groupings of voices and instruments. The inconsistency of the transcription forces us, however, to consider whether there are other types of instruments on which the array of pitches could be realized. The spacing of the pitches does suggest instruments whose tones are the harmonics of a fundamental pitch. Two such instruments are the trumpet and the tromba marina, which brings us back to our point of departure. The four-octave harmonic series which most closely incorporates our array of pitches is shown in Example 9. This series does not, however, include the note e^1, and the f is a low f^1, not an $f\#^1$. The f might have been coaxed to sound somewhat higher than its true pitch as a harmonic, and, according to Cecil Adkins in the *New Grove*, a tone between the sixth and seventh harmonics (here the e^1 we have assigned to the figure 6) was sometimes employed by the tromba marina as an auxiliary pitch—frequently in duets, where it was always approached by scale step (which, however, is not often the case in the tablature pieces we have considered).

The repertory (hardly magnificent or martial), the array of pitches, the basic nature of tablature notation—all of these factors argue against the use of the trumpet. The tromba marina was rarely built with G as the fundamental pitch that would generate as harmonics most of the pitches in my transcriptions. However, I would not rule out absolutely the possibility of performance on the tromba marina. There is a tradition that pairs of marine trumpets were played by nuns (hence the instrument's nickname, *Nonnengeige*), although documentary evidence of such a practice seems to be lacking. I consider it more likely that the music was played on instruments descended from the medieval fidel or rebec. The rebec—obsolescent by the early seventeenth century—was a bowed instrument with three strings,

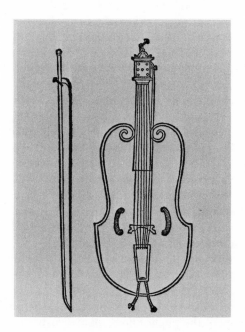

The lira da braccio. Frontispiece illustration from Edward Heron-Allen's *De Fidiculus Bibliographia*, vol. 1 (London: Griffith Farran and Co., 1890). *HRC Collections.*

tuned in fifths, producing a pungent, rather nasal tone quality.[14] Milton's reference to "the jocund rebecks sound" as an accompaniment to dancing characterizes its nature and use.[15] Another instrument for which the tablature might have been intended was the lira da braccio (a descendant of the medieval fidel).[16] This bowed instrument usually had seven strings, of which two were drones; in the sixteenth century a hybrid type was developed with only three strings. No extant written music is known for the lira da braccio, which was used in improvisation.

Thurston Dart's suggestions concerning the provenance of the manuscript seem well supported by my listing of the repertory. The inclusion of the "Miserere del Dentice," first published in 1593 but remaining popular during the first two decades of the seventeenth century, as well as the emphasis on settings of the Ruggiero and Fedele patterns, popular during these same decades, support ca. 1620 as a reasonable time of origin. This repertory and the use of the Italian language within the manuscript clearly support Italy as the country of origin. The tablature still presents many unanswered questions concerning transcription, instruments, and use of the repertory, but future study of the Fedele settings may shed more light on this unique and tantalizing musical remnant from the early seventeenth century.

[14] See David D. Boyden, *The History of Violin Playing from Its Origins to 1761 and Its Relationship to the Violin and Violin Music* (London: Oxford University Press, 1965), pp. 9 and 119.

[15] John Milton, "L'Allegro," line 94.

[16] See Boyden, p. 10, and Emanuel Winternitz, "Lira da braccio," *Die Musik in Geschichte und Gegenwart*, vol. 8, cols. 935–54.

Original terra-cotta mask of Claude Debussy by the French sculptor Louise Ochsé. 26 × 18.2 cm. This mask was commissioned by the impressario Gabriel Astruc for an international Debussy festival held in Paris in 1932. *HRC Collections*.

Debussy's Settings of Verlaine's "En sourdine"

By Marie Rolf

The way in which composers refashion their works is a fascinating process. By studying subsequent versions of a single piece, we can often catch a glimpse of an artist's unique approach to the act of composition as well as subtle developments in his style. In the uncommon case where completely different versions of the same work exist, a comparative examination can be especially revealing. Such extraordinary possibilities occur in Claude Debussy's two settings of Paul Verlaine's poem "En sourdine."[1]

The dates of completion for Debussy's two versions of this song—1882 and 1892—circumscribe a period of rapid personal and professional growth for the composer. These years witnessed his inner turmoil while living at the Medici Villa in Rome as a winner of the coveted Prix de Rome, and his concerted attempts to free himself from the rigid academic training he had received at the Conservatoire in Paris. The same years also saw Debussy making several pilgrimages to Bayreuth and becoming instantly fascinated with the music of Richard Wagner. Late in the decade, at the Paris Exhibition of 1889, Debussy first encountered the music and dances of Java, the traveling theatre from Cochin, China, the decorative arts of the Orient, and some of the earliest manifestations of the Art Nouveau movement—all under the shadow of the Eiffel Tower along the Champ de Mars. At the same time, the composer was associating with some of the leaders of the Symbolist movement in Paris, most notably the literary artists. He attended Stéphane Mallarmé's famous *mardis* at the poet's apartment on the rue de Rome, and he frequented Edmond Bailly's Librairie de l'Art Indépéndant, a meeting place for many of the Symbolists on the rue de la Chaussée d'Antin. Debussy's assimilation of these events and experiences naturally contributed to the development of his musical esthetic and to the gradual emergence of his unique musical vocabulary and style. Both elements eventually coalesced in 1894 with his celebrated masterpiece, *Prélude à l'après-midi d'un faune*, based on the Symbolist poem of that title by Mallarmé.

---

[1] "En sourdine" is one of twenty-two poems in Verlaine's collection *Fêtes galantes*, first published as a group in 1869 by Alphonse Lemerre.

The two settings of Verlaine's "En sourdine"—composed at the beginning and at the end of this pivotal period in Debussy's life—offer evidence of a solidification of the composer's musical vocabulary and esthetic. For these two versions there exist no fewer than seven manuscripts; indeed, more manuscripts survive for this work than for any other by Debussy except those for his opera *Pelléas et Mélisande* (1902) and for "Ibéria" (1910) from the orchestral *Images*. While five of the seven "En sourdine" manuscripts are of the 1882 version, which was never published during Debussy's lifetime,[2] the remaining two are of the 1892 version, which was not published until 1903. Questions regarding their precise identification, chronology, and content have gone largely unanswered during the century that has lapsed since their creation. The location and description of all seven manuscripts are shown below:

1882 version	*1892 version*
Piatigorsky Collection	Humanities Research Center
3 pp., black ink,	(The University of Texas at Austin)
signed and dated at end:	4 pp., black ink,
"Vienne 16.Sep.82"	signed and dated at end: "Mai 92"
12-staved paper,	26-staved paper,
Lard Esnault stamp	Litolff stamp
Vasnier Songbook	Robert Owen Lehman Collection
(Bibliothèque Nationale Ms.	(on deposit at the Pierpont Morgan
17716 [1–9])	Library)
cover page and 47 pp. of ms.,	3 pp., black ink,
black ink,	signed,
13 songs bound together,	30-staved paper
several dates and signatures,	
12-staved paper	
Houghton Library	
(Harvard University)	
4 pp., black ink,	
music for 2 songs (incomplete),	
text for 3 Verlaine poems,	
signed,	
18-staved paper,	
Lard Esnault stamp	

[2] The 1882 version was published posthumously in facsimile in a volume entitled *Inédits sur Claude Debussy* in 1942, and in an edition by Elkan-Vogel in 1944 with the title "Calmes dans le demi-jour / (En sourdine) / In Undertones."

The Pierpont Morgan Library
(provenance Cobb)
  4 pp., black ink,
  15-staved paper,
  Lard Esnault stamp

Jobert Collection
  8 pp., ink,
  title page, "En sourdine" (2 pp.),
  "Clair de lune" (2 pp.), and
  "Fantoches" (3 pp.),
  signed and dated "91"
  26-staved paper,
  Litolff stamp

Variants among the "En sourdine" manuscripts, even among those of the same version, reflect Debussy's lifelong habit of continually revising a piece. Some of these manuscript copies were presented to various friends or performers and were written in haste, quite possibly from the composer's memory, which would explain minor differences in articulation, texture, and dynamics. Other changes doubtlessly came to Debussy's mind after hearing performances of the piece. In a sense, Debussy never really "finished" a work, if one defines that act as a complete conclusion, beyond desire for further alteration.[3] Furthermore, maddening as it may be for us, the composer sometimes even refused to acknowledge autograph changes in his works as improvements; for instance, when asked which corrections were valid in a heavily annotated score of the *Nocturnes* that Debussy gave to the conductor Ernest Ansermet, the composer replied, "I am no longer sure. They are all possibilities. Take this score and use those which seem good to you."[4] Debussy clearly believed that one could never and should never feel a piece of music in the same way from one day to the next, an attitude that is demon-

[3] In an article in a special issue of *La Revue musicale* ("La Jeunesse de Claude Debussy" [May 1926]: 48), Maurice Emmanuel, Debussy's classmate at the Conservatoire, remarked, "With a constant care for perfecting and for scruples that one can call admirable, he would love to perfect his works and to revise them in detail. One can say that only his death could render definitively the orchestral text of *Pelléas et Mélisande*" ("Avec un souci constant de la mise au point et des scrupules que l'on peut dire admirables, il aimait à perfectionner son oeuvre et à en réviser le détail. On peut dire que, seule, sa mort a pu rendre définitif le texte orchestral de *Pelléas et Mélisande*"). All translations are my own.

[4] Quoted in Arbie Orenstein, *Ravel: Man and Musician* (New York: Columbia University Press, 1975), p. 127, footnote 24 from Ernest Ansermet, *Entretiens sur la musique* (Neuchâtel, 1963), p. 37.

strated by his differing notations of the same piece.[5] The various states of each version of "En sourdine" reflect this compositional posture. Comparison of the early with the later setting, however, reveals a definite progression in terms of Debussy's technical skill and the crystallization of his esthetic philosophy.

THE 1882 VERSION

Debussy's first setting of "En sourdine" was written expressly for Madame Eugène-Henry Vasnier, an amateur singer whom the composer accompanied on piano and whom he obviously adored. One of Debussy's part-time positions while he was a student at the Conservatoire was as accompanist for the pupils of Madame Moreau-Sainti, and it is in this context that he met the woman who was to be the inspiration for at least twenty-five of his songs. Madame Vasnier possessed a high soprano voice evidently capable of negotiating coloratura passages with ease. These special vocal qualities were fully accommodated in the melodies that Debussy wrote for her.

Before departing for Rome in January 1885, Debussy presented a small volume of "chansons" to Madame Vasnier. This "Vasnier Songbook" contained thirteen songs, written between 1881 and 1884, and was dedicated on the title page "to Madame Vasnier. These songs which have lived only through her and which would lose their charming grace were they nevermore to issue from her melodious fairy mouth. the author eternally grateful. CD."[6] The first five songs in the volume are collectively entitled *Fêtes galantes*.[7] Their order as notated by Debussy is given below, followed by my

---

[5] This philosophy has been corroborated independently by Debussy's step-daughter, Mme Gaston de Tinan, and by M. Fernand Gillet, an oboist who performed at the premiere of *La Mer* and who reported that when Debussy had suggested a faster tempo to the conductor, Camille Chevillard, at a rehearsal, Chevillard said: "mon cher ami, yesterday you gave me the tempo we have just played. Debussy looked at him with intense reflection in his eyes and said: but I *don't feel music the same way every day*" (personal letter to the author dated 17 March 1974).

[6] "à Madame Vasnier. / Ces chansons qui n'ont jamais / vécu que par elle, et qui perdront / leur grace charmeresse—si jamais plus / elles ne passent par sa bouche / de fée mélodieuse. / l'auteur éternellement / reconnaissant. / CD." This dedication was probably written just before the composer left for Rome; the fact that Debussy signed his name as "CD" indicates a time period later than the application of the other signatures on the general title page and also on the title page for *Fêtes galantes*, which are "Ach. Debussy" and "A. Debussy" respectively. Christened as Claude-Achille, Debussy was called Achille until the early 1890s, when he became known as Claude.

[7] Although Debussy eventually set eight of the twenty-two poems in Verlaine's collection of *Fêtes galantes*, he toyed with several different groupings of these songs. (Debussy's *Fêtes galantes*, series 1, published in 1903, included "En sourdine," "Fantoches," and "Clair de lune," while his series 2, published in 1904, was comprised of "Les Ingénus," "Le Faune," and "Colloque sentimental.") Later in his life Debussy contemplated writing an opera-ballet based on *Fêtes galantes*, but although some sketches exist for this project, it apparently never materialized. For details see Robert Orledge, *Debussy and the Theatre* (Cambridge: Cambridge University Press, 1982), pp. 204–216, 326.

208

brackets to indicate the order in which the poems originally appeared in Verlaine's first edition of *Fêtes galantes*.[8]

Vasnier Songbook

1° Pantomime [II]
2° En Sourdine [XXI]
3° Mandoline [XV]
4° Clair de lune [I]
5° Fantoches [XI]

It is likely that Debussy himself played from this score when accompanying Madame Vasnier, a possibility which is strengthened by the absence of details of musical notation in the manuscript—phrase markings, accidentals before pitches, dynamic markings, etc. (Naturally, Debussy would have retained such items in his head and would have had no reason to indicate them on the score.) That others eventually used this particular copy is clear from additions, in a hand other than Debussy's, that have been penciled over the original black-ink notation.

Since the setting of "En sourdine" in the Vasnier Songbook contains a number of important improvements over the Piatigorsky manuscript in linear and rhythmic motion, harmony, and register, the Vasnier setting is probably a revision of the Piatigorsky.[9] Like the Vasnier manuscript, the Piatigorsky includes only occasional dynamic and articulation markings, with a number of accidentals added in pencil over the original black-ink score. Debussy's signature is also similar in both the Piatigorsky and the Vasnier sources: "Ach. Debussy." Unlike the Vasnier Songbook, however, the Piatigorsky score is dated 16 September 1882, and the place of composition is cited by Debussy as "Vienne."[10]

The Houghton Library manuscript, though undated, probably succeeds the Vasnier Songbook since its title page lists a song which Debussy began

[8] By 1882, Verlaine's work was still relatively unknown to the general public. It is possible that Debussy met Verlaine as early as 1871, when he studied piano with the poet's mother-in-law, Madame Mauté. (For a full account of this relationship, see Edward Lockspeiser, *Debussy: His Life and Mind*, vol. 1 [Cambridge: Cambridge University Press, 1978], pp. 17–23.) In any case, Debussy must have used the first edition of Verlaine's *Fêtes galantes* as the basis for his text settings, since the second edition, which contained some alterations in the texts of the poems, did not appear until 1886, four years after Debussy had already set "En sourdine."

[9] The Piatigorsky manuscript is the principal source for the 1944 publication by Elkan-Vogel.

[10] During September 1882, Debussy was traveling with the family of Madame von Meck, the well-known patroness of Tchaikovsky, who employed Debussy during the summers of 1880, 1881, and 1882. According to Lockspeiser, however, Madame von Meck and her entourage spent September 1882 in Moscow, and they did not go to Vienna until October of that year. See Lockspeiser, *Debussy: His Life and Mind*, vol. 1, pp. 41–42.

composing in 1885, "Chevaux de bois."[11] That Debussy was immersed in the works of Verlaine and that he was experimenting with new groupings of poems from the collection of *Fêtes galantes* are clear from the title page of the Houghton manuscript, which is transcribed below:

Poèmes de Paul Verlaine

Fêtes Galantes

1° Mandoline
2° En Sourdine
3° Pantomime
4° Paysage sentimental
5° Pierrot

Romances sans Paroles

1° Paysage
2° Chevaux de bois

A. Debussy

Unfortunately, this manuscript is incomplete; following the composer's notation of "Mandoline," there exists only one page (16 measures) of "En sourdine" and no music whatsoever for any of the remaining songs.[12] Furthermore, the text underlay for the first page of "En sourdine" is lacking, indicating the likelihood that Debussy actually stopped writing at this point, though it is possible that more pages of this manuscript exist elsewhere.

Contrary to the Piatigorsky and Vasnier documents, the Houghton manuscript contains many details of articulation, tempo, and dynamics, and appears to be a clean copy written out by Debussy for someone else's use. Thus, even though it is essentially a musical duplicate of the Piatigorsky score, the Houghton manuscript seems to be one step removed from the immediate circumstances of composition, i.e., from Debussy's own performances with Madame Vasnier.

The paper used for the Houghton manuscript is similar to that of the Piatigorsky and Cobb manuscripts in size and in its distinctive stationer's mark—Lard Esnault/Paris/25 rue Feydeau—which Debussy used for many

---

[11] A manuscript of Debussy's 1885 setting of "Chevaux de bois" exists, as yet unpublished, in the Bibliothèque Nationale. This setting must have been from Verlaine's early version of the poem, published in 1877 as part of his *Romances sans paroles*. Verlaine reworked his poem in 1881, publishing it without a title in his collection *Sagesse*, and Debussy also set this later version to music, incorporating it into his *Ariettes, paysages belges et aquarelles*, published in 1888 and reissued in 1903 as the *Ariettes oubliées*. See Margaret G. Cobb, *The Poetic Debussy* (Boston: Northeastern University Press, 1982), pp. 82–83, 94–95.

[12] The last page of the Houghton manuscript contains the texts of three of Verlaine's poems: "Mandoline"; "Fantoches," which he mistakenly titled as "Pantomime"; and "Pantomime," which he mistakenly titled as "Pierrot." For a facsimile of this page, see the second illustration following p. 148 in Cobb, *The Poetic Debussy*.

210

of his subsequent works. However, the Piatigorsky contains only twelve staves per page while the Cobb has fifteen and the Houghton eighteen. Because Debussy's handwriting became smaller as he matured, in general he used manuscript paper that had smaller staves, and thus more staves per page, for his later works. This fact reinforces the argument that the Houghton manuscript postdates the Piatigorsky and perhaps even the undated Cobb as well.

Before tackling the problem of dating the Cobb manuscript, it is important to note its ties with the earlier scores. Like the Houghton manuscript, the Cobb is a clean copy, rich in performance indications. The back page of the Cobb contains Debussy's notation of the first nine measures of "Mandoline," linking this source to the Vasnier and Houghton manuscripts, both of which contain indications for other songs from Verlaine's *Fêtes galantes*. Regarding the relative date of the Cobb score, several points should be made. First, even though the Cobb manuscript has fewer staves per page than the Houghton score, Debussy's handwriting is actually smaller in the Cobb, hinting at a later time period. Second, even though the musical text of the Cobb is closer to that of the Vasnier than to that of the Piatigorsky or Houghton manuscripts, several rhythmic changes, improvements in voice leading, and a postlude of tighter construction in the Cobb all suggest a later date.

None of the above evidence can establish conclusively that the Cobb manuscript succeeds any of the other manuscripts mentioned so far, but an extramusical clue does tip the scale in favor of this supposition. A curious array of encircled numbers written over the original musical notation appears on each page of the Cobb score. The logic of their placement becomes apparent only when the folios are opened up and two leaves are viewed at once. The page of "Mandoline" and page 1 of "En sourdine" can thus be read together, as can pages 2 and 3 of "En sourdine." The numbers are placed in a circular arrangement as shown below:

Cobb Manuscript

Pages 4 and 1   Pages 2 and 3

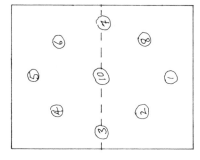

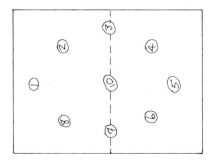

To my knowledge, no other manuscript in Debussy's entire oeuvre contains analogous annotations. What can they mean? Perhaps some scholar in the future will be able to decipher them more precisely than I, but my best guess is that they are in some way related to Debussy's occult activities at the bookshop of Edmond Bailly, the Librairie de l'Art Indépendant, which the composer frequented during the early 1890s.

Bailly opened his shop in 1890 and published a number of literary and musical works by authors such as Pierre Louÿs, Stéphane Mallarmé, Henri de Régnier, Villiers de l'Isle-Adam, André Gide, and Oscar Wilde, and by composers such as Chausson and Debussy. The latter's *Cinq Poèmes de Charles Baudelaire* and his *La Damoiselle élue* appeared in 1890 and 1893 respectively. The manuscript of *La Damoiselle élue*, now in the Robert Owen Lehman Collection in the Pierpont Morgan Library, carries the following dedication: "This manuscript is offered to Bailly in remembrance of much between 5:00 and 7:00 which was and always will be to me *a precious esthetic* [my emphasis], and also for your sincere friendship / Claude Debussy./ May 93" ("Ce manuscrit est offert à Bailly / en souvenir de beaucoup de 5ʰ à 7ʰ / qui me furent et me seront toujours / de précieuse esthétique, et aussi pour / la sincère amitié / Claude Debussy. / mai. 93"). As one of the principal meeting places for the Symbolist writers, painters, and musicians, Bailly's bookshop offered a number of esoteric, yet lavish, publications geared to their elitist circle. Bailly himself was not only a publisher, poet, and musician, but he also dabbled in the occult. He and his wife sold "portable turning tables" at the bookshop, and their black cat Aziza was a medium for calling up the spirit of Bakoun, who often "advised" clients on purchases of books available at the shop.[13]

In addition, several artists associated with the cultlike Rosicrucian movement, including Erik Satie, Henri de Régnier, and Catulle Mendès, were often seen at the Librairie de l'Art Indépendant. Debussy interacted with all three men, though not in any especially mystical context. The astrologer Ely Star, whose association with matters of the occult is documented, frequented the shop as well, although his direct influence on Debussy is virtually unrecorded.[14] We do know, however, that Villiers de l'Isle-Adam, Catulle Mendès, Odilon Redon, and Debussy—all regulars *chez* Bailly—revered the teachings of Eliphas Lévi as they were propounded in his influ-

---

[13] See André Lebey, *Jean de Tinan: Souvenirs et correspondances* (Paris: H. Floury, 1922), pp. 5–8 for a description of Bailly's bookshop and the "spiritual sessions" held there. I am grateful to Ross Wood for pointing out this source. See also Henri de Régnier's account of Debussy's activities at the Librairie de l'Art Indépendant in his "Souvenirs sur Debussy," *La Revue musicale* (May 1926): 89–91.

[14] Jean Pierrot, *The Decadent Imagination: 1880–1900*, trans. Derek Coltman (Chicago and London: University of Chicago Press, 1981), p. 117.

Paul Verlaine in the Café François I, n.d. Photograph by "Dornac" as it appears in "Album de photographies dans l'intimité de personnages illustrés, 1845–1890." Gernsheim Collection, *HRC Photography Collection.* Below the photograph, a handwritten passage in French by the unknown compiler of the photo album describes Verlaine: "With Ronsard, one of the two greatest inventors of rhythm in the French language. With Baudelaire, one of the two living poets whose verses the young recite by heart. Knew days without bread and nights without lodging. Today, goes from disreputable hotel to hospital, from brothel to confessional, without deportment and without dignity, but [at one time] translated into poetry, with his delicate touch, the aristocratic dream of our eighteenth century better than the Watteaus and the Fragonards. Imperishable poet. (November 1891)."

ential book, *Dogme et rituel de la haute magie*.[15] Debussy's flirtation with the occult and the supernatural can be established most concretely in his relationship with Jules Bois, a writer whose work was published by Bailly and for whose *Les Noces de Sathan* Debussy himself was to provide incidental music. At the last minute, the composer evidently withdrew from this collaboration, but his brush with these secretive, ritualistic, mystical elements was real enough.[16]

Debussy's vulnerability to these forces is suggested in his unusual tempo indication in the Cobb manuscript, which is completely unlike that of any of the other manuscripts: "Lent—dans une sonorité très voilée" ("Slow—in a very veiled [or muffled, or obscured] quality of sound").[17] The circular set of numerals may have had some special, secret meaning known only to those members of the elite milieu associated with Bailly's bookshop. The figures on pages 2 and 3 of the Cobb score are much larger than those on pages 1 and 4, and they are written in pencil as opposed to the black ink of pages 1 and 4. The handwriting on pages 1 and 4 could be Debussy's, although the hand on pages 2 and 3 is absolutely not his. Perhaps he was discussing a "magic circle" with one of his confrères, looking at the various possible positions of the numbers within the circle, and hence the two variations. Indeed, the numbers could be seen as an attempt to illustrate a mod 10 system, since the sums of each two-digit set, when the circular configurations are viewed back to back, are 10 in every case, except for the pair of 1's (e.g., $2 + 8$, $3 + 7$, $4 + 6$, etc., with 10 in the center). Pairs of sums and differences, among other symmetrical and proportional phenomena, had been discussed at length by Charles Henry, the well-known author of *Le Cercle chromatique* in 1888.[18] It is also possible that the numbers were being employed to illustrate some of Lévi's concepts. In his *Dogme et rituel de la haute magie*, Lévi mentions a "quadrature of the circle" in which four equal

[15] This work, published in 1855, was read by Villiers in 1866 and apparently formed the basis for the occult content in Villiers's play *Axel*, published in 1872. Part 3 of the play is entitled "Le Monde occulte," and other parts of the work employ symbols and music associated with the Rosicrucians. Obviously fascinated with *Axel*, Debussy set one of its scenes, but unfortunately his manuscript is now lost. For further details, see Orledge, *Debussy and the Theatre*, p. 17.

[16] For a more complete discussion of Debussy and the occult, see Lockspeiser, *Debussy: His Life and Mind*, vol. 2, pp. 272–77.

[17] A similar instruction to play "dans une sonorité douce et voilée jusqu'à la fin et toujours très calme" ("with a sweet and veiled quality of sound to the end and always very calm") appears thirty measures before the end of *Pelléas et Mélisande*, a score with which Debussy was intensely occupied from 1893 to 1895 and which he subsequently refined.

[18] Although there is no documentation of Debussy ever meeting Charles Henry, the latter's ideas had an undeniable effect on the Symbolists. For a general explanation of Henry's writings, see José A. Argüelles, *Charles Henry and the Formation of a Psychophysical Aesthetic* (Chicago: University of Chicago Press, 1972), and for a more specific discussion of Henry's influence *vis-à-vis* Debussy and the Symbolists, see Roy Howat, *Debussy in Proportion* (Cambridge: Cambridge University Press, 1983), pp. 164–68.

angles move in a circle about a central point.[19] His wheels of Pythagoras and Ezekiel contain eight equidistant points around the perimeter of a circle,[20] just as in the configurations in Debussy's manuscript. Lévi also explains the concept of perpetual motion with a circle that is read "forwards and backwards,"[21] if you will, which could elucidate the numerical permutations found on Debussy's score. In any case, the Cobb manuscript of "En sourdine" may have been copied out by Debussy for one of his acquaintances at the bookshop—possibly Satie or even Bailly himself. This hypothesis is not inconceivable, especially since there was a piano on the premises and Debussy is known to have played it.[22] If the above speculations are accurate, they would point to a date of around 1890 for this score, which is clearly later than the dates of the other manuscripts mentioned thus far.

The Jobert manuscript (provenance Fromont) is a fair copy, a clean score given to the publisher for the purpose of engraving.[23] It is both signed, "Cl. Debussy," and dated, "91." Collectively entitled *Fêtes galantes*, this manuscript begins with "En sourdine" and continues with settings of "Clair de lune" and "Fantoches." Even though it is dated twelve years before publication, this score would appear to be the fair copy for Debussy's *Fêtes galantes*, series 1, published in 1903 by the firm of Fromont,[24] which utilized revised settings of all three songs. However, the Jobert manuscript contains the 1882 versions of both "En sourdine" and "Fantoches," along with a variant of the 1891 version of "Clair de lune" (in effect, a key piece of evidence illustrating the gradual genesis of *Fêtes galantes*, series 1, as it emerged from earlier settings all begun in the 1880s). Furthermore, this early version of "En sourdine" is now transposed down a whole tone to the key of D major. Since the song was no longer intended solely for the voice of Madame Vasnier, Debussy was attempting to bring the tessitura within more reasonable vocal limits. Perhaps he realized that the range, an octave and a tritone, was still extremely wide; perhaps he felt dissatisfied with his treatment of the text. In any event, Debussy eventually scrapped this version altogether and composed the setting of "En sourdine" that we know today.

Before discussing the second version of "En sourdine," let us consider some of the more dramatic changes—alterations in pitch, harmony, register,

---

[19] Eliphas Lévi [Alphonse Louis Constant], *Transcendental Magic*, trans. A.E. Waite (York Beach, Maine: Samuel Weiser, 1981), p. 37ff.

[20] Ibid., pp. 160–61.

[21] Ibid., p. 56ff.

[22] Victor-Émile Michelet, *Les Compagnons de la hiérophanie* (Paris: Dorbon-Aîné, 1937), p. 74. A full chapter in Michelet's book is devoted specifically to Bailly's bookshop; see pp. 65–78.

[23] The Jobert manuscript is reproduced in facsimile in *Inédits sur Claude Debussy*.

[24] Debussy's early works appearing under the imprint of Fromont were in fact published by Georges Hartmann, with whom Fromont was associated. Hartmann, whom Debussy had met in 1890, was a benevolent patron of the composer, providing him with an annual salary from 1894 until Hartmann's death in 1900.

linear and rhythmic motion, and tempo—made among the various manuscripts for the first version of the song. If the presently proposed chronology of the sources for the early "En sourdine" is accepted, the tempo markings become progressively slower, as indicated below:

Piatigorsky	Vasnier	Houghton	Cobb	Jobert
(no tempo indication)	*Andante*	*Rêveusement*	*Lent-dans une sonorité très voilée*	*Très Lent*

While the Jobert score maintains the slowest pulse, Debussy has taken some pains to improve its surface rhythmic motion by adding the constant eighth notes in measure 10, which appeared in every score postdating the original Piatigorsky (see Figure 1). The Cobb manuscript already reflected the composer's efforts to continue the surface rhythm in measure 5, where the B was restruck on the second beat (this was employed earlier in measure 3 in both the Houghton and Cobb manuscripts and in the postlude of the Piatigorsky score. Linear motion in the Jobert score is refined and enhanced in measures 6, 7, and 8 by the moving bass line.

The concept of surface rhythmic motion in the accompaniment is closely linked with octave doublings and register in the next excerpt (see Figure 2). No two manuscripts are alike in these details in measure 13, and the Jobert score continues to differ in register through measure 16. By doubling the voice at the unison in the right hand of the piano in measure 13 of the Jobert,

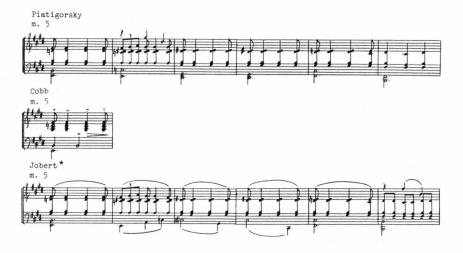

*N.b. that for purposes of easy comparison, the Jobert score, originally notated in the key of D major, will be transposed to E major in all of the following musical excerpts.

Fig. 1

Debussy accentuates the high leap to the a#² on the word "extasiés"; he then allows the piano, along with the voice, to fall gradually in its tessitura to the end of the phrase "des pins et des arbousiers." In this way Debussy further sets up a descending line in the bass, beginning in measure 15 and continuing in measure 16, that flows quite logically into the bass in measure 17. An octave-by-octave transfer of register in measure 18—a technique that becomes a trademark of Debussy's mature style, especially in transitional passages in his works—appears in all subsequent copies of this version of the song (see Figure 2).

The composer's concern for harmonic clarity is illustrated in Figure 2 as well. The sonority in the piano in measures 15 and 16 functions as a D#⁷ chord, eventually moving to the B chord in measure 18. In the earlier

Fig. 2

Piatigorsky and Vasnier scores, Debussy notated this chord enharmonically as an $E\flat^7$, simply to avoid the awkward notation of an fx and to facilitate reading; the function of this chord is made explicit, however, in its notation as $D\sharp^7$ in the three later scores. Finally, the implied $F\sharp^7$ sonority on beat three of measure 17 is stated only in the Jobert manuscript, with the thirteenth added to accommodate a smooth soprano line.

Changes in octave register and in harmony appear again in measures 37 and 41–42 (see Figure 3). The right hand in measure 37 carries an 8– – – sign in all scores after the Piatigorsky, and since there is no musical reason for the pianist to jump the octave for this single measure (this passage occurs in measure 35 as well), the 8– – – should be retained. The harmonic change

Fig. 3

on beat two of measure 41 is relatively inconsequential, although it should be noted that Debussy consistently preferred the lusher sound of the added seventh in sources written after the Piatigorsky. Similarly, he chose the stronger resolution to the A major chord in measure 42 in all scores (emphasized with an octave in the left hand in the Jobert) over the deceptive resolution notated in the Vasnier.

Perhaps the most interesting alterations revealed in Figure 3 involve the rhythm of the text setting in the voice. A slight lift occurs after the words "quand" and "solennel," and Debussy initially notated rests at those points to enhance that natural inflection. He subsequently realized that a good singer would articulate such inflections anyway and that his rests only broke up the line, and so removed them. In measure 40 in the Jobert score, he modified the rhythm to a triplet in the process of adding an extra pitch for a word, "noirs," from Verlaine's original poem which he had inadvertently omitted in all his earlier scores (see Figure 3).

Pitch changes made to accommodate new text are clear-cut issues, but other variants in pitch are more subtle and often depend on the composer's regularity in notating accidentals. Unfortunately, Debussy was never consistent in this aspect of composition, and as a result, a number of errors in pitch have been perpetuated in many of his scores. Measures 45 and 46 are a case in point (see Figure 4). The Piatigorsky manuscript originally contained no accidentals for these measures in the piano part, but the natural signs in measure 46 were later added in pencil. If d♯'s are assumed for the entire bar, an augmented chord results—a sonority which Debussy would exploit with marvelous effect in his later works but which is out of context in this setting and especially at this late juncture of the song. In fact, all subsequent scores of this version of "En sourdine" include the accidentals as shown in Figure 4, creating an exact parallel to measures 22 and 23.[25] The pitch discrepancy in the outer voices on beat three of measure 46 in the Cobb was probably due to a momentary slip of Debussy's pen; he surely was planning a chromatically ascending line on the second and third beats of this bar.

The postludes of all the sources are given in Figure 5. Two important conclusions can be drawn from their comparison. First, in polishing the final measures, Debussy eventually decided to truncate his material, a procedure which he followed for nearly all of his future works. Second, in reworking the harmony, Debussy chose to accentuate by prolongation the dissonant, colorful chords (measures 52–53 in the Vasnier and the Cobb, measures 50–51 in the Jobert) and to understate their final resolution. These subtle refinements occur on an even larger scale in the second version of "En sourdine."

[25] The Piatigorsky lacks a sharp on e¹ on beat two of measure 22.

Fig. 4

Fig. 5

By the time Debussy was resetting "En sourdine," his relationship with Madame Vasnier had dissolved, and he was involved romantically with Catherine Stevens, daughter of the Belgian painter Alfred Stevens. The composer proposed to her in 1895, but she refused him.[26] Both extant manuscripts for the second version of "En sourdine" were inscribed to her, although the first edition of the song, which appeared eleven years later, was dedicated to Madame Robert Godet, the wife of Debussy's lifelong Swiss friend.

The manuscript now in the Humanities Research Center was originally presented "to Miss Catherine Stevens in homage and in order to mark a little of the joy I have in being your affectionately devoted / CADebussy."[27] The date of "Mai 92" is entered just after the final bars of music, and the twenty-six-staved manuscript paper used for this score is identical to that of the Jobert score of the early version of "En sourdine," dated 1891.[28] The Lehman manuscript (provenance Jobert), though undated, evidently succeeds the HRC manuscript, for it is a fair copy used by the engraver. Thirty-staved paper is used, and a formal dedication "à Mademoiselle Stevens" appears on the title page. Both the HRC and Lehman manuscripts are detailed, clean copies, suggesting that other sketches or drafts preceded them. Their musical texts are virtually identical, though they differ in some essential ways from the published edition of the song. Since eleven years elapsed between the composition of this second version of "En sourdine" in 1892 and its publication in 1903, such discrepancies are to be expected.

One type of change involves a refining of the text setting. By altering the rhythm on the words "silence profond" in measure 9 (see Figure 6a), Debussy was able to reiterate in augmentation the rhythmic pattern heard in the accompaniment on beats two to three of that bar: ♫ ♪. In measure 21, he followed more closely the natural duration of the words "Et de ton" by changing the value of "Et" to an eighth note. This in turn facilitated his elision of text on the words "sur ton sein" across the barline (see Figure 6b). This passage continues with the words "Et de ton coeur endormi / Chasse à jamais tout dessein," on which the melodic line is modified (see Figure 7).

---

[26] Debussy's lack of financial stability may have been a large factor in her refusal. For further details on their relationship, see Marcel Dietschy, *La Passion de Claude Debussy* (Neuchâtel: Éditions de la Baconnière, 1962), pp. 118–20.

[27] "à Mademoiselle Catherine Stevens / en Hommage / et pour marquer un peu de ma joie / d'être ton affectueusement dévoué / CADebussy." This inscription bears a marked resemblance to the dedication of the short score of the *Nocturnes*, now in the Library of Congress, in which Debussy wrote to his then wife, "This manuscript belongs to my little Lilly-Lilo, all rights reserved, it also shows the profound and passionate joy that I have in being her husband / Claude Debussy" ("Ce manuscrit appartient à ma petite Lilly-Lilo, / tous droits réservés, il marque aussi la joie / profonde et passionnée que j'ai d'être / son mari / Claude Debussy").

[28] Of German origin, the paper bears the mark of Litolff/Braunschweig.

1892 manuscripts
m. 9

len - ce pro - fond

1903 edition
m. 9

len-ce pro - fond

Fig. 6a

1892 manuscripts
m. 20

bras sur ton sein, Et de ton

1903 edition
m. 20

bras sur ton sein, Et de ton

Fig. 6b

1892 manuscripts
m. 22

coeur en- dor - mi_{chasse} à ja-mais_{tout} des-sein.

1903 edition
m. 22

coeur en- dor - mi_{chasse} à ja-mais_{tout} des-sein.

Fig. 7

Catherine Stevens, to whom Debussy dedicated the HRC manuscript of "En sourdine.

The tessitura in the manuscripts soars even higher than in the earlier line on the word "extasiés"; by omitting the high f♯^{2} on the word "endormi" and by saving it for the last phrase of text—"Voix de notre désespoir"—in the published version, Debussy underscores the textual climax of the poem.

The greatest melodic divergence between the sources is found in measures 26–31 (see Figure 8). Once again, the motion to a higher register is delayed, placing greater emphasis on the end of the phrase. By remaining constant on the low d♮^{1} for the words "Laissons nous persuader," Debussy intensifies the feeling of intimacy in this passage.

One of the magical moments in the published version of the song occurs in the piano interlude before the entry of the voice for the final stanza of the poem (see Figure 9). Debussy skillfully continues the chromatic, triplet arabesque in the left hand while he introduces the syncopated g♯^{2} in the right, which in turn prepares the arrival in measure 33 of the nightingale motive that had opened the song. The subtle intermingling of these three elements was perfected only in the published version of the piece. In this version the sensation of a pulsating g♯ in measure 31 is implied without literally repeating the pattern of measure 32, and the deceptively resolving seventh chords in measure 32 are heard without being duplicated exactly in measure 33. The change to a lower register in the left hand in measure 31 articulates the end of this verse of the poem, and the subsequent move to treble clef in measure 32 and then its gradual shift to bass clef in the next bar parallel the falling arabesque figure heard in the right hand in measure 33.

Measure 33 begins the last stanza of the poem, in which the first phrase, "Et quand, solennel, le soir / Des chênes noirs tombera," is merely preliminary to the climax, "Voix de notre désespoir, / Le rossignol chantera." As a result, Debussy maintains a constant eighth-note motion in the voice so as not to detract from the all-important following phrase (see Figure 10). The progressively ascending melodic gesture of the published version serves this anticipatory function more precisely than the meandering line of the manuscript sources.

Fig. 8

1892 manuscripts
m. 31

1903 edition
m. 31

Fig. 9

1892 manuscripts
m. 33

Et quand, so-len-nel, le soir des chê-nes noirs tom- be- ra,

1903 edition
m. 33

Et quand, so- len- nel, le soir des chê-nes noirs tom- be- ra,

Fig. 10

Lehman manuscript
m. 35

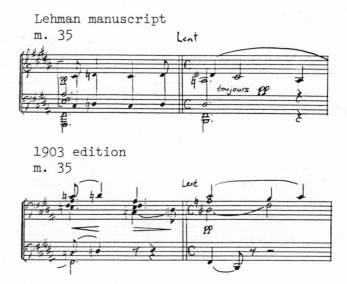

1903 edition
m. 35

Fig. 11

1892 manuscripts
m. 39

1903 edition
m. 39

Fig. 12

The piano accompaniment prepares for the crucial words "Voix de notre désespoir" as well by its hint of a whole-tone scalar basis in measure 35 and its cessation of rhythmic motion on the downbeat of measure 36, which changes both tempo and meter signature. This halt on beat one is more abrupt in the published version, where the top voice of the piano moves immediately to $c\sharp^1$ instead of delaying its resolution from $d\sharp^1$ (see Figure 11). In addition, the slightly thinner texture of the published version allows for maximum clarity in the text declamation and helps to balance the understated dynamics of the final phrase.

An atmosphere of *mystère* is preserved throughout the postlude as the nightingale reiterates its song in the piano part. As in the closing measures of the sources for the first version of "En sourdine," Debussy increases the number of dissonant elements in his revision without detracting from the passage's basic tonality (see Figure 12). Instead of employing the predictable B tonic pedals in the last five bars of the song, as he did in the manuscript sources for this version, Debussy surprises the listener with a B♯ in measure 39 that moves to a C♯ (II), an F♯ (V), and finally, at the last moment, a B (I). Over this B, however, he continues the dissonant sixth of $g\sharp^1$ as opposed to the earlier resolution to the chord tone, $d\sharp^1$. Such a deliberate and artful clouding of tonality distinguishes the second version of "En sourdine" from the first.

COMPARISON OF TEXT SETTINGS

Debussy apparently was attracted to the poetry of Paul Verlaine even before the latter became well known in Parisian circles. Eventually, his poetry would be set by a number of French composers, including Fauré, but Debussy's early settings of 1882 were quite progressive for their time. His later setting of "En sourdine," however, reflects not only a growing musical sophistication but also a deeper understanding of the Symbolist esthetic as it is portrayed in Verlaine's poem. The composer's perception of Symbolist ideals, fostered by his literary confrères, had a direct effect on his approach to text setting and is clearly demonstrated in the 1892 version of "En sourdine." Indeed, no composer of his time was more absorbed with Symbolist philosophy or more devoted to the application of these ideals to musical creations.

The essential purpose of the Symbolist artists was to suggest rather than to describe, and they often relied on a symbol or image to convey this suggestion. Poets like Verlaine and Mallarmé employed words for their coloristic qualities as well as for their provocative, inherent multiplicity of meanings. Elements of the Unconscious—mysticism, dreams, hallucinogenic or other uncontrolled experiences—played a major role in much of Symbolist art, which attempted to communicate the inexpressible or the intangible. Debussy clearly believed that the Symbolist esthetic was most naturally revealed in music, for he said "music begins where words are powerless. . . .

227

[It] is made for the inexpressible. What I would wish is that it should seem to emerge from the shadows and retire again from time to time, and that its role should always be a discreet one."[29]

Before examining Debussy's attempts to realize the above ideals in his setting of "En sourdine," we would do well to review Verlaine's poem:

En sourdine
Muted

Calmes dans le demi-jour
   Calm in the half-light
Que les branches hautes font,
   Made by the lofty branches,
Pénétrons bien notre amour
   Let us permeate our love
De ce silence profond.
   With this deep silence.

Fondons nos âmes, nos coeurs
   Let us mingle our souls, our hearts
Et nos sens extasiés,
   And our entranced senses,
Parmi les vagues langueurs
   Among the vague murmurings
Des pins et des arbousiers.
   Of the pines and arbutus trees.

Ferme tes yeux à demi,
   Half close your eyes,
Croise tes bras sur ton sein,
   Fold your arms across your breast,
Et de ton coeur endormi
   And from your sleeping heart
Chasse à jamais tout dessein.
   Banish all thought forever.

Laissons nous persuader
   Let us be wooed
Au souffle berceur et doux
   By the lulling and gentle breeze

---

[29] "La musique commence là où la parole est impuissante. . . . [Elle] est faite pour l'inexprimable; je voudrais qu'elle eût l'air de sortir de l'ombre et que, par instants, elle y rentrât; que toujours elle fût discrète personne." Quoted from Maurice Emmanuel, *Pelléas et Mélisande de Debussy. Étude historique et critique. Analyse musicale* (Paris: Paul Mellottée, 1926), p. 35.

Qui vient à tes pieds rider
    That wrinkles at your feet
Les ondes de gazon roux.
    The waves of russet grass.

Et quand, solennel, le soir
    And when, solemnly, evening
Des chênes noirs tombera,
    Descends from the dark oaks,
Voix de notre désespoir,
    Voice of our despair,
Le rossignol chantera.
    The nightingale will sing.

Paul Verlaine à l'hopital, ca. 1890. Lithograph by Fredillo after a painting by F. A. Cazals in the Museum of Luxembourg. Image 12.4 × 8.4 cm. *HRC Iconography Collection.*

Suggestive images permeate the text. The "half-light" and "deep silence" provide an ethereal atmosphere—"muted"—in which "souls," "hearts," and "entranced senses" mingle. We are encouraged to allow ourselves to sink into nothingness, permanently banishing all thoughts and feelings. Stanzas of vague reverie are alternated with stanzas of subtle motion; the restful state of verses 1, 3, and 5 contrasts with the faint rustlings of nature—the trees and the grass—in verses 2 and 4. These pastoral images are juxtaposed rather abruptly with the last lines of the poem, "Voix de notre désespoir, / Le rossignol chantera." This crucial phrase is filled with irony and ambiguity. Instead of its usual association with an expectant, hopeful lover, the nightingale's song here symbolizes the despair of the two persons. The calm, muted silence of evening has been shattered by the voice of distress.

Debussy's sensitivity to the equivocal character and the implied, yet unstated, elements of Verlaine's text reveals itself far more profoundly in his later version of "En sourdine." The ambiguous nature of the poem is mirrored in Debussy's consistent avoidance of the tonic key in his 1892 setting, as illustrated below:

1882 version: E tonic

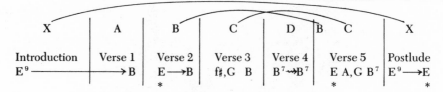

1892 version: B tonic

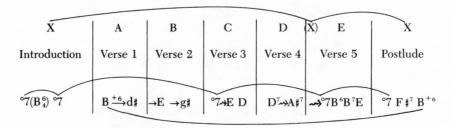

Although the beginning of both versions already clouds the tonal center, the 1892 setting starts farther away than the 1882 setting (°7 of the dominant as opposed to a tonic ninth chord). Moreover, it continues to stray farther afield throughout the remainder of the song; each verse of the 1892 version cadences on a different harmony, while verses 1–5 of the 1882 version cadence consistently on B, the dominant of E. Instead of the more conventional key relationships by fifths, as in the 1882 setting, the 1892 version explores third relationships, to d♯ (iii) and g♯ (vi), on either side of the tonic. While the early setting arrives solidly in its tonic of E three times, as indicated by the asterisks in the chart above, the later version of "En sourdine" rarely even touches on its tonic of B, and Debussy always obscures it—even in the final chord of the piece—by placing it in an inversion or by adding a sixth to it. Debussy's technique of delaying chordal resolutions, as we saw in the postludes of both versions of "En sourdine" (see Figures 5 and 12 again), has now been applied to an entire song. By consistently avoiding and clouding the sense of a tonic key in the 1892 setting, Debussy is mirroring musically the intangible and ambiguous nature of Verlaine's poem. Tonality is implied but never stated; it is suggested but never described.

The essence of Verlaine's poem is portrayed far better in Debussy's 1892 setting of the last critical phrase, "Voix de notre désespoir, / Le rossignol chantera." The composer saves the highest note of the song for the word "Voix" and he prepares it with a low tessitura on the phrase "Et quand, solennel, le soir / Des chênes noirs tombera" and a cessation of rhythmic motion in the accompaniment just before the final phrase (see Figures 10 and 11 again). The early version, on the other hand, retained the same melodic material for the phrase "Voix de notre désespoir, / Le rossignol chantera" that Debussy used on the words in the third verse, "Ferme tes yeux à demi, / Croise tes bras sur ton sein." This repetition not only detracts from the singularity of the final line, but it also necessitates reiteration of the words "Voix de notre désespoir, / Le rossignol chantera" in order to balance musically the second phrase from the third verse, "Et de ton coeur endormi / Chasse à jamais tout dessein." By foregoing such textual license in his later setting of "En sourdine," Debussy shows his sensitivity to Verlaine's use of irony and understatement at the end of his poem.

By relegating the final phrase to a single, unique statement in the 1892 version, Debussy not only gives it more impact, he also makes the entire song more compact. This truncation, combined with a slight compression of material before the entry of the last verse, results in a 43-measure song instead of a 54-measure piece (using the Piatigorsky manuscript, the earliest source, as a basis for the length of the first version). Debussy's habit of tightening his material in his revisions, shown already in his reworking of the postlude for the 1882 version (see Figure 5 again), is here seen on a larger scale.

The concept of subtle understatement—so much a part of the Symbolist esthetic—is exercised in the later setting in Debussy's use of a consistently low tessitura for the voice and in his frequent employment of a single pitch to deliver entire lines of text, such as on the words "Calmes dans le demi-jour" or "Laissons nous persuader." No longer do we find such a dramatic leap for the word "extasiés," for example, as in the early version. Nor do we discover as many interior passages that are treated as musical sequences; rather, the later version utilizes a technique of continual spinning out or subtle variation of the melodic line, a device that becomes a permanent component of Debussy's mature compositional style. At last, Debussy is considering the Symbolist text first and allowing his melodic line to be shaped by it rather than fitting the words to a preconceived tune.

Simultaneous with his developing sensitivity to the text, Debussy's own unique approach to melodic writing is emerging. First of all, his freedom from the exigencies surrounding the composition of the early setting, i.e., Madame Vasnier and her exceptional vocal qualities, has allowed the composer to experiment with a lower, darker melody that is more responsive to the ethereal, suggestive text. The vocal range of the 1892 setting is between

m. 1

Fig. 13

1882 version
m. 5

| Que les branches hautes | font, | | Pénétrons bien notre a- | mour | de | ce silence profond. |

1892 version
m. 5

| | Que les | branches hautes font, Pénétrons | bien notre a- | mour De ce si- | lence profond. | |

Fig. 14

b and e^2, while the range of the 1882 version is from e^1 to $a\sharp^2$. Secondly, the straightforward harmonic underpinning of the first version supports a correspondingly straightforward melody comprised largely of triadic outlines and stepwise motion; the more elusive harmonic plan of the later version, on the other hand, can accommodate a more unconventional melody. A three-note set of a whole step followed by a minor third permeates this setting; it suggests a pentatonic scalar basis. In measure 35, the whole-tone scale of e-f$\sharp$-g$\sharp$-a$\sharp$ (completed with c and d in the piano) helps to cloud the sense of tonality altogether. Finally, the triplet arabesque that is so characteristic of Debussy's mature melodic designs emerges in the 1892 setting as an integral element of not only the vocal part but also the piano accompaniment, whose interaction with the voice is more substantial than in the earlier version. The opening motive of the nightingale ideally exemplifies this quality of arabesque (see Figure 13); it is reiterated in the piano in measures 5–6, 7–8, 9, 10, and 14 within the first two verses of the poem, and again in measures 33, 34, 40, and 41 within the final stanza and postlude, thus providing an element of unity to the entire song. No similar symbolic melody opens and closes the earlier version, although it begins and ends with identical accompanimental patterns.

Careful attention is given to the text declamation and natural rhythmic accent in both settings, although the later version shifts the most important words to stronger metric positions (see Figure 14). The accompaniments provide a supple, rhythmic undulation with fairly consistent harmonic changes as backgrounds for the text. In the case of the 1882 setting, these accompanimental patterns change precisely with the beginning of each new stanza of the poem, producing the overall structure shown earlier. The accompaniment of the 1892 setting, on the other hand, subtly elides over several of these textual divisions, creating a stronger sense of rhythmic fluidity and a smoother progression of continuing thoughts. The resultant form is more cohesive and organic, and less sectional than that of the 1882 version.

Each text setting ultimately reflects the time period in which it was composed. The early version from Debussy's student years demonstrates his budding fascination with the poetry of Paul Verlaine but his deference to the voice of Madame Vasnier as the major inspiration for his music. The later version, written while Debussy's attraction to Symbolist ideals was in full bloom, displays a keener perception and a deeper response to their values. Further, a personal and distinctive musical vocabulary—one that is expanded upon but never abandoned for the rest of his life—emerges as compelling proof of his artistic genius.

This article is dedicated to Margaret G. Cobb, who provided the inspiration for the project.

NOTES ON CONTRIBUTORS

RONALD D. CLINTON received his doctorate in piano performance from The University of Texas at Austin in 1983. He has concertized extensively throughout Texas and the Southwest and has been a top-prize winner in numerous piano competitions, including the Three Rivers Southwest Regional, National Young Artists, and the Shreveport Young Artists Competitions.

STEWART R. CRAGGS is a reader services librarian at Sunderland Polytechnic, Tyne and Wear, England. In 1973 he produced a bibliographical study of Sir William Walton for his Library Association Fellowship thesis, which was subsequently extended and published as a Walton thematic catalogue by Oxford University Press in 1977. He recently completed his doctor of philosophy degree at the University of Strathclyde in Glasgow, Scotland, where he made a comprehensive study of the music of Sir Arthur Bliss (1891–1975), Master of the Queen's Musick.

ARCHIE HENDERSON received his Ph.D. in English from UCLA, where he wrote his dissertation on Ezra Pound's musical activities in the 1920s, emphasizing Pound's relationship with the American composer George Antheil. He has contributed several articles to *Paideuma* on various aspects of Pound studies.

DELL HOLLINGSWORTH received an M.M. in musicology from Texas Christian University in 1979 and is currently responsible for cataloguing music scores, books, and recordings at the Humanities Research Center. Her special field of interest is musical performance practice in the baroque period.

RICHARD LAWN is Associate Professor and Director of Jazz Studies in the Department of Music at The University of Texas at Austin. He attended the Eastman School of Music and played with the Eastman Wind Ensemble and the Jazz Ensemble and recorded with the Nova Saxophone Quartet. From 1976–1980 he directed the jazz program at the University of Northern Iowa, where he developed several award-winning jazz ensembles. He has played professionally with such jazz greats as Lionel Hampton, Dizzy Gillespie, and Chuck and Gap Mangione.

BENNETT LERNER, pianist, received his B.M. and M.M. from the Manhattan School of Music. In addition to his concert work in the United States and Europe, he is an active figure in New York's contemporary music scene, hav-

234

ing given numerous first performances of works by major American composers such as Copland, Thomson, Bowles, Leuning, and Ramey. His formative studies at the piano were with Claudio Arrau, Rafael de Silva, German Diez, and Robert Helps, and he is the winner of an award from the Martha Baird Rockefeller Fund for Music.

ROBERT B. LYNN is an Associate Professor of Music History and Literature at the University of Houston. He received his Ph.D. from Indiana University with a dissertation entitled "Renaissance Organ Music for the Proper of the Mass in Continental Tablatures." He is known for his harpsichord and organ performances as well as for his musicological studies.

ROBERT ORLEDGE was educated at Clare College, Cambridge, and is now Senior Lecturer in Music at the University of Liverpool. He is the author of *Gabriel Fauré* (Eulenburg, 1979) and *Debussy and the Theatre* (Cambridge University Press, 1982), as well as of numerous articles on French music in the period 1860–1930. His latest book is on the life and works of composer Charles Koechlin.

WILLIAM PENN is an adjunct lecturer of film scoring and commercial music at The University of Texas at Austin. He received a Ph.D. from Michigan State University and taught music theory and composition at the Eastman School of Music from 1971–78. He has composed original scores for the Folger Shakespeare Theatre and Smithsonian Institution in Washington D.C., the New York Shakespeare Festival, the Wisconsin Shakespeare Festival, and the Williamstown Theatre Festival; and his music has appeared on programs in Carnegie Hall, Lincoln Center, and on National Public Television.

MARIE ROLF received her Ph.D. in music theory from the Eastman School of Music of the University of Rochester and is presently an Assistant Professor of Music Theory at that institution. She is the American member of the international editorial board of the *Oeuvres complètes de Claude Debussy*, the ongoing critical edition of all of Debussy's works, published in France. She has been the recipient of grants from the National Endowment for the Humanities, the American Council of Learned Societies, and the Mellon Foundation, and her articles have appeared in *The Musical Quarterly*, *Haydn Studies*, *19th Century Music*, and *Notes*, among others.

SUSAN YOUENS received her Ph.D. in musicology from Harvard University. She is an Assistant Professor of Music at Ithaca College and has written articles on Debussy, Schubert, Wolf, Mahler, Verdi, and Stravinsky for *The Musical Quarterly*, *Music & Letters*, *The Journal of Musicology*, *The Opera Quarterly*, and others.